D0914132

Eye-Deep in Hell

Eye-Deep in Hell

A Memoir
of the Liberation
of the Philippines,
1944–45

William A. Owens

Southern Methodist University Press

First edition, 1989
Requests for permission to reprint material from this work
should be sent to:
    Permissions
    Southern Methodist University Press
    Box 415
    Dallas, Texas 75275

Library of Congress Cataloging-in-Publication Data
Owens, William A., 1905–
    Eye-deep in hell.

    Includes index.
    1. Owens, William A., 1905–   .   2. United
States. Army. Counter Intelligence Corps—History.
3. World War, 1939–1945—Military intelligence—
United States.   4. World War, 1939–1945—
Campaigns—Philippines.   5. World War,
1939–1945—Military intelligence—United
States.   6. Intelligence officers—United States—
Biography.   I. Title.
D810.S8094   1988   940.54'86'73   88-42637
ISBN 0-87074-279-5

The epigraph and title of this book are drawn from the
poem *Hugh Selwyn Mauberley*, in *Personae: The
Collected Poems of Ezra Pound*. Copyright © 1926 by
Ezra Pound. Reprinted by permission of New Directions
Publishing Corporation.

Design by Whitehead & Whitehead

For Duval Edwards
My compatriot, *mi compadre*

These fought in any case,
   and some believing,
      pro domo, in any case . . .
Some quick to arm,
some for adventure,
some from fear of weakness,
some from fear of censure,
some for love of slaughter, in imagination,
learning later . . .
some in fear, learning love of slaughter;

Died some, pro patria,
   non "dulce" non "et decor" . . .
walked eye-deep in hell. . . .
   —Ezra Pound, *Hugh Selwyn Mauberley*

And some—the enemy—fought for *Hakko Ichiu,* the belief that Japan was divinely ordained to bring the world under one roof, with the Emperor at the roof pole. This belief was sentimentally and fanatically proclaimed in a Japanese soldiers' song:

> I wish I could dye with my blood
> The Rising Sun of the flag
> And conquer the whole world!

> Today in Berlin and tomorrow in Moscow,
> And I shall feel no discomfort
> In snowy Siberia!

> As I will piss from the top of the Great Wall,
> A rainbow will rise
> Above the Desert of Gobi!

The War in the Pacific, mid-1944–45

1944:

19–21 June	Battle of the Philippine Sea, prelude to the U.S. invasion of the Philippine Islands. The Japanese suffer heavy naval losses, particularly in irreplaceable trained air crews.
15 September	U.S. landings on the islands of Morotai and Peleliu to establish forward bases for the invasion of the Philippines.
20–22 October	U.S. landings on Leyte.
23–26 October	The Battle for Leyte Gulf (Second Battle of the Philippine Sea). In the largest naval battle in history, the Japanese fleet is destroyed as an organized fighting force.
28 October	First U.S. B-29 mission from the Marianas. Final strategic air offensive against Japan begins 24 November.
10 December	Limon and Ormoc on Leyte taken by the U.S.
15 December	U.S. landing on Mindoro, south of Luzon, to establish an advance air base for the assault on Luzon.

25 December	Organized Japanese resistance ends on Leyte.
1945:	
January-August	Allied offensives in Burma, China, New Guinea, and the Netherlands Indies.
9 January	U.S. landing at Lingayen on the island of Luzon.
30 January	Two amphibious landings north and south of Manila by General Eichelberger's Eighth Army. XI Corps in the Subic Bay area seizes Olonpago to help seal off the Bataan Peninsula.
3 February– 4 March	Battle for Manila.
16 February– 17 April	Clearing of Manila Bay: Corregidor, Fort Drum, and Caballo Island.
February-August	Liberation of the remaining Philippine Islands, including Mindanao.
19 February	U.S. invasion of Iwo Jima. (Organized Japanese resistance ends 16 March.)
22 February	Japanese garrison in Manila driven into the old walled city (Intramuros), isolated from main forces.
4 March	Organized Japanese resistance ends in Manila.
9–10 March	The great fire bomb raid on Tokyo (the most destructive air raid in history).
15 March– 15 August	U.S. assaults against Japanese mountain defenses on Luzon end with the surrender of General Yamashita and 50,000 Japanese.
1 April	Invasion of Okinawa by U.S. marines and army troops. (Organized Japanese resistance ends 22 June.)
8 May	Unconditional surrender of Germany.
May-August	Shattering series of U.S. air raids against the Japanese home islands and remaining Japanese naval assets and merchant marine.
June-August	Preparations for U.S. invasion of Japan.

6 August	Atomic bomb dropped on Hiroshima. (Three days later, second atomic bomb dropped on Nagasaki.)
8 August	The Soviet Union declares war on Japan.
10 August	Japan offers to surrender.
15 August	Japan declares a cease-fire, ordering its armed forces to lay down their arms.
2 September	Official Japanese surrender aboard battleship U.S.S. *Missouri*.

ONE

DAYLIGHT came at last—the dawn we had feared, the dawn of A-day, 20 October 1944, the day we would meet the Japs on the beaches of Leyte Island. The sky was clear except for scattered clouds, the water smooth, glassy, stirred lightly by slow-moving ships gliding into place, the largest task force ever assembled—a thousand-ship convoy ending the thousand-mile journey up from the Admiralty Islands, coming in on time and on target. Ours was the *George F. Clymer,* a troopship. Soldiers in green or camouflage fatigues crowded the rails, stem to stern. I stood among them, relieved that the predicted typhoon had held off long enough for us to hit the beaches.

It was a day to celebrate: MacArthur's "I shall return" would become "We have returned." It had been a long struggle—three years lacking three weeks since the "day of infamy" at Pearl Harbor. We had fought our way up from Down Under, island-hopping from Guadalcanal to New Guinea and now to a stretch of beach in the Philippines, with many a landing in between. At last we would pay the yellowbellies back for Pearl Harbor, for Bataan and Corregidor. But there was no celebration on our deck—only soldiers with sober faces, some fresh from basic training, some with eyes that had already seen too much of bloody battle, some in anger braced to kill, kill, kill, some with faces lifted heavenward, as if there could never be enough of prayer.

My eyes were on the panorama before us. Ten months I had spent in intensive preparation for this day, first in the Philippine Islands section of the San Francisco Public Library, second in the Counter Intelligence Corps headquarters in Brisbane, researching captured Japanese documents and reporting enemy intelligence organizations. Now I could identify details I had known only on maps. To the right rose the mountains of Samar Island, a rugged barrier hemming in one side of Leyte Gulf. Straight ahead, in dim outline, lay the landing beaches we would hit—Orange, Violet, Blue, Yellow. Back of the beach and to our right, Catmon Hill rose fourteen hundred feet, an enemy fortress with artillery trained on the beaches we had to take. On beach and mountain they waited, entrenched, holding the advantage, ready to make of us a massive slaughter for the Emperor. Our decks were quiet as we watched six battle wagons move slowly into an elongated oval formation between convoy and beach.

0600. The battleships moved faster in their pattern; as they reached the beach side of the oval they boomed ear-numbing salvos at Dulag, at airfields near Dulag and beyond, at no targets at all in indiscriminate firing. Already softened up by two days of attack from underwater demolition crews, Dulag was flattened in minutes. The church fell in a rubble of stone and sheet iron. Of the municipal building only some pieces of concrete wall were left standing. Tall coconut palms shuddered and fell, cut off like weeds halfway up. A lone Zero, flaunting a rusty red sun on a yellowish green background, cut past the first line of ships at chilling speed, banked and turned back, untouched by obscene yelling, apparently untouched also by the black-smoke bursts of ack-ack.

0800. The grind of our anchor being let out. Zeros or not, we would be ready for the landing.

0900. The battleships stopped firing and moved out to form a line across the entrance to Leyte Gulf—their answer to rumors and sightings of a Japanese fleet bearing down to bottle us up. Cruisers and destroyers took up patterns of firing, but closer in. On board, soldiers, the first wave, now in battle gear, lined the portside rails and stared down landing nets—inch-thick rope mesh, each square a foot. Landing craft, fast-moving targets, circled the ship and formed a zigzag oval. The first wave waited, no sense of panic, only of inevitability, a sense born of the knowledge that some would never make it to the beach.

1000. H-hour. Time to go over the side. A white-faced lieutenant with infantry pack and slung rifle ran along the deck yelling, "Get your asses in gear. Go."

They went, silent, grim-faced under their helmets, with a heft over the rail, a tight grip on a rung of the ladder. As though running an obstacle course, they lowered themselves boot and hand till they could drop into a bobbing craft. As the boats filled they moved out from the ship in an oval that spread wider and wider— each boat no more than a dot-like target for a Zero. When the last was loaded the oval became a straight line, speeding as if in a race. The sea was smooth, the sun brilliant. After a time we could see only a line of spray and hear machine gun fire from their escorts. A silence like death hung over the *George F. Clymer.*

Just before 1200, when the second wave was gathering, we saw a ragged line of landing craft returning across heat-shimmering water. One spurted ahead and came toward us. As it approached, a windlass whirred—a loading net was being lowered. A young naval officer watched sailors guiding the landing craft to the net. Then he ran among us yelling, "Stand back, goddamn it, stand back." No one stood back. We jammed against each other trying to see. The net was raised slowly, as if someone was trying not to jolt the cargo.

"Don't look," the officer yelled. "For Christ's sake, don't look. Get back. Give us room."

Second-wave soldiers would not be pushed back. They had to see, to know. The net came even with the rail and we saw the cargo—bodies of young soldiers who never made it to the beach, broken bodies, parts of bodies, dripping blood as the net settled to the deck. A hand and arm, white tinged with red-blond hair, hung outside the net. Gently, the naval officer pushed it back. The first war dead we saw were our own.

"Goddamn it to hell," men swore. "Sons-o'-bitching Japs."

Stern-faced, soldiers of the second wave looked with hard eyes at the dead and gathered silently at the rail. Not one stayed back. As silently, when the command came they hoisted themselves over the rail and, pack-laden acrobats, scrambled down the swinging ladder.

I gripped the rail and watched. Three more hours and I would follow them to the beach and, if I made it, proceed alone to the CIC rendezvous near the western base of Catmon Hill. Captain Harold Frederick, our officer in charge, would be waiting. With a handshake and a light-voiced "See you there," he had gone down to the first boat with the first wave. He meant what he said.

We had worked together twice the afternoon before. The first time, I had stood on a canopied foredeck with fifty or more soldiers standing at ease before me, waiting for one more lecture on the mission of the Counter Intelligence Corps. Captain Frederick stood behind them, relaxed, listening. A month earlier he had seen to my transfer from fat-cat living at headquarters in Brisbane to combat duty with the XXIV Corps. There was an implied understanding— captain and sergeant, we would stick together.

It was a canned lecture, a "Zip Your Lip" talk, written by men who had been no closer to combat than Australia, and no closer to enemy minds than rumor: Japanese soldiers are fanatic, self-professed soldier-gods, eager to die for their divine Emperor, to eat human flesh in order to overcome the enemy. My lecture ended with a lesson learned from Pearl Harbor: "The Nipponese, because of their inherent capacity for deceit, trickery, double-crossing, take as naturally to espionage or spying as ducks to water."

This I believed from my study of captured documents and from trying to define *Tokumu Kikan,* an elusive intelligence organization with secret members deployed throughout the military. Their agents spied on foe and friend alike, on enlisted men and officers. In my military training at Camp Ritchie I had encountered no Allied organization with their power, physical or psychological.

I ended my part of the talk with two morale-building orders taken from captured documents:

4

To bring about certain destruction to the United States troops, it has been decided that hereafter the following terms of imprecation will be employed. Each unit will recite them at roll calls morning and night, or at other times as necessary.

Procedure: Close the eyes, raise one or both hands to the forehead, and then bellow out "Damnation." Thus will Yankee courage be sapped. In addition, the ranking present will shout "Let's do it!" and all the others will follow in chorus with "We will do it!"

Finally, take a saber in the right hand, and in a rigid stance of steely determination to cut down between the shoulders of the enemy, shout "Cut a thousand men!"

And these instructions, given to Japanese soldiers on a troopship approaching New Guinea:

When sinking, remain calm until the water touches the feet, and when in the water take necessary precautions. In contrast to this, those who hurriedly jump into the sea will drown themselves. When in the water, sections and platoons should gather together and sing military songs.

My GI audience laughed, but it was not a laughing matter. Japanese soldiers were not inscrutable. Neither were they unemotional. Out of such rituals came the fanaticism that made them deadly.

Later, the last night out at sea, Captain Frederick and I were in a wardroom crowded with first-line officers, lieutenants and captains, infantry and medics, one group there to lead an advance echelon, the other to patch up the wounded in a station hospital, and all tense with anxiety as we moved toward morning. Medics wanted to know about malaria: none on Leyte. Others wanted to know about the Filipinos: How many pro-Japanese? How many loyal to America?

No one knew. Guerrilla reports that got through to Brisbane were often sketchy; too often the numbers of the loyal were too great to be realistic. A few things were clear. We were going to fight an enemy on territory that was ours by conquest, on the island that had held out longest against us, among Filipinos who had lived for more than three years under the Japanese with their slogan "Asia for Asians, the Orient for Orientals." We could expect Filipino spies to infiltrate our lines, Filipino guerrillas to be our eyes and ears as well as our weapon bearers. A problem was time. We had not been given enough time to prepare for meeting unknown enemies on thirty-five miles of beaches.

Conversation became speculation, stretched out in a reluctance to go, as though lingering together would bolster us for the morning.

1400. *Now hear this.* A call for the third wave to get in battle gear. I tested again my Colt .38 and carbine and the rounds and clips in my ammunition belt. With GIs around me doing the same, I unrolled and rerolled my infantry pack after a final check of the landing list: a change of clothes, K rations for two days, two canteens of water, an infantry shovel for digging foxholes. Warned that the Japanese would shoot or behead me if they captured me with my CIC credential and badge, I put them in my fatigue jacket pocket, then decided to carry them in my hand—easier to toss them away. I read again my search permit: "Owens, W. A., T/sgt, is hereby authorized to search enemy dead and installations for documents and material."

We were sworn to treat the enemy, living or dead, according to the rules of the Geneva Convention. We were at a disadvantage. Japan did not recognize the Geneva Convention; hospitals and hospital ships had no protection from an attack, nor did the captured Allied soldier from a beheading in the Samurai tradition.

From basic training on, I had watched soldiers finger the dog tags hanging inside their shirts—their one identification in the mass of government issue, and in the anonymity of death. I unbuttoned my shirt. They were there—aluminum ovals, skin-polished, embossed with name, serial number, P for Protestant—my link with the world I had left behind . . . or a souvenir for some Jap soldier.

1500. We still waited, burdened with battle gear, with no word of why we were waiting, only rumors. We watched phosphorous shells exploding white on Catmon Hill. The Japs were still there. Landing craft ran like water bugs in frenzied patterns toward the beach. The landing was not going well, we told each other, and we paced the deck, eagerly listening to opinions that immediately became rumors: we had underestimated the Japs; we were being pushed back into the sea.

I stopped by a soldier half my age sitting with his back against a bulkhead, his rifle across his knees, his cleaning kit open. He was crying. I reached out to touch him on the shoulder but drew back. Army regulations made no distinction between a pat on the shoulder and a sock to the jaw. I leaned close and said, "Don't be afraid."

He said nothing.

Now hear this.

The sound was ominous, rumor became fact. Landing operations were being held in abeyance. All personnel would remain on board that night. Orders increased our anxiety. Complete blackout would be observed: no lighted matches, no cigarettes on deck. It was a night of the bombers' moon. A smoke screen would have to be laid down. The voice stopped. No word from the beaches. The fact for us was that the *George F. Clymer* was a sitting duck.

In a tropical twilight, smoke machines spread a gray, oily-smelling fog that screened out the shoreline and ships close to us. It closed us in from sight and sound, in total isolation. It penetrated troop decks with a fear of blackness, blindness. Soldiers stumbled against each other on deck and ladder and swore and bitched: "Better be bombed than choked to death."

Heat and stench unbearable below, soldiers crowded topside and bedded down, bodies inches from bodies, like slaves on a slave deck, sweating in battle gear, shifting with each roll of the ship, bitching, bitching. They were there because of the goddamned Krauts, goddamned Eyties, goddamned Japs.

"I say, goddamn my draft board."

The words hung for a moment in the midst of groaning and laughing.

I lay with my nose close to the deck, with a hand cupped over my face to form a pocket of air. The soldier to my front lay the same, until he turned flat on his back to ask a question: "You drafted?"

"No."

"Enlisted?"

"Yes."

"Son-of-a-bitch. How come?"

I could have said out of loyalty to my country. He would not have believed me; no draftee would. I could have said out of boredom from teaching freshman English classes. He would not have known what that boredom was.

There had to be something more. This time I opened to truth. Pearl Harbor left me more angry than I had known. I wanted to fight. Then in May 1942 the Japanese hung out a banner boasting the surrender of Corregidor. At the same time they started the inhumane Death March. On 23 June I went to Fort Sam Houston and enlisted.

The soldier next to me touched my hand and then gripped it. A voice from farther down deck interrupted with an old Army joke: "Say, soldier, whatcha gonna be when you grow up?"

Relaxed a little by the laughter, I covered my nose with a handkerchief, put my face against the deck, and spent the hours sleeping and waking.

Now hear this.

Smoke and darkness had lifted and we were in the dawn of another day—A plus 1. Terse communiqués followed. Our beachheads had held. Our headquarters had been established in Tacloban, capital of Leyte. General MacArthur had broadcast his "I have returned" message around the world. Everything sounded up and up, but we still had to hit the beaches. Enemy fire had been heavy around Dulag and airfields to the north throughout the night. White smoke from phosphorous shells still dotted the slopes of Catmon Hill. Jap guns were still trained on the beach where we would land.

While I was oiling and testing the action on my pistol and carbine there was another *Now hear this*. The wave scheduled for 1500 on A-day would go at 1500 on A plus 1. We would leave our barracks bags on deck; they would catch up with us later. I repacked mine. From Australia to New Guinea to the Admiralty Islands and now to Leyte I had kept my blue suit and tie, my white shirts and black shoes, ready to switch from soldier to civilian on order. This time I packed them at the bottom, and with them the U.S. patches that would identify me as a civilian employee of the military. Between civilian clothes and GI uniforms I hid the diaries I had kept from the day I embarked in San Francisco—my record of a soldier's life.

Chow time over, our wave, again in battle dress, was hustled to the rail. The sky had turned blustery, the water turbulent, an oval of landing craft bucking the waves. An officer ran among us, yelling "Up and over." Soldiers ahead of me swung over and climbed down. My turn came. I had to get my stocky, thirty-eight-year-old body, my weapons and pack up, over, down. With all my strength I pulled myself up and clung to the rail long enough to catch my breath. Don't look down, we had been told, but I did— at the helmets of soldiers scrambling ahead of me, at the tiny craft, cork-like in the rough water. Clinging only by my hands I lowered myself till I found a foothold in the net. There was no stopping. Combat boots of soldiers behind me grazed my hands. I had to move fast or have my fingers crushed. Like a living thing, the net jerked under weight and movement, swung far out and then back against the hull—a blotched wall against which I swung my feet to keep from being smashed.

When I thought my grip would hold no longer, hands grabbed my legs and pulled me into the boat with a "Hurry up, goddamn it." When the last man was in, the boat turned with a lurch that threw us against each other. There was little room to fall in, and no place to spit the rising nausea. Then we were in a circling pattern, waiting for the formation to be complete, turning and turning in whitecaps that threw spray over us. The soldier I had told not to be afraid was afraid. He was pushed so close to me that my carbine rested at high port against his shoulders. The pallor in his cheeks was from seasickness—seasickness mixed with fear. He leaned his head back and I could see tears in his eyes, drool on his lips. In a kind of controlled hysteria he said, "Oh, God, oh, God," till someone told him to shut up. With a blowing out of breath he went limp and slid down. Bodies closed over him, boots rested on him, and there was no way to help him—a casualty before combat.

9

I was with an infantry detachment, our orders the same. It would be a wet landing. The craft would stop but not anchor. The ramp would swing down. We would hit the water running and keep running zigzag till we found cover. It was every man for himself.

In water up to my thighs, I followed the others to the beach and hit the sand running zigzag, keeping low to fall to the ground at the zing of a bullet. Somewhere beyond the beach road I would come to the XXIV Corps headquarters. Still running zigzag I crossed the road and worked my way into a strip of bombing debris and tropical undergrowth. At the cough of a mortar I instinctively hit the dirt. As instinctively, I began creeping and crawling—the right knee forward, reach out, left knee forward, reach out, of basic training. Belly to dirt I reached a line of coconut palms slashed and broken by shelling. Past them, on my knees now, I saw the green of Army fatigues, the shapes of soldiers gathering. I crossed the last strip standing up.

As I came closer I saw Captain Frederick standing out from the others. He saw me and gave me the raised-fist, lowered-fist infantry signal for on-the-double. He came toward me, fresh shaved, his fatigues clean and unwrinkled.

"You made it."

His greeting was as cool, as casual as if I had come in from a stroll.

"Yes, sir."

I was too out of breath to talk, and too scared. A mortar coughed on the slope of Catmon Hill and I hit the dirt. The shell exploded close but undershot. No one else hit the dirt. After twenty-four hours under fire, they had learned to judge the trajectory of a shell by its whine.

Captain Frederick was matter-of-fact.

"Better dig in. It may get rough. It was rough as hell last night. Rougher than anything I saw on Los Negros."

Neither in Brisbane nor on the convoy up had he mentioned landing with the First Cavalry Division on Los Negros, officer in charge of the first CIC combat team in the Pacific, or the Silver Star awarded him for bravery in action.

10

He said dig in and we dug in. Alexander Bakewell, a special agent from St. Louis, and I decided to dig in together, not in a shallow foxhole but in a round hole so deep that only a direct hit would get us. Unwittingly, the XXIV had landed in a swamp. Digging was easy. We dug a well shoulder deep, and stopped only when water began seeping in. Captain Frederick watched us but said nothing. He had made a foxhole for himself as long and as wide but not as deep as a grave. He lined it with a blanket, spread down two white sheets and another blanket. We carried K rations because an army travels on its stomach; for him, morale traveled on a clean body.

I was ten years older, but he did not let years make a difference. He was the officer, I the soldier, and he kept it that way. With him I had no complaint. If a general could be a soldier's general, then he was a soldier's captain.

Bakewell and I had no choice but to sit face to face, knees interlocking, human warmth passing one to the other. Water rose to our ammunition belts and the warmth was gone. Mortar shells came sporadically, some exploding close enough to shake the earth around us.

"Goddamned Japs," Bakewell said. "Goddamned Japs. They've already sent more than two years of my life down the drain. God knows how many more."

TWO

AT FIRST LIGHT I crawled out of the hole, water-shriveled in flesh, shriveled in spirit by the night-long shelling, by the reality that the enemy was out there ready for attack, by doubt that when I came face to face with a Jap I could pull the trigger, in spite of the sheath of hatred Army propaganda had encased me in. The camp was coming alive, not in military order but in a confusion of commands and countercommands in loud, edgy voices. Soldiers juggled rifles and trenching tools and K-ration biscuits and chocolate bars trying to keep up with the commands. Farther away, toward enemy lines, others pushed ahead till they were mired in mud. An infantry outfit passed us and moved along the foot of Catmon Hill, carrying the attack where weapons carriers could not go.

Captain Frederick talked anxiously about what we would do. He now had four agents. Ed Gorman from Brooklyn and Miles Matsumoto from Hawaii had made it in. From Brisbane we had been designated a combat detachment with the double mission of combat and counterintelligence. But from XXIV Corps headquarters there was no directive. Corps claimed that nothing had come from GHQ. To Corps officers we were dogfaces and would be used like dogfaces. Captain Frederick argued the high quality of our education—an average of two university degrees among us— and our special Army training. The major answered his argument with a question: If we were so well educated and trained, why were we sergeants, enlisted men? To that, Captain Frederick had only a lame answer. This was something decided by the Army when the Counter Intelligence Corps replaced the old Corps of Intelligence Police. In the end there was no hope, even from General John R. Hodge, Corps Commander. We were caught in another Army snafu.

Locating Corps headquarters in a swamp was an obvious miscalculation. There was higher, dryer land nearby, but the general refused to deviate from the original plans. We would dig in where we were. Soldiers began digging square holes waist deep and setting up pyramidal tents. The hole for General Hodge's tent was closer to neck deep. Captain Frederick took one look at the piece of swamp assigned to the CIC and sent me to Dulag to find a house—any house would be better than a hole in the ground, and better still if it was out of sight of Corps headquarters.

The stretch of Violet beach between us and the center of Dulag had become a jam of men and vehicles and supplies. In their rush to comply with reversed orders, ship-to-shore crews had unloaded rear echelon supplies ahead of ammunition and rations for frontline troops. Landing craft with rams lowered edged up on the sand. Soldiers working with conveyor belts built mountains of rations cartons, gasoline drums, ammunition cases. Trucks and jeeps with drivers but no cargoes idled just above the tidemark. It was clear that plans had gone awry. One Japanese bomber could immobilize a division or two.

I met my first Filipinos on Highway One at the edge of Dulag. They had fled inland when the shelling started. Now they were straggling back, half-naked, looking half-starved, men and women carrying and leading children, old men and women, some disfigured by leprosy—pathetic victims of Karl von Clausewitz's legacy, total war. Dazedly they searched for their houses, but the land was now covered by the materiel of war and, defenseless, they were driven away.

Navy guns had done their work on Dulag. In what had once

14

been the center of town little was left: crumbling walls of the church and *convento*—the sheet-iron roof caved in; parts of concrete walls and steps that had been the municipal building; and across the road a nipa palm hut with roof and walls half-flattened. Farther along the highway there was a frame house, windowless, a shell hole in the wall toward the water. I asked about it.

"*Kempei Tai,* ser," Filipinos told me. "Very bad, ser." *Kempei Tai,* Japanese military police. Ironic. From that house they had kept watch over Filipino civilians. In our own way, we wanted to do the same.

The house faced across the road to the beach. Near it another road ran inland, toward the Dulag airstrip, still under bombardment from our cannon. Built on stilts, the house was high enough above ground for me to walk under it upright. I went inside. Desks and chairs were in place, but there were no desk drawers. In their haste the Japanese had taken them. The rooms would do for our offices. We could set up cots under the house. I told the Filipinos trying to move in that they would have to leave.

"But, ser," they begged, "we have no place to go. Everything is gone."

We had to have the house. As gently as I could I herded them toward the area between the church and the beach, where other refugees milled about or rested on the sand. They went, but I could see resentment in their eyes.

I had landed in the Ninety-sixth Infantry sector. Now I was in the Seventh, near the dividing line of the two, and near the field hospital set up for both, a brown canvas tent with red crosses painted on the top. Beyond the hospital I could hear the rattle of machine guns.

"How far to the fighting?" I asked Filipinos on the road.

They pointed north.

"No so far, ser. We have only come from there. Much fighting, ser. Many dead *Japones.*"

They had come through the lines at daylight, past a command post the Japs had deserted in the night. It was a nipa hut, off the road, not far from the Dulag airstrip. I could find it, they said. I had to find it, I thought.

I reported to Captain Frederick and went on to search the

15

command post. It was farther than I expected, and there were dead Japanese along the way. Most had been stripped of their uniforms. One, small and pitiful in his cheap cotton shirt and trousers, lay in fresh blood. I felt nausea at touching him but my orders were to search. I took his wallet and diary from his pockets and with my Boy Scout knife cut from the front band of his trousers the tags that bore his name and unit. From captured documents I knew there were other items to look for: the *omamori*, a card from the shrine of his clan; the *seninbari haramaki,* the thousand-stitch belt; a Rising Sun flag signed by relatives and friends at his leave-taking. He had his *omamori* in his wallet, but no flag or thousand-stitch belt. I left him face down in his own blood.

The command post was on a path a short distance from the road. A few feet in I saw a thin black thread stretched across the path. The place was rigged with a clumsily made booby trap. Each end of the thread was tied to the detonating mechanism of an anti-tank mine, the kind that suicide squads slapped against enemy tanks. The explosion could destroy the tank; it would certainly kill the soldier. I stepped over the thread and entered a hut as clumsily booby-trapped with hand grenades. I left the traps in place but took the few scattered papers and a pocket diary.

Close to sunset I was on my way back to Dulag. Before I came to the beach road I heard a plane and saw a Zero skimming over the mountains to the west and coming straight toward me. It banked to the left, toward Tacloban, and again I saw the rusty red circle on a blotchy green fuselage. I crouched in a ditch and the plane passed on, close enough for me to see the pilot's face—and to hate it.

Shaken, I climbed out of the ditch and hiked on to the house, now identified with a CIC sign, black on white. Captain Frederick was on his way to Corps to file a report. The other agents had moved in. So had Mendoza. Captain Frederick had found Mendoza, or Mendoza had found Captain Frederick. Either way, Mendoza was our boy—not handsome, not quick on the trigger, but willing and energetic. He would clean our house. He would find a *lavandera* to wash our clothes. He would get the *tuba* when there was nothing better to drink.

The diary was our first captured document. We sat with Matsumoto around a Coleman lantern while he translated. Like a scholar he deciphered and wrote. Suddenly he laughed and began translating out loud: "Don't sit under the apple tree with anyone else but me. . . ."

"Christ," someone said, "he's been listening to Tokyo Rose."

Somewhere, if not from Tokyo Rose, the diarist had acquired a taste for the West, or at least for one Western song. There was nothing in the Army propaganda I had listened to that prepared me for this. Our propaganda had allowed no room for contrast or complexity in the Japanese soldier: he was inscrutable and brutal. In his diaries I had found him sentimental and brutal, and matter-of-fact. A diary entry I had read in Brisbane stuck in my mind:

> 25 September 1942. Guadalcanal. Discovered and captured the two prisoners who escaped last night in the jungle, and let the Guard Company guard them. To prevent their escape a second time, pistols were fired at their feet, but it was difficult to hit them. The two prisoners were dissected while still alive by Medical Officer Yamaji and their livers were taken out, and for the first time I saw the internal organs of a human being. It was very informative.

An official-looking document I had brought back from the command post showed another facet of the Japanese soldier's military character—the compulsion to record everything in writing and to carry his records with him. It was a list of names and addresses of a Japanese spy network in Burma. For intelligence at GHQ it was a remarkable find. For us it was a clue to operations of similar networks on Leyte. No doubt they had their spies among the refugees crowding into Dulag.

Ten thousand refugees, the Army estimated—ten thousand in two days, with no food, no water, no shelter, in tropical darkness with a monsoon setting in. There was no control. Leaders of the puppet government had fled with the Japanese or gone into hiding. The prewar Commonwealth Government was still to be reorganized. Manuel Quezon, president when war broke out, was dead in the States. Sergio Osmeña, his successor, was in Tacloban with his staff and an advance unit of the Philippines Civilian Affairs Unit, all helpless. The Army designated a section of the beach for a refugee camp. It was overrun before the end of the first day.

Families with crying children surrounded our house and touched us to get our attention. A few in Spanish, more in English, most in the soft syllables of Visayan begged for food.

"Ser, you have the rice for the children?"

We did not have rice. We did have a few cases of C rations, only enough, when handed out, to bring more people running. When everything had been given out, our house was still surrounded by people waiting for morning.

From early hours till midnight a young Filipino waited to talk to me.

"Ser," he said when the people were quiet, "you will have the woman?"

"The woman?"

"You will have the woman? *La puta?*"

"Are they near here?"

"Only there, ser, at the beach."

"Friends of the *Kempei Tai?*"

"Very good friends of the *Kempei Tai*. They came often to this house."

"What are their names?"

There were three that would please me. "Purificación, Concepción, and Expectación."

I laughed.

"Very young," he urged.

"Can you bring them early in the morning?"

He could. I did not say that I would arrest them as spies for the *Kempei Tai*.

Rain late at night, intermittent and then steady, left water standing on the flats and running in ditches. The morning report made out, Captain Frederick sent me to Corps headquarters to deliver it. Headquarters was a tent city drying in the sun, the tents hanging slack, soldiers' gear strung out on guy ropes. Water stood about four feet deep in the general's tent. Soldiers stood in mud eating their C rations, the field kitchen not yet in operation. Soldiers squished in mud in the tent where I delivered the report.

Near the general's tent a detail of soldiers splashed and dug, shaping drainage ditches. As I went past, a colonel yelled at me: "Soldier, grab a shovel. Get digging."

I stared at him, my blood rising. He was not considering either my mind or my mission—my B.A., M.A., Ph.D., my counter-intelligence training at the Chicago school, my combat intelligence training at Camp Ritchie, my work rounding up Jap and Filipino infiltrators. Why should I help dig out a general who stayed in a swamp when there was higher ground nearby? I did not question him but I did show him the CIC badge pinned under the lapel of my fatigue jacket. He became abusive. Did that give me the right to question an order? I was a soldier, in uniform. My mind slipped back to Camp Wallace, to basic training, to a sergeant giving a lecture on military courtesy. "Suppose you meet a black lieutenant on the street. You gonna salute? Fucking right you gonna salute. You ain't salutin' a nigger. You're salutin' the uniform."

The colonel was used to making judgments on uniform, on insignia. It was the military way. He pointed to a shovel. "Now get going."

I knew I had to grab it. Not to was insubordination and the stockade. I had seen GIs in stockades. I knew what a court-martial for insubordination in a combat zone could mean. I stooped toward the shovel.

"Colonel, sir," someone called, and he turned away. That was enough time. I rounded the tent and fell in with a detail policing up. My uniform became my cover. One dogface looks like another. Out of the colonel's sight, I ran—angry, my pride cut to the quick—till I could not run anymore. I got back to Dulag out of breath but with my mind made up: I would, by God, soldier in my own way. An old saying from Pin Hook flickered in my mind: They can kill me but they sho' God cain't eat me.

Hearing my story, Captain Frederick was shaken. Then he tried to find explanations. The XXIV Corps had come straight from Hawaii, from one command to another. Perhaps the briefing had not been adequate. Perhaps General Hodge's staff did not know

19

the confidence General MacArthur had placed in the CIC mission. He ended up looking on the darker side. What had happened to me might happen to any other agent. They could order us out on KP, if they ever got their kitchen set up, or to digging slit trenches. We bitched. He went to Corps headquarters.

In less than an hour we saw him striding back on the beach road and knew that he had failed. He strode up to our front steps, his face angry red under his Atabrine yellow, and, in language rare for him, told us how badly he had failed. He had seen the general, but the colonel had gotten to him first. There had been a charge of insubordination of an unidentified CIC agent. That charge would be dropped, but the general had issued a vocal order: CIC or not, a soldier had to follow orders or get the book thrown at him. As far as the XXIV Corps was concerned there was nothing special about a special agent. Our bitching came close to disaffection. Calling ourselves the Corps of Indignant Corporals was mild beside it.

Captain Frederick told the others to carry on and took me for a walk. His voice was quiet, angry.

"I asked them to get a directive from Tacloban—GHQ, anybody. They turned me down. I asked for permission to call myself. They threatened me with court-martial if I did. They've got us in a bind. Any message I send now would have to go through the scrambler. It would be stopped there."

He did not blame me for hauling ass when I did, but my troubles were not over. They did not have my name but they could get me, or get the whole outfit for protecting me. A whole CIC detachment in the stockade was an absurdity but nothing to be laughed at. That was a battle we would lose. He never said what he was leading up to, but I knew. Somebody had to take our message to Garcia, and I was picked. He knew the consequences if I got caught. So did I. At the least I would be busted to private and transferred to something like the ship-and-shore crew, or I would sweat out the war in a barbed-wire stockade. But we were in this together. I saw him as my commanding officer, and also as a man I respected and trusted. He was indispensable. Better my ass than his. I stopped and faced him. "Do you want me to go to Tacloban?"

There was relief in his voice. "I am not ordering you to go," he said earnestly. "Too risky for all of us."

There would be no orders, verbal or written. What I did I would do on my own.

At Corps headquarters he had studied the situation map. Japanese forces still held a strip of shoreline between Dulag and Tacloban. "Chances are you would never get through," he said quietly.

We came to the edge of the civilian squatter camp, to the thousands of homeless, their homes destroyed not by Japanese enemies but by American friends. Among so many there had to be the disaffected, the spies, the remnants of a fifth column that had worked against us at Bataan and Corregidor. Our work was there, searching out the enemy within. It was worth the risk. Hell, I had taken the main risk when I joined up. "I will go to Tacloban. I don't see any other way."

He was abrupt, almost antagonistic. "You can do what you damn please. I don't want to hear anything about it." His voice softened. "Colonel Irwin and Major Labatt are in Tacloban."

He meant for me to report to them. I knew them and knew they would listen. Colonel John N. Irwin was second in command of the CIC in the Southwest Pacific. I had seen him often in the office in Brisbane. Major Blair Labatt was in charge of the Sixth Army CIC. We had come in together on the *George F. Clymer.*

There was nothing more to be said. I would go, but not alone. I went to Ed Gorman, a special agent from Brooklyn. He was Irish, husky, and angrily disaffected, and more than willing to take the risk.

Unexpectedly we were saved from going by night through enemy lines. Two naval officers arrived at the CIC with a Japanese pilot they had pulled from plane wreckage in the water. They had been ordered to get rid of him. Could the Army help? We could. We had an excuse to go not by land but by water.

With no word to Captain Frederick or to anyone else, we marched the pilot to the beach and to a crew unloading an LCVP. We took the bos'n aside and showed him our badges. Same as the FBI, we told him. Then Gorman spoke firmly and to the point. We were going to take the Jap to General MacArthur's headquarters, in

21

his boat. Military intelligence would find out what field he took off from. Our bombers would blast hell out of it. The bos'n understood but said no. He would be court-martialed for taking a boat without orders. We threatened him with court-martial if he did not. Afraid to go, more afraid not to go, he went, with his machine gun in place, his gunner tense beside it.

The Jap was young and scared, and he knew no English. Aboard, Gorman and I stood, one on either side of him with pistols in holsters, carbines at sling, badges and credentials in hand, ready to be dropped in the drink if we were attacked. The Jap was not the inscrutable enemy of Army lectures. From the look in his eyes he might have been counting the lines of tanks and trucks moving slowly inland. The bos'n raised the ramp and piloted us through a maze of Liberty ships and landing craft. The Jap blinked his eyes and moved his lips but made no sound. He might have been taking inventory of all the ships at sea.

Gorman wanted to know what we might expect from Colonel Irwin. I did not know. I did know that while I was still in Brisbane, General Eichelberger, CO of I Corps, had asked for me by name, with a promise of a commission and a place on his staff. The request for transfer was turned down—by Colonel Irwin, if I could believe the scuttlebutt. I could say only one thing to Gorman: "He's got to look out for us."

An hour or so later, with the Jap-held strip of Leyte close on our left, the mountains of Samar far to our right, Gorman and I realized we were lost—we were circling in a sea of ships, lost. The bos'n did not know how to get to Tacloban. Toward Samar there was a troopship with a ladder down. We pulled up to the ladder.

"Which way to Tacloban?" the bos'n yelled.

Sailors at the rail waved straight ahead and then one yelled, "They've got a goddamned Nip down there."

That set the sailors to running and yelling. "Gut him!" "Nut him!"

They did neither. He was a prisoner of war. I asked for chow. They brought ham sandwiches for Gorman and me. I looked up at the sailors. "Cne for the Nip?"

Their manner changed. He was the enemy, but they had seen

22

him up close and no longer feared him. They handed down another sandwich.

"What's gonna happen to him?" they asked.

It was my turn to be bitter. "He'll get the number one treatment. They'll interrogate him and then put him up in quarters like a hotel and feed him three squares a day. He'll get more rice in a day than he's used to in a week."

We were on our way again and I was hating him, not for himself but for what he stood for, for the atrocities I had read in captured documents, for the starving, the torturing, the beheading of Allied prisoners of war.

Well past mid-afternoon the bos'n began to worry. "We've got to turn back. Dark comes fast here. I'll be in one hell of a mess if I don't report in before dark."

We persuaded him to go a little farther. That was far enough. A DUKW with two black soldiers aboard crossed our bow. They objected. There was not room enough for the Jap and them on board. We commandeered it anyway.

We reached the beach, and what had been a boat became a land vehicle. The driver worked our way into the traffic of what seemed to be the main street, and moved slowly toward what he thought was GHQ.

"Bill! Bill!"

Colonel Irwin and Major Labatt were leaning out a second-story window, smiling, waving, beckoning. The driver stopped.

"Come on up."

The welcome was better than we had expected. The Jap between us, we climbed the stairs.

"God, it's good to see you." Strange words from a commanding officer to two soldiers insubordinate and AWOL. But they had heard nothing from Dulag.

MPs took the Jap away. Gorman and I sat on a cot and told them why we were there and how we had used the Jap to get there. We had decided to tell the story straight, and we did—insubordinate, absent without leave. They looked stunned. Either was a crime subject to the death penalty, if some judge advocate wanted to throw the book at us. Any mitigating circumstances? I told them

23

about the order to dig ditches and Captain Frederick's argument with Corps, and Corps threats to him.

"Captain Frederick gave no orders," I said. "We came on our own."

They understood. They also understood that covertly or overtly this was an attack on the CIC. Suddenly we were in a conspiracy: two sergeants, a captain, a major, and a colonel against a major general and his staff. Our talk grew hushed. All of it came back to Colonel Irwin. He was the ranking CIC officer on Leyte. He had to straighten out XXIV Corps. He had to cover for us.

"I'll do what I can," he said. "You stay here tonight. I'll go with you to Dulag in the morning."

A kind of bargain had been struck. We were all in this together, officers and enlisted men, officers who were also gentlemen quietly covering for enlisted men.

A driver in a jeep took us to the CIC tent in a tent city. Two agents on duty, Jim English and Woonha Park, showed us where to dig our foxholes. We would need them. Japanese planes still controlled the air over Tacloban.

Dug in, we sat in the dark and talked about the Japanese pilot's good luck. One of us captured would not have such luck. Three from the West, one Western-born Oriental, we talked about contrasts. I could quote from research I had done in Japanese documents: "Do not fall captive even if the alternative is death. Bear in mind the fact that to be captured not only means disgracing the Army, but also your parents and family will never be able to hold up their heads again. Always save the last round for yourself."

That was the code of *Bushido,* the code of the warrior, the basis for Japanese treatment of prisoners of war. A soldier who surrendered was a weakling and to be beheaded in the tradition of *Bushido*—unless he had special skills in the operation and repair of radios and motor vehicles. Then his life would be spared as long as he was useful.

The question of cannibalism came up.

"You have any proof?" they asked me.

"Only in captured photographs and documents."

I had in mind a photograph of naked Fuzzy-Wuzzies hanging

in the shed, the fingers cut off, strips of flesh cut from the thighs. I wanted to shock them as I had been shocked, to show them that we were too soft on Japanese prisoners.

"Would you like a recipe for cooking human flesh? For making it taste like pork?"

"God, no."

"They say fingers are the greatest delicacy. White or Japanese. We have captured Japanese with fingers in their pockets."

We were interrupted by the broadcast of communiqués to America—heroic accounts of our progress written for people back home, not for GIs in foxholes. We bitched at the glossing over. Ironically, air raid warnings opened up. We heard the drone of planes, saw tracer bullets rising over the airstrip, and felt the quake of bombs exploding. We were under a major attack and could do nothing but sweat it out, hugging the dirt in a foxhole through a long, long night.

In the quiet of daylight Colonel Irwin and Major Labatt met us. They were shaken, and with reason. A bomb had hit an officer's tent. For one of their friends, the war was over.

Gorman and I went with Colonel Irwin to the beach, where he had ordered a motor launch. In measured stride he led the way, Princetonian, Oxonian, New York lawyer—only by circumstance a military man. We followed, single file, in dirty, slept-in fatigues. In a supply dump we saw stacks of C rations. I swung a case up on my shoulder and kept going, in a kind of parody of a boy totin' for his master.

At Dulag Colonel Irwin and Captain Frederick went at once to XXIV Corps headquarters. Gorman and I checked the morning report. Our names were on it. Someone had covered for us.

At noon or later Colonel Irwin and Captain Frederick came back from Corps. We never knew what orders from GHQ, if any, they had taken with them, or what bargaining had gone on. We did know that from then on our mission was intelligence and nothing else. We would never again be ordered to dig ditches.

Colonel Irwin decided to sleep that night on a cot in our office. Corps was still on C rations. So were we. I worried about breakfast. C rations did not seem good enough for a colonel who

25

had fought for us and won. I asked Mendoza to find a chicken. The best he could do was try.

At daylight Mendoza woke me. "Ser," he said in a low voice, "the rooster she lay the egg."

Later, someone made our cover-up official:

441st Situation Report Oct 44

Two members 224 (Owens, Gorman) arrived at 6th Army HQ, Tacloban . . . reported bombardment, bombing of ammo dumps, 10,000 civilian refugees, *Kempei Tai* office occupied by CIC.

• • •

On the third and fourth days of the invasion the Seventh and Ninety-sixth pushed their beachheads inland, but the battle for Leyte had hardly started. Back-up men and materiel were crowded on narrow strips on the east coast. Japanese forces held the remainder of the island, including Ormoc and Ormoc Bay on the west coast. Allied commanders, basing their judgment on sketchy and inaccurate intelligence reports, had expected the main defense to be on Luzon. They had misjudged. The heaviest concentration of Japanese troops and materiel was in the Ormoc Bay area, and there was a steady flow of reinforcements.

Zeros and bombers tested our defenses. We had only the airstrips we had captured, and they were small, primitive, and, except for the one at Tacloban, useless for our planes. The Japanese had to know, as we knew, that our carrier planes were being pulled back. Battleships, carriers, cruisers silently moved out of Leyte Gulf to counter attacks from the sea. The Army was left exposed on the beach, with no place to pull back, with Filipino refugees clogging roads and beaches and slowing any military movement.

Our situation at Dulag was as precarious as any. Japanese troops still held Catmon Hill. From their caves and coconut-log fortifications they could train their artillery on targets at random. Zero attacks were relentless and undiscriminating. The station hospital, between us and the Dulag airstrip, was a random target. In the middle of a sunny day we watched Rising Sun planes drop shells on the hospital, undeterred by red crosses, undeterred by our ack-ack that peppered the sky with puffs of black smoke but could not reach the planes.

Night of the fourth day came, soft and warm, the moon riding high, bright enough to cast shadows. We were in total blackout, except for the moon.

"Bomber's moon," we said to each other, half-joking. We were lined up on a coconut log at the front of our house, talking, daring to boast that we had survived another day, dreading the insecurity of the night, counting on waking to another dawn.

Captain Frederick called the names of guards for the night. Mine was the midnight shift. At 0800 I left the log, crawled into my cot, and closed the mosquito net tight around me, uniform and all. The guard on duty, walking a post no more than thirty feet from me, would wake me.

I came awake at an ear-piercing hiss and men yelling, "Bomb! Bomb! Look out! Take cover!"

Before I could untangle myself, one bomb hit, and another, so close that the impact threw me several feet off the cot and against a piling. My shoulders and knees struck the wood, and a shaving mirror came down on me, the edge of the frame heavy on my head and neck. My first thought was to get out and get away from there. Then I heard men screaming, "Help me! Oh, God, help me!" A burst of flame glowed bright enough to cast light under the house. The gasoline dump had been hit. Oh, no. Next to it hundreds of soldiers were bivouacked.

"Help! Help!"

I hit the road, running as hard as I could toward the yelling. The gold of moonlight had turned to the angry red of gasoline flames. Men like black shadows ran toward the flames, then back from the flames, and then circled like addled ants. An officer came running on the road yelling, "Get back! Get back! Take cover!" Others were running up behind me. "For God's sake," he yelled, "I order you to take cover. You can't do anything. The ammunition dump's going next."

I took cover in a Japanese pillbox across from our house. It was crowded with our agents and with strangers, but they let me push in, ass-end first, my head out, turtle-like. Flames oiled up. A steel barrel of gasoline rose flaming and burst with a bomb-like explosion that shook the coconut logs in the shelter and sifted sand over us. We waited and shivered and hoped the shelter would not cave in.

The ammunition dump caught next. First there was the sound of small-arms fire and bullets whizzing as if we were in a big fire fight. Then the big shells, the 155s, began exploding. Almost as if timed, they rose high in the air, burst, and rained shrapnel down on men and materiel. We could comprehend only quantitatively: so many troops, so much machinery of war, victims of one lone bomber.

As what had become a holocaust spread, our pillbox became a trap. Logs separated, dirt poured down. We could be buried alive. We talked about the stone wall at the back of the church. It would be safer, if we could get to it. Several shells exploded at once. "I'm going," I yelled. Then I was on the road running, stooping, zigzagging, hitting the dirt in shell craters to catch my breath.

When I was near the church an ambulance driving blackout swung close. "Hang on," someone yelled.

I managed to get my hands on a door handle, my feet on a bumper. The ambulance was running with blue lights, the driver needing no more light in the glare. We swerved and swerved again, traveling short distances west, north, east, to the station hospital. When we stopped I could hear cries of wounded in the ambulance, cries of wounded in a blacked-out tent. On one side of the tent there were soldiers stretched out, dead. Near the entrance there were others, wounded, waiting for help. A corpsman with a flashlight spoke to me and let me go. I was battered but not wounded enough to be taken in at the moment.

He told me to take cover in a Japanese trench near the hospital, a trench that, waist deep, zigzagged out into the darkness. From it I could watch barrel after barrel of gasoline rise and burst. The whine of shrapnel from exploding shells did not reach as far as the hospital. Other soldiers came in and we crowded together, but there was little feeling of safety, even after a combat detail went out to reconnoiter.

Toward midnight the attack came, with shouts of "*Banzai! Banzai!*" shrill in the midst of fire and explosion. Japanese soldiers were down the trench, fighting with bayonets. No one knew how many, but we heard someone begging for help, and American soldiers crowded back on us in the trench. They had left one man dead, with a bayonet in his back.

"Yellow-bellied sons-o'-bitches. Attacking a hospital."

In minutes the enemy struck and pulled back. In minutes more, Americans were creeping and crawling down the trench. No place for me, with only a pistol and no helmet. I swung onto an ambulance. It stopped near the church, and I walked to our house in eerie light and silence. Supply dumps still burned but there was no sound of shrapnel.

Captain Frederick had ordered us to take cover. Now he was waiting on the front steps, checking us in. I was the last, and the only one with a scratch, and that not enough to qualify for a Purple Heart.

At daylight we saw the damage done. "He'll damned sure be decorated," we said of the pilot. For him the mission had been easy. He had come over the mountains from the direction of Ormoc, dipped too low to be picked up by radar, cut his engines until he was on target, dropped his bombs, cut his engines back on. All with no shots fired at him.

We walked in anger and hatred and terror at the devastation wrought by two bombs dropped by one plane—and in the knowledge that the Japs had so many planes while we had so few. We still had no landing strips for our P38s. The bombs had hit at the center of dumps and bivouac areas. They had raised a mounded hill of sand with arms and legs sticking out, with no one knew how many soldiers inside, buried alive. A hundred? Two hundred? A whole unit destroyed, and blackened earth and debris where gasoline barrels and ammunition cases had been stacked.

Percussion had done its damage. Men sleeping in foxholes had died. I came across a young clerk from Corps headquarters staring into a foxhole. I looked down and saw a dead man on his back, his face distorted by a force so strong that it had burst his jacket pockets open. I picked up a square piece of paper and read

29

in blue-ink writing: "This is Duke in his new uniform. I did not have time to get the sleeves and legs altered." I turned it over. It was a picture of a boy in military school uniform. The sleeves and legs were too long. I handed it to the clerk and left him standing there.

Morale sagged. Soldiers became either despondent or trigger-happy. Civilians huddled on the beaches or roamed the military areas. The campaign just started moved relentlessly on, to end God only knew when or where. My patrol for the day was up the beach toward San José and through squatter camps beyond Corps headquarters. In a coconut grove not far from Corps I came upon a field shower: two gasoline barrels punched with holes and set on stilts with a ladder for carrying water up. Under a barrel that had run dry a young soldier stood, naked, motionless, crying silently. I did not stop.

Late in the afternoon, after I had seen more misery among the squatters than I had ever thought possible, I was returning along the beach when a plane came from the direction of Tacloban. I hit the dirt but got up again. It was a Navy plane from one of our carriers. The pilot was hugging the beach, obviously looking for a place to land. As he passed over the Ninety-sixth area, I heard a burst of antiaircraft fire and saw scattered tracer bullets. The plane shuddered, but he kept straight ahead. He had no escape. There was a spume of flame and then smoke trailing black and boiling. Cheers echoed up and down the beach, turning to "Oh, no! Oh, God, no!" in the sudden knowledge that we had shot down one of our own. Not every plane was an enemy plane.

In a twilight noisy with tanks on the road, Gorman and I sat on our steps watching Filipinos struggling toward the squatter camps on the beach near the church. A cry rose among them: "*Japon! Japon! Espía!*" A Jap. We saw him running in the crowd and went after him. Gorman got to him first and threw him to the ground. I grabbed his legs and together we took three live grenades from his pockets. We held him to the ground, a short, scrawny, terrified piece of humanity that in my anger I could not think of as human. He was the enemy—a spy hiding in Filipino clothing. He could have killed us. He meant to see that many of us would be killed.

We could have killed him but did not—not from compassion but for the use we could make of him. He was worth more to us alive than dead. We would make him talk. After that he might get the death penalty, but we doubted it. More likely he would go to a life of safety in a prisoner of war camp.

The MPs took him away. My pistol was still in the holster. I had not fired a shot.

• • •

From the day I enlisted I was pounded with the belief that there were two kinds of generals: the soldier's and all the others. For his general the soldier fought in loyalty and respect; for all the others, he fought because the Articles of War said he must. On the beach at Hollandia, New Guinea, I heard over and over again that General Walter Krueger, Commanding General of the Sixth Army, was a soldier's general. Soldiers who had been through the New Guinea campaign respected him as a fighting man. They loved him because, not a West Pointer, he had worked his way up through the ranks—private, corporal, sergeant—and knew what it was to be an enlisted man. His office was always open to enlisted men—to any soldier who had a serious personal problem or felt he had been done an injustice, but not to the goldbrickers or malingerers. CIC agents had their gripes at being used as combat soldiers but their gripes were not directed at General Krueger.

A story they told may have had some basis in fact. As in other outfits, Sixth Army agents were efficient at scrounging—moonlight "requisitioning." They had made buddies of soldiers in supply, the kitchen, the motor pool. One night at the end of the New Guinea campaign they decided to have a party. A sergeant from supply came with a case of beer; the cook from an officers' mess brought steaks, all trimmed, ready for broiling. Tropical night had dropped dark as a hood. Outside the tent there was the glow of a cooking fire; inside, the white light of a gasoline lantern. Beer loosened the men to laughing and singing. Without warning, a tent flap was pushed aside and an officer stood before them, an officer with stars. General Krueger. The men came to attention and saluted but they could not hide their steaks and beer. The general smiled.

"At ease, men. Carry on. I like to see my men enjoy themselves when they can." As they relaxed he asked, "May I join you?"

With that he took off his stars and, sitting on a cot like any other GI, joined in the eating, drinking, and talking. He could have court-martialed them. Another general might have, but not Krueger.

The story became a legend, told and retold by soldiers on islands Krueger touched, and he touched most of them from New Guinea north. The teller, as if by rote, inevitably ended with "I'd go through hell for him."

We knew that General Krueger was a strong supporter of the CIC. He was in Tacloban. We liked to believe that he had intervened in our behalf at XXIV Corps.

Whether through intervention or circumstances, we were shifted from combat intelligence to counterintelligence among Filipino civilians. As Allied ground troops pushed the Japanese farther inland, security in our rear action areas became more critical. Day and night, Filipinos came through the lines and made their way to refugee camps on the beaches. There was no way for us to tell who among them was friend, who foe, who a Japanese soldier in civilian clothing, who a Filipino infiltrator working for the Japanese. Filipinos with hand-printed identifications were allowed to come and go among military installations, usually without challenge. One of our passwords was "lullaby lane." We never expected it to come back "rurraby rane." It never did.

Early one morning soldiers were setting up a situation map, not at Corps headquarters but in front of the Dulag church, a most unlikely place except for photographing. It was a large map, large enough for the ragged battle line to be visible to the curious on the road. Artillerymen brought up a battery of Long Toms and placed them on the road near the church, the muzzles pointing inland, toward the battle lines.

Before noon we knew that the "I have returned" drama already staged at Tacloban would be reenacted at Dulag. From our front steps we watched several landing craft approach and lower their ramps. I got to the beach in time to see the general himself, Douglas MacArthur, followed by a flutter of aides, step out at water's edge and make the symbolic wade ashore. A crowd was gathering in front of the church. I found myself walking among Filipinos who shouted "*Mabuhay!*"—"Long live!"—to the general. Cameramen moved in, grinding out pictures of the wrecked church, the flattened nipa hut, and a woman near the ruins of the municipal building washing clothes in a fluted tin pan. It was like a professionally arranged tableau.

When I was almost under the muzzles of the Long Toms, the guns let out volleys that shook the earth and sent shells in a trajectory visible all the way to targets in the vicinity of the San Pablo, Buri, and Bayug airstrips, or the road between Burauen and Dagami. The firing appeared staged for the cameras, but it was not wasted. The fight for the airstrips was not over.

As the general approached the situation map, a colonel with a movie camera set up in a personnel carrier tested for light and focus. A colonel with a long pointer touched the combat line where it reached toward Abuyog. The general took a stance I had seen at the Lennon Hotel in Brisbane and in news photographs from around the world.

The shelling stopped. In the silence that followed, a rifle shot sounded and a bullet whizzed through the crowd. I hit the dirt in a dive that threw me against a piece of the municipal building wall. There were more shots, more bullets whizzing. They were coming from under the nipa hut—Japanese guns, Japanese infiltrators; our security breached. American soldiers fired back. A brief firefight, and all was silent. It had been a suicide attack, and it was over. I raised my head. Hundreds of Americans and Filipinos had hit the dirt. Only two were left standing: the general, calmly surveying the situation map, his stance unchanged, and the woman, as calmly washing her clothes.

I have returned. GIs around me were angry. So was I. The pictures, the communiqués, would go out, carefully edited. The world would never know what had happened. There would be stories again of the loyal Filipino people, but no account of how Japanese soldiers had infiltrated so effectively, no conjecture on how they had known the exact time, no speculation on the impact a single bullet could have had on the course of the war. Word would pass

33

on and on that the general was fearless, that he had ice water in his veins. Cameras ground again, and he departed as quickly as he had come. It had been a good show but one not likely to inspire a soldier to say, "I'd go through hell for him."

The breach of security left us at CIC frightened and worried. It had been too easy for the enemy. We watched refugees straggling along the road from Burauen. We would have to inspect more closely, make judgments for or against them, let them go on to the refugee camps or send them to a barbed-wire stockade. Little brown brothers, hell. Word passed around: "You got to keep an eye on the goddamned gooks." We were hardened by the fear of enemy infiltration, and by the soft attitude toward Filipinos set forth in directives from GHQ. Only Filipinos with guerrilla identifications could enter military installations. We knew that any Filipino could declare himself a guerrilla and write his own identification. Directives hastily drawn became ambiguous, ambivalent, contradictory. Agents were forced into snap judgments, some of which they came to regret.

One night I was in charge of quarters when MPs brought in a young Filipino who claimed to be a guerrilla. They had found him wandering around within our perimeter asking for something to eat and a place to sleep. They were afraid to trust his guerrilla card, but afraid not to. Could the CIC give him clearance or should they send him to a stockade?

He stood across the desk from me, not much more than a silhouette against the light of a gasoline lantern. I questioned him about his credentials and the connections of his guerrilla unit. He was indeed a brevet captain as the paper said, he insisted. He had been recruited by Colonel Ruperto Kangleon, the commander of the Leyte guerrillas. His story seemed plausible in every way, but I hesitated.

He leaned toward me. "Ser, only let me stay."

I looked up and saw a circle of raised skin on his cheek, a circle that marred his young, handsome face.

"What's that on your cheek?" I demanded.

There was sorrow in his voice. "Ser, I am a leper."

I believed him and wanted to give him a place to sleep, but a leper? We had no instructions on how to deal with a leper. I asked headquarters medics.

"A leper? God, no. Get rid of him."

I handed him a can of C rations. "You can't stay here. You will have to go."

"But, ser, where can I go tonight? I fight for the Americans but they do not give me a place to sleep." There were tears in his eyes, pleading in his voice. "Ser, only for tonight."

The medics said no. I had to say no. I told him about the refugee camps on the beach. He would find a place there. I sent him, knowing the only bed he would have would be the sand.

He put out his hand but I did not take it. Revulsion rising from Bible stories, revulsion from the sight of a woman's noseless face among the refugees, fear of contamination, fear that his presence contaminated the air I breathed—all of these were part of why I ordered him out into the night.

• • •

A-day plus four. Gloom hung over our part of the beach. Through the night and part of the day before, a naval battle had been echoing outside the entrance to Leyte Gulf and up the east coast of Samar. From one outfit on the beach to another, rumors spread that the Allies were being outclassed and outmaneuvered north and south on the Philippines Sea. The land situation was desperate enough without an attack from the sea. Because of the earlier confusion in landing orders, supply shortages were so acute that the Ninety-sixth had to delay action. The Japanese still held Catmon Hill, with enough firepower to keep combat units pinned down on the beach. A naval commander attached to our unit made his way out to a communications ship and back. Our situation was worse than the rumors. Two, perhaps three, carriers and one cruiser had been lost. Navy pilots were forced to ditch on the beach. Everything seemed to favor the Japanese. He talked anxiously, and then sat on the coconut log in front of our house with his head in his hands.

A runner came from the Ninety-sixth CIC. The Division, still in short supply, still held up by rough terrain and heavy shelling,

35

had been ordered to bypass Catmon Hill and push on into Leyte Valley. The CIC stockade at San José was full of Filipinos under investigation. Corps would have to take over. Their frustrations equaled ours: they did not know which Filipinos to trust; there had been no adequate directive from GHQ on disposition of collaboration cases. The question was sensitive, we all admitted. In public statements the Filipinos were our loyal friends. In reality, they had been under Japanese occupation for three years, and under a Japanese puppet government almost as long. Directives on handling collaboration cases were slow in coming, were political, expedient, and subject to change as situations changed.

Captain Frederick gave a verbal order that made the civilian problem my special problem. He sent me to San José. With my gear on my back and a case of ten-in-one rations on my shoulder I hitched a ride a mile or so up the beach, to a point where military traffic made walking faster than riding. LSTs with their ramps pushed up on the sand poured men, weapons, and supplies on an already overcrowded beach. Rear action soldiers, freshly landed, struggled to get their land legs and keep up with their units. Farther along, artillery outfits, pulled back from the front lines, had stationed their Long Toms under cover of coconut palms. They had trained the muzzles out to sea, to where enemy ships might round the point of Samar.

My ride ended, I hiked past a temporary cemetery with its lines of white crosses and Stars of David, with its new lines of fresh-dug graves. Farther on toward Catmon Hill I came to San José. Dulag was poor. San José, a *barrio* of Dulag, was poorer. In a row of shell-torn nipa palm houses I found the one the Ninety-sixth had left. A Filipino family had moved in. A woman was cooking a handful of rice over a fire on a tray of sand on a raised platform. I told her the house belonged to the CIC and she would have to go. She spoke only Visayan and did not understand. Her husband spoke a little English, enough to say that it was not good for me to stay there, but the reason was not clear. Something about the half-destroyed house next door. When I let my temper show they took their pot of rice and went to find shelter wherever they could.

Faustino, who had been boy for the Ninety-sixth, came and

set up my cot and mosquito net. He brought a bloody Japanese flag and hung it out on the wall to dry. It was mine to take with me. I hung a hand-printed CIC sign on the front and walked through the four rooms, curious at the split-bamboo floors, the bamboo rafters and laths under a nipa-thatch roof. Through it all was what I came to know as the fecal smell of the Orient.

Up the beach toward Catmon Hill an infantry company was probing into a jungly lower slope; another was pulling back, retreating under sniper fire. I came face to face with a soldier with his helmet slung on his shoulder and a red flower sticking straight up from his fatigue hat.

"How was it?" I asked.

"Hell. Cain't see the sons-o'-bitches."

The stockade, barbed wire stretched on bamboo poles, was between Highway One and the water. One MP guarded the gate. Forty or fifty Filipinos—boys, young men, old men—sat or lay in the hot sand, shading themselves as well as they could with palm-frond umbrellas and *abaca* shirts hung on bamboo poles. When they saw me they pushed against the fence begging for food, cigarettes, chocolate bars.

"What you got there?" I asked the MP.

"Bunch of goddamned gooks. You want 'em? You can have 'em."

They were mine all right, at least for a preliminary investigation. The Ninety-sixth agents had been busy. They had assumed that any official in the puppet government was a Japanese collaborator. In the belief that it was better to arrest first and investigate later, they had indiscriminately arrested *población* mayors, *barrio tenientes*—almost anyone accused by anyone else. Only one investigation had been completed, the suspect freed. He was a *barrio teniente* from San José, with convincing guerrilla connections.

The MP let me inside and prisoners crowded around me. "Investigate me. Investigate me," they begged. They pleaded loyalty to the Americans. They hated and feared the *Japones*. "Only investigate me and you will know, ser."

An older man, much older than the others, sat in the sand ten paces or so from me. I ordered the others to sit in rows to wait their turn and went to him. He stood and bowed. With no other greeting he said, "I think the Americans are in great danger."

"How do you know?"

"I have watched them point their guns to the sea. They fear an attack from the sea. I have seen planes land on the beach."

I did not challenge him. So had I. Suspect or not, he was different from the others. I took out my notepad.

"Name and occupation?"

He spoke slowly, quietly, his English marked slightly with an accent that might have been Spanish, or one of the dozens of Filipino dialects.

"I am Mayor Pundavela. The Japanese made me mayor of Tolosa. I did not want to be mayor but the people feared the Japanese and begged me. I am not a spy. I am not what you call a collaborator—"

"Why are you here?"

"I was walking on the road looking for my son. Japanese soldiers took him when they left Tolosa. I was going to Dulag to look for him. In the stockade they began yelling at me and calling me *espía*. The CIC took me and put me in the stockade."

"When?"

"Yesterday morning. I slept on the sand last night. The air off the water was cold and damp, and I have had the tuberculosis. I will be sick."

He looked sick. His body was thin and bent, his face bony and lined. His eyes were feverish. If he was not released soon he would die in the stockade. His answers to my questions were short and too straightforward to be wholly dishonest. He was born while the Philippines were still ruled by the Spaniards. He was a young man when José Rizal was urging independence from Spain. He thought it was good when Emilio Aguinaldo led the revolt against Spain. He was sad when Aguinaldo led the insurrection against the Americans. The Americans were good to the people. The Japanese took too much from them.

His life was a review of fifty years of Filipino history.

"What was your occupation when the Japanese came?"

"Commissioner of Education for the Province of Leyte."

I let him talk.

"When the Americans first came to Leyte there was much fighting, much bloodshed, till General Leonard Wood came. He was good. I went to him and became his boy. I learned English and he made me his interpreter. I took care of his quarters and washed his uniforms—"

Tears showed in his eyes.

"The Americans were good to me. They gave me an education. They let me work with my people. When the Japanese came I still had to work for my people. I am not a collaborator. You do not call me a collaborator, sir?"

I did not answer. My job was to gather information and make recommendations.

"I pity my family," he said. "They need me. My wife does not like to be left alone. My mother is old. She will not understand. Sir, could I send them word?"

The MPs were not strict. They let him send word by a man passing on the road.

Through the afternoon he was my interpreter from Visayan to English, my helper in locating places with strange names like Alangalang and Tabongtabong. He wanted me to understand his people, the Visayans, the people on Leyte. They were poorer and not so well educated as the Tagalogs on Luzon. They had to look to Manila when they needed help. Even the senator who represented them lived on Luzon.

At dark I left the prisoners with the MPs and went to my hut. Faustino had bartered for pink rice, cleaned the rooms, turned away refugees who begged to stay there just for the night. The area was in total blackout. Faustino stuck a strand of coconut oil in half a coconut shell and made a shade with a shelter half. While I wrote reports he watched the house and sky. When tracer bullets rose north or south we took cover in a ditch.

My report on Mayor Pundavela was long and somewhat ambivalent. The Army had not defined the difference between a collaborator who was pro-Japanese and one who collaborated because he saw no other way. I was convinced that Mayor Pundavela was the latter. I ended my report with a plea that in view of his health and prior service to the Americans he be released, or at least placed under house arrest.

When I arrived at the stockade the next morning Mayor Pundavela came to me at once. He spoke, and there was concern in his voice. "I have heard where you sleep. It is not good."

"Why?"

"The man in the house beside you is a leper. The Japanese released him from the colony on Palawan. It is not good to live so near a leper."

I sent word to the *barrio teniente* to turn the leper over to the Army. I also sent word to Faustino to clean the house again with soap and an aerosol bomb.

Between interrogations I talked to Mayor Pundavela about the puppet government, about José Laurel, the puppet president, and his collaboration. Conversations and interrogations were frequently interrupted by refugees wandering up the beach toward Tanauan, down the beach toward Dulag. Prisoners in the stockade studied them intently as they passed. Again and again prisoners pointed out a man or boy and yelled *"Espía!"* "Ser, you must investigate him. I know him. I saw him with the Japanese."

Some I arrested and held for investigation. After a while I no longer trusted their yelling. After a while there was no more room in the stockade.

By nightfall, though I had heard nothing official, I sensed that our situation was better. There were few details, only that the enemy had been pushed back. Faustino met me on the road. The leper had been taken away, not by the Americans but by his family. His family would never let him be taken back to Palawan.

The next morning there were changes in San José and along the road. A bulldozer was pushing the leper's house aside to widen the road. The Long Toms had been taken in the night back to the front. The stockade was gone, vanished, with nothing but a litter of palm fronds on the sand to show where it had been. Infantry soldiers, after having been beaten back so often, were gradually pushing their way up Catmon Hill. On a slope they had taken, I passed a Japanese medical supply dump, poorly equipped, pitifully small. An American dispensary would have much more.

At Dulag Captain Frederick gave me a short briefing. The Navy had won the Battle of the Philippine Sea, and we were no longer under threat of being pushed into the water. The Seventh Division, with the airstrips at Burauen declared secure, had moved west into the Leyte Valley and south as far as Abuyog. The stockade had been moved to Abuyog. My assignment was there, twenty-five miles down the coast, and I would get there any way I could. He gave me a new set of regulations for civilians: they were barred from military areas, forbidden to wear Army issue clothing, prohibited from carrying arms.

It was now 1 November, and we were running behind schedule. Resistance had been unexpectedly strong in some areas. The rainy season had set in, and the roads were soft mud that boiled around truck wheels and tractor treads and flowed like lava into ditches. Streams overflowed. Bridges had been bombed out. Amphibious vehicles became ferries. I hitched and walked the twenty-five miles. It was my thirty-ninth birthday.

Not a heavily fortified town, Abuyog had suffered little from shelling. *Kempei Tai* guards had fled inland when the invasion began. People were living in their houses. On the main street, in front of what had been the *convento*, the priest's house, I found the CIC sign left by the Seventh. It was a large frame house with tiny windowpanes of translucent shells. The rooms were spacious, the bedrooms furnished with beds of bamboo strips woven on mahogany frames, the toilet a back room where the priest could take his comfort in a rocking chair. The priest had fled, to Manila some parishioners thought. There was ample room for me and a radio unit.

The battle line had moved inland, but was close enough for us to see flashes of fire and hear shells exploding. Our communication with advance command posts was by a radio powered by a bicycle unit. Through the night we took turns at guard duty and at pedaling what looked like an exercise machine. Filipino volunteers located Japanese troop concentrations on a situation map. We radioed the information in and watched artillery fire cover the area.

Near midnight Filipinos came to tell us that Japanese soldiers had infiltrated to the edge of town. We doubled our guards and changed our password from "lullaby lane" to "apple dumplings." My post was on a front balcony ten or twelve feet above the street. The night was luminous with tropical light. Just below, thousands of fireflies covered the leaves and branches of a small tree, adding enough glow for me to see Japs, for them to see me if they came. They never came. The sounds of fighting moved farther west.

The Seventh CIC had left their suspects in the municipal jail, among them a woman who had run an "entertainment house" for Japanese soldiers. I found her alone in a cell, angry, profane, bitterly anti-American. Never before had she been in jail. She refused to talk about her Japanese customers. I could see her house for myself—I would find it well run and her girls the best in town— if I would only go with her. I would not. She demanded and then begged to be let out of jail. Following orders, I left her there and closed her house.

The prisoners from San José arrived, and a pavilion near the beach became their stockade. A lieutenant came with them and moved in with the CIC.

"How about Mayor Pundavela?" I asked him.

"He's in the stockade."

"Can he be released? The captain wants to know."

"Not yet. The bastard's lying through his teeth."

"Can you prove it?"

"Hell, yes." He paused. "Not yet but I will."

"Is it all right for me to see him?"

"Yes, Sergeant." He had used my rank as a reminder. "Don't interrogate him. I want some answers to my questions." He wrote an order to the MP guards. "Here. Bring him here now. I'll report to the captain."

I took the order and went to a wooden pavilion on the *luneta*. A wind was blowing mist almost as heavy as rain, wetting the building and the prisoners, who had huddled as close as they could to the landward side. Among them was Mayor Pundavela, looking older, more dispirited. He was wrapped in an Army blanket. I took his hand.

"I thought you would be freed."

He shook his head. "They brought me here."

"How are you?"

I knew without asking. If the tuberculosis had been arrested before, it was no longer so. His skin was dry and burned with fever.

"I am not well. How can I be? When the wind blows, the rain comes under the roof. We have not enough rice. We have the slit trench but the men are not made to use it. We live in filth."

"The lieutenant is waiting to see you," I told him. "Come with me."

Together we walked to the priest's house. While we waited for the lieutenant we sat by a fire on a dirt hearth in the kitchen. A Filipino boy made hot chocolate. The wait was long and we talked. I asked again about General Aguinaldo.

Mayor Pundavela spoke earnestly. General Aguinaldo had been too ambitious, even after his defeat by the Americans. He had signed the loyalty oath but remained the enemy of the Americans. He had welcomed the Japanese invaders, and they had given him a place of great honor.

"How about José Laurel?"

"He was also too ambitious. He wanted to be president of the Philippines. Even from a young man that was his ambition. The Japanese gave him his wish. He is their puppet."

The lieutenant came and read Mayor Pundavela a part of my interrogation report. "Are these statements correct?" he demanded.

"They are, sir."

"Then how in hell could you collaborate with the Japs? Americans have been damned good to you—"

"It is as I said, sir, I did not collaborate—"

"Like hell you didn't. You had to collaborate to be mayor. You sold out. You spied. You—"

He stopped in the rage he had built up.

"Sir—"

"Shut up."

Mayor Pundavela looked at me helplessly. I shook my head. It would be foolish for a sergeant to try to intervene. The lieutenant kept pressing. "All you have to do is admit you were a spy."

"Sir—"

"Admit it."

43

The lieutenant stood up and leaned over him. The mayor was pleading. "Sir, what I did I did for my people."

"Were you a spy?"

"No, sir."

The lieutenant swung his hand. The palm hit one cheek, the back the other. The mayor cringed.

"Sir." I had to intervene.

The lieutenant turned on me. "Get the goddamned gook out of here."

Out in the street I took the mayor's arm and supported him as we walked back to the pavilion. I gave him another blanket and a shelter half and, with a half-embrace, left him.

Later the lieutenant, his manner still belligerent, called me in. "What do you want to do with him?"

"Take him back to Dulag. Ask the captain to run a quick check on him in Tolosa. He could die here. We would have some explaining to do."

"The roads are flooded. How'll you take him?"

"Hitch rides on the beach. Grab anything that comes along."

"What if he escapes?"

"He won't."

"Sergeant, you assume full responsibility?"

"Yes, sir."

"O.K. Sign him out. It's your ass—"

In Dulag I took Mayor Pundavela to Captain Frederick and asked for an immediate review of the case. He listened to my account and said we would skip the review. He would arrange for a release.

At the station hospital I persuaded a medical officer to have Mayor Pundavela admitted for diagnosis. The admitting officer spent a few minutes with him and called me aside. "It looks bad. What's he in for?"

"Charged with collaboration."

"Goddamned Flips."

His response was automatic. I did not argue. "Can I leave him?"

"You can leave him. He won't escape in his condition." He

looked at his notes again. "You'd better notify his family to come."

I sent word by Filipinos on the road. Before the afternoon was over his daughter came on an Army truck. The driver was kind, she told me. A son came and we sat together by his cot. The son was angry. Americans were no better than the Japs, even worse. Dispiritedly I tried to defend the Americans but he would not listen. All he would say was "Look at my father."

Before the release could be secured a Filipino came to the office with a message from the mayor. He wanted to make his deathbed statement in the form of an affidavit. He wanted Captain Frederick to come, but Captain Frederick had been sent to Hollandia as CIC planning officer for the Luzon invasions. He had been replaced by Captain Daniel McGillicuddy, who was willing for me to take the statement.

The mayor was obviously weaker but firm in his determination to clear his name. He dictated slowly while I typed. It was a long statement—a page and a half or so—addressed to the Commanding General, Douglas MacArthur. It was the humble statement of a man who had chosen to change his allegiance from the Spaniards to the Americans. It was a passionate denial that he had ever yielded that allegiance to the Japanese. What he had done he had done for his people.

I typed clean copies and he signed it, the signature witnessed by the captain, who assured him that it would go to General Headquarters at once.

"Is there anything else I can do for you?" the captain asked.

"Yes, sir. You can let me die at home."

The captain read through the affidavit again. "You can go tomorrow morning. I will give the order." To me he said, "You will take him?"

It was about the least I could do.

When I arrived at his cot the next morning Mayor Pundavela was dressed in a fresh *barong Tagalog* shirt and white cotton pants. On the trip his spirits were good and he wanted to talk—about how sad he was to see Japanese invaders overrun the land, and how glad he was to see the Americans again.

We came to a frame house on the edge of Tolosa.

"My home," he said.

We stopped in the road and I helped him down. There was a sound of doors opening and running feet.

The first to come out was the son who had been taken by the Japs and later rescued by soldiers from X Corps. He took the mayor in his arms and sobbed, "Papá, Papá." Two daughters knelt to kiss his hands and then put their arms around him. The son threw himself to the ground and rolled and cried. Two women came out, his wife and mother, the younger supporting the older. His wife kissed his hands and embraced him. With a wailing cry his mother circled the jeep and came close to him.

His son and I half-carried him up the steps, through a large living room, and into a bedroom. Gently we laid him down on a bamboo-slat bed. Gently we undressed him and covered him with blankets. The son stood at his side, kissing his father's hand over and over. The daughters stood by the doorway crying. His wife and mother knelt, one on either side of him, beads in their hands, praying.

I leaned over to say goodbye. He held my hand and spoke to his family. "You must not feel against him. In all this, he has been my friend."

This did not dispel their resentment, but they shook my hand, and the son went with me to the jeep.

Two days later I stopped the jeep at his house. The son came out alone, his eyes red and swollen.

"My father is dead," he said bitterly. "We buried him yesterday."

"I am sorry," I said and tried to take his hand.

He gripped his hands together and walked away. At the steps he turned. "It is hard to lose a father."

His mother, in black dress and mantilla, came and stood beside him but did not speak.

Again I said, "I am sorry."

There was nothing more to do except to mark his file "case closed."

• • •

Like most American soldiers, I had come to the Pacific Theater with *banzai* and *hara-kiri* in my vocabulary and with contempt in my mind for the little, yellow-bellied, slant-eyed soldiers who were the enemy. Like most Americans I judged a man by his size and not by the power of the gun he held, or the metal in the sword he carried. From the few training films that we had seen, we knew that both gun and sword were pot metal. That knowledge faded in places like Guadalcanal and New Guinea. By the time of the Leyte landing, we had learned that pot metal rifles and pistols can kill. We had also learned that the Japanese would keep on fighting with nothing but a bamboo spear and for nothing but fanatic devotion to the Emperor.

An ancient samurai wrote in his diary, "I am setting out today without a regret, as an unsightly shield for the Emperor," a sentiment I found repeated in diary after diary. American soldiers came to fear but not understand enemies whose psychological makeup was completely foreign, whose motivation was political and military, and at the same time religious and moral. Japanese soldiers were shaped by the requirements of traditions Americans did not know and could not understand. American soldiers had to memorize the general orders and read the Articles of War. Japanese soldiers had to memorize five sections of the "Imperial Rescript" set forth in 1889. Soldiers were made to believe that these five articles, divine words of the Emperor, were the grand way to heaven and the universal law of humanity. In fact, these articles had opened the way for the political and military expansion that began with the march into Manchuria and erupted in World War II.

Tenno Heika! Banzai!—the cry of warriors going into battle—"Long live, Oh, Emperor Most High, Heavenly King." It was the war cry across Manchuria and into China. It was the final command in the code used for the attack on Pearl Harbor. It was ritualistic and religious, subverted by the military, made fanatically patriotic, made eternally rewarding. Enshrinement at Yasukuni Shrine on Kudan Hill in Tokyo was the glorious reward for those killed in combat. They immediately became soldier-gods. Before battle they could bolster each other with the admonition "Hold death light as a feather." They could cling together in the belief that their struggle against the enemy would be continued after death. One soldier wrote in his diary on 13 October 1943:

Those detestable American forces! I will not settle it just by killing them alone. If I should be so unfortunate to die from an enemy bullet, my soul will positively chew to death the American forces. Until the American forces surrender, I will not be able to go to Yasukuni Shrine feeling at ease.

Disgrace, loss of face, would be his lot if he failed to overcome the enemy; a greater disgrace would fall on him and his family if he surrendered to the enemy. He was given a general order: save the last bullet for yourself. This was the tradition of *Bushido,* the way of the ancient Japanese warrior, now the code of the soldier of lowest rank.

Hara-kiri, often called "harrycarry," is the word Americans use for the Japanese *seppuku,* suicide by disembowelment. It was a samurai tradition practiced in the Southwest Pacific, either to show disgrace over failure in battle or to avoid being taken prisoner or to atone for some ephemeral sense of disrespect to the Emperor. It was a cult of the sword, or the bayonet if a sword was not available, or a bullet as a last resort.

Kamikaze, suicide attack by plane, was born in desperation in the summer of 1944, born in the belief of divine intervention. According to legend, when Kublai Khan tried to invade Japan in 1274 and again in 1281, the gods sent a divine wind in the shape of a typhoon that destroyed all the enemy ships. The *Kamikaze* attack, named for that wind, originated among navy pilots and was a mixture of Emperor worship, loyalty to the homeland, and desire for an honorable death in the tradition of *Bushido. Kamikaze* was a special task force, with volunteers preferred, and its members had to go through purification training in the Shinto manner. Their expressed aim was to sacrifice life and plane to bolster Japanese morale and inspire terror in the enemy. In the latter goal they succeeded.

Ordered to duty 19 October 1944, the *Kamikaze* made their

first official attack on 25 October 1944. I may have seen it. I certainly saw one of the earliest. In Dulag in the middle of an afternoon I heard a plane coming from over the mountains, coming directly toward us at less than a thousand feet up. It was Japanese but not a Zero. It was coming at an angle that would take it directly into a troop ship anchored offshore. It came closer, so close that I could see the pilot's face, the set of his jaw, the white ceremonial scarf around his neck. His machine gun was strafing troops and dumps, so near that I could see where bullets kicked up dirt. With a whistle of wings cutting through wind he crossed the beach. He kept on target and with a crash of metal on metal went nose first into the transport. Flame and smoke rose, first from the plane and then from the ship. Soldiers swung themselves over the rails and into the water. In a few minutes no more came over the rails. In a few minutes more the steel plates amidships were a shimmering red. A funeral pyre, the ship was gutted to the waterline. If sacrifice was a way to Yasukuni, the pilot had made it. Soldiers who reached the shore would not talk to me. They wandered in a daze, their words disconnected mutterings of fear and grief and hatred.

A plane had been traded for a ship, one life for hundreds of lives, in a kind of action for which Americans had no understanding, no psychological defenses, nothing but angry determination to kill, kill, kill, and never take a prisoner. American soldiers relied on man and machine and vaguely perceived principles of loyalty and morality in a world in which the individual counted. Japanese soldiers lived and fought and died under strict thought control, their minds filled with memorized slogans such as "Liberalism and individualism are the dirt which must be removed," teachings dutifully set down in diaries and repeated in assemblies of any size.

Morning or distant worship was a daily reinforcement. In formation Japanese soldiers faced the east, or the Emperor's palace, or the traveling shrine that housed photographs of the Emperor and Empress, if their unit had one. Then with sharp claps of their hands they summoned their gods, as in some cultures servants are summoned. The commanding officer or someone appointed by him read the Imperial Rescript declaring war. Thus they fortified their belief that divine guidance was with them and that divine destiny to create the Greater East Asia Co-Prosperity Sphere had been set for them.

A spirit similar to that of the *Kamikaze* developed among soldiers of the parachute forces, though suicide was not a required part of their mission. "The Attack Song of the Parachute Force" ends not in sacrificial death but in a boast of victory:

Suddenly they pour out of a rain of rapid fire,
And resolutely attack. Now in the blood-spattered stronghold
The sun flag is raised. The day is theirs.

At Dulag we were attacked first by the *Kamikaze* and then by the parachutists, the first without warning, the second with warnings too lightly taken. From captured documents we knew that Japanese parachutists planned attacks on the airstrips around Burauen, but XXIV Corps intelligence officers chose to question our own intelligence reports and to belittle Japanese capabilities. The Corps had other priorities: to push on with the drive that would end with the capture of the main Japanese forces at Ormoc and to restore captured airfields and make them operable. Both had been slowed and hampered by rain that toward the end of November fell on an average of an inch a day. While we fought mud, the Japanese were able to bring heavy reinforcements to Ormoc by sea.

Four of the airstrips—Dulag, San Pablo, Bayug, and Buri—lay on or near the road from Dulag to Burauen, the farthest six miles or so from Dulag. Heavy equipment churned the road into a lake of mud; engineers fought mud on the runways with metal mats and gravel. Costs in man-hours and equipment seemed excessive, results dubious, but there were shouts along the beach when the first P-38 came in. Other planes landed. Units of the Eleventh Airborne Division were moved in to protect operations.

The Japanese command read the situation correctly. If this buildup was allowed to continue, communication between their southern forces and Japan would be cut. In desperation they planned a combined ground troops and parachutists attack for the night of 6 December. By 27 November, XXIV Corps knew their plans in detail, but decided that the Japanese would not be able to put them into effect. Parachutists could be dropped, but they could not coordinate with ground troops. The XXIV Corps decision was to put the troops at the airfields on alert and order them to have arms and helmets ready at all times. They misread Japanese desperation, Japanese willingness to sacrifice themselves in a suicide attack.

At 0245 on 27 November three transport planes attacked. One crashed in the water, one on the beach, the third on the Buri airstrip. XXIV Corps decided that this was a suicide mission and diversionary only. Our combat intelligence units, concentrating on the drive toward Ormoc, had not discovered that Japanese ground troops were converging on the airfields. There were some air attacks, so accurate that we suspected that they were getting spot signals from the ground, from pro-Japanese Filipinos. We alerted some selected guerrillas, tightened our own security, and waited. Tension increased. More soldiers went to Mass.

Just before dark on 6 December we were sitting outside when we heard planes over the airfields and saw parachutes opening— the white blossoms of the parachutists' song. There were yells of "Take cover!" and "Put out that goddamned light!" We piled under the house, bumping each other, falling on each other, thrashing for space. A bomber came over the Dulag strip, headed in our direction.

Matsumoto, who had been translating diaries upstairs, came down quietly and crouched near the steps. For an instant he turned on his flashlight.

"I knew it," an officer yelled. "Signaling. Goddamned Jap." He threw himself at Matsumoto. "Give me that flashlight."

"No. No." Our voices were low, intense. "Not Miles."

Abruptly the officer released him and we huddled together. The plane swept past, machine guns spraying, and crashed in the water down the beach. Bombers and transports and fighter escorts circled in patterns that brought them over us. Antiaircraft batteries opened up along the beach. Red and green tracer bullets rose like water in a fountain. Still the planes came. One strafed the beach, so close that we could see the bursts of machine gun fire and hear the splat of bullets. We hugged the ground and waited. Suddenly

Matsumoto could no longer take the strain. He ran out, a slender silhouette in flashing fire, shaking his fist, yelling "Goddamned Japs." As quickly, he ran back.

Planes went down, some in flames, some not. Bombs hit P-38s on the ground and left them burning a lurid light. Parachutists caught soldiers asleep and bayoneted them in their blankets. Parachutists who missed their targets came down away from the fields, either to die or be captured. Japanese ground troops fought their way in and held parts of the field.

Within an hour runners brought captured documents to our office. Anxiously we watched while Matsumoto, a stunned look still on his face, put pieces of maps together. He soon knew that each parachutist had been given a piece of a map and an attack plan dittoed on rice paper. Patiently he put maps and then orders together. There were to be three attacks: the first at 1800, the second at 2400, the third at 0600 the next morning. The information went to Corps. We could only wait and watch and listen for the next attack. It never came, but there were enough Japanese on the airfields to destroy planes and rout American defenders, in an attack well planned, in a manner desperate but arrogant.

A large detachment had descended on the San Pablo strip, a smaller one on Buri. Those on San Pablo ran up and down the field yelling not "*Banzai!*" but, in English, "Hello, where are your machine guns?" At Buri, American soldiers, service troops, not prepared for such an attack, fled, leaving guns and ammunition behind. Soon Japanese soldiers were firing American weapons at American soldiers. There was no way for anyone to tell friend from foe. Relentlessly, the Japanese attacked. Doggedly, Americans held on to what they could, waiting for daylight and reinforcements.

At daylight 7 December—Pearl Harbor three years past—I went down the beach to search the crashed bomber and Japanese pilot. Two soldiers in a small boat helped me get the pilot out of the cockpit and to the beach. His gear, strapped to his body, weighed as much as he did. He was armed with a Luger-like pistol and a kind of rifle I had not seen before, with belts of ammunition for each. The rifle, broken down, was strapped to his legs, barrel on one leg, stock on the other, with ingenious locks for rapid assembly. On top of his parachute pack he had strapped three Molotov cocktails, glass jars that looked like elongated Mason jars. They had cracked; gasoline shone irridescent over him.

With my Boy Scout knife I cut his belt in front and ripped identification tags from his uniform. Carefully I untied his thousand-stitch belt, the stitches uneven crosses, red on white, sewn by family and friends as a talisman against the kind of fate that had befallen him. Pressed under his tunic I found a Navy flag, white with a red sun and rays reaching out like spokes on a wheel. Then I rolled him over, ripped open his back pockets, and took out his wallet and diary. Soldiers angrily demanded and got the yen notes in his wallet. I left him on the beach and went straight to G-2. Officers broke their huddle over a situation map and took the things I had brought. The parachutist's rifle was the first of its kind to be reported. It would be forwarded to Sixth Army at once. They needed information on the plane.

Back to the beach I went. Filipinos had stripped the pilot bare. An American sailor, they told me, had cut off his genitals and taken them for a souvenir. He lay there in the sun, stocky of build, light of skin, with only the slightest tinge of the yellowbelly. I got the plane dragged to shore but I might as well have left it in the water, for American souvenir hunters defied me and crawled all over it, ripping off strips of aluminum and copper wire to be made into jewelry. What I could take back to G-2 had no intelligence value.

No matter how much I hated the Jap, I felt that he could not be left there to rot between a Filipino refugee camp and the Seventy-seventh Division area. I commandeered a six-by-six and with the help of the soldier drivers lifted him in. They did not like the job. They touched him with loathing. At graves registration, the only place I knew to go, the noncoms in charge wanted no enemy dead, under any circumstances. For all they cared he could be dumped in a ditch. "Take him away, goddamn it." I was stuck with a dead Jap, two angry soldiers, and no authority to appeal to. The soldiers had a way out. They knew another place and would take him there. I would not have to go. They may have been lying. I watched them drive away and hiked back to Dulag.

Not until the next morning were the Americans able to organize an effective offensive. By then the Japs had dug themselves in and the going was tough, but the Americans had the advantage in men and materiel. Any help the Japs expected never came. At the last it was a genuine suicide attack, with most of the Japs dead, only a few taken prisoner.

By then we were convinced that pro-Japanese Filipinos had done their work. From guerrillas we learned that a Filipino down the road toward Abuyog had been seen flashing a light the night of the parachute attack. A guerrilla took me aside. "Ser," he said, "if you will only go with me we will find him."

We crossed the Daguitan River on a temporary ferry and hiked across swamps and rice paddies till we came to a nipa hut half-hidden by banana palms. The man was sullen, suspicious. His English was not good but good enough for him to tell me how much he hated the *Japones*. He said he was a guerrilla. I did not believe him. I searched his house but found no flashlight—only pieces of American Army uniforms, enough that he might pass as a guerrilla. He claimed that American soldiers had given them to him. When he said that he knew nothing about the flashing lights I arrested him. I told him that he was lying and that he would have to go with me. He protested. I threatened. His wife and children crowded around him touching him and crying. He begged for pity. I had no pity for him. I had to take him. The guerrilla took one arm, I took the other, and we dragged him till he was willing to walk.

In a back room at the office I carried on an interrogation that was long and frustrating. He knew too much—the *Kempei Tai* and the house we were in—but there was no way to connect him with the signal lights except to force him to confess. He would not, no matter how much I promised or threatened. I called the guerrilla in but he was no help. He wanted me to use methods used by the *Kempei Tai*: hanging by wrists or ankles, driving bamboo splinters under fingernails, forcing the prisoner to drink water till he vomited. At dusk I gave the Filipino a can of C rations and handcuffed him to a tent pole. He might change his mind by morning, or I might find someone who would testify against him.

When we were in total blackout a plane came over, flying low, searching for a target. I took cover under the house, near the captain. When the plane had gone the captain spoke sharply. "He might have been killed in the strafing. Did you think about that?"

I had not.

"It would have been an atrocity. You could have been court-martialed for an atrocity against a civilian. It would have gone hard with you."

The captain, as I had seen him, was religious, moral, and strict in interpreting the law. In this case I knew he was right. I took the cuffs off but the man did not run away. The guerrillas took him.

On 10 December the Japanese made what was their final attack on the airfield. The Americans were ready and drove them back with heavy losses. For the Americans the attack was costly. For the Japanese it was more so in suicides alone.

11 December 1944. The battle for the airstrips was over, Ormoc was under Allied control, GIs with flamethrowers were burning Japanese soldiers out of their caves and pillboxes in the mountains. Japanese stragglers and deserters hid in the jungles, escaping the Americans, escaping the Filipinos, reduced as they had been in New Guinea to surviving on leaves and roots and each other's flesh. One campaign had ended. We were waiting for the next to begin.

Waiting and working. I was assigned to work with a civilian population that was disoriented, dispossessed, disillusioned, in many cases angry, bitter, sullenly silent over what had happened to them. Not since the Aguinaldo insurrection against the Americans had there been fighting in Leyte. Never had there been so much death and destruction. The Americans had returned, but at what cost? Better to have lived under the Japanese, anti-Americans said.

The fighting over, refugees drifted away from the beach camps back to their rice paddies and nipa palm huts. In monsoon rain they waded barefoot in mud and water, scantily clothed, sheltered by banana palm leaf umbrellas. On patrol to *población* and *barrio*, to church and government building, I saw the sadness of families as they returned home. Sometimes there was nothing left—not a house, not a carabao, not a pig, not a chicken—the crops ground to slush under the treads of Army vehicles. They searched in grief for what they had lost, the grief greater if the loss included death. I saw sadness change to despair at what lay before them. They could build a new hut in a few days, but the rice and banana crops were lost for the season. Without rice there was only starvation. I walked among them, sympathized with them, all the while feeling alien among people who had been under the same flag with me for forty years.

Our work was serious but haphazard, the problems of numbers too great, the military directives ill-defined. The few directives we had were sketchy and had been written under the assumption that local government would be intact. In the areas where I worked, government both civil and religious had broken down completely. I never found a priest to interrogate. Mayors and *barrio tenientes,* victims of early arrest, wore out their days in stockades, waiting for someone to hear their cases. Officials who could have remained in their government posts went into hiding or joined guerrillas to keep from being arrested by the CIC. Civilian control was left in the hands of temporary police and guerrillas.

Guerrilla power became a problem, not major but a problem nevertheless. On 28 October 1944 President Osmeña had by executive order decreed that members of recognized guerrilla units would become members of the Philippine Army. They would be called to active duty by the United States Armed Forces in the Far East, the USAFFE. Their ranks would be recognized by the United States Army and they would receive United States Army pay. The question of rank and pay became more than irritating to American soldiers. It was galling to me that a Filipino who had seen neither military training nor service could with a scrap of paper outrank me and draw double my pay. Bonafide guerrillas with a genuine claim to recognition were soon outnumbered by peso guerrillas, who demanded that the inflated peso be backed by the American dollar. Japanese invasion money—"monkey" or "Mickey Mouse" to American soldiers—had become so inflated that one egg might cost a hundred pesos or more. Americans had added to the inflation by an operation that backfired. They had counterfeited millions of pesos in Japanese invasion notes and dropped them from submarines in drums to float to any island shore.

The Army from the Commanding General down, for political or other reasons, was too soft on the guerrillas. A man of little standing could appoint himself a guerrilla rank and enlist his friends and neighbors in his company. The Filipino sociopolitical system aided him. In pre-Spanish times local control was in the hands of a *datu,* or boss. Spaniards found this system compatible with their own and called the boss the *cacique.* Unhappily this *caciquism* was inherited by the Americans, and was too embedded to be eradicated by their attempts to enforce democratic voting. In guerrilla outfits the *cacique* usually gave himself brevet rank in grade from captain to colonel. The arrogance of one transferred easily to the arrogance of the other. With either, the CIC agent was at a disadvantage.

Unbriefed as we were, we landed on Leyte calling all Filipinos Tagalogs—which we pronounced "Tag-a-logs"—and expecting a Westernized and Christianized culture within the fringes of the Orient. We had to learn that Leyte was one of the Visayan Islands, a chain that lies like a belt between the two large islands of the archipelago—the largely Christian Luzon and the largely Muslim Mindanao. Ethnically and linguistically the people were Visayan; culturally they were still close to the Malayan-Polynesian migrants who were their ancestors, but with thin veneers of the Spanish and American. For three and a half centuries Spanish officials and priests alike had tried to reshape them on the more accessible model of colonial Mexico—accessible because Spanish galleons sailed from Acapulco with Mexican silver to be traded for Chinese silks and spices in Manila, accessible because Spain governed state and church with officials and priests domiciled in Mexico. Whether in church or state, the Spanish attitude was superior and authoritarian, and their efforts at acculturation touched large numbers but with slight impact. Americans, dedicated nationally more to democraticizing, had more impact, but not a great deal more. Japanese, Orientals, operated largely through the military, also with little impact. Under all three the *datu-cacique*-boss system persisted. He was now a guerrilla, backed by the power of the United States Army.

Language was often an insurmountable barrier between Army and people. The CIC was furnished interpreters—Filipino soldiers recruited in the United States, most of them either Tagalogs from around Manila or Ilocanos from northern Luzon. The Visayan language of Leyte was as strange to them as it was to me. In the *población* I tried to speak Spanish but it was of little help. Spoken by no more than 10 percent of Filipinos at the end of the Spanish occupation, it had been reduced to the language of the social and political elite, with the center in Manila. Americans claimed that in one generation they had taught 25 percent of Filipinos to speak English, a figure greatly exaggerated on Leyte. Few in the *población* spoke it well enough to serve as interpreters. In the *barrio* my investigations usually ended at the blank wall of noncommunication. But the Americans had tried. From the beginning of their occupation they had required English of anyone who wanted a civil job. They sent thousands of American teachers, religious and secular, whose mission was to teach English language and American culture through a school system modeled after the American. Japanese officials destroyed American schoolbooks and substituted books in simplified Japanese. In an abandoned *barrio* school I found a fifth-grade Elson and reread "The King of the Golden River." It seemed as much out of place as the Japanese propaganda book in which faces of Filipino children had a Japanese look. Tools of conflicting cultures, both had been left to disintegrate.

Poverty was an impediment to our work in *población* and *barrio*. Leyte had been a poor province under the Spaniards, Americans, and Japanese, and was no more prosperous under the developing rule of the Commonwealth Government. Prospects for a richer life through the independence to be granted 4 July 1946 appeared slender. Under the election system Leyte was treated like a colony. The senator, the chief representative, was elected at large. He was not required to be from Leyte, or to live in Leyte. Intentional or not, it was a way to keep the people poor, the way of life primitive, the moment drowned in *betel* or *tuba* or some other sedative.

Escape was cheap and easy in the drink called *tuba*. Early in the morning a man carrying a bamboo bottle climbed a coconut palm. He cut a notch in a flower stalk and hung the bottle to catch the drip. Late in the afternoon he brought the bottle down full of fermented juice that to some tasted like ambrosia but to Americans more like tannic acid. The effect of a few drinks was numbness and euphoria.

A sense of futility spread among the CIC agents, futility and depression from living and working day after day in heat and dampness that mildewed the soul. They carried investigations as far as they could. The more disaffected signed off with "Leave the Flips to the Flips." As far as they were concerned the Leyte campaign was over. The Luzon campaign was coming up and, dangerous or not, soldiers looked forward to it. The season would be dry. Manila was there. Luzon might be bad but it was not the pits of Leyte.

Christmas Eve came—time to celebrate. We stood in line for our ration of beer, scrounged food from a GI kitchen, traded souvenirs to medics for a bottle of grain alcohol. We sent Mendoza for a Christmas tree. He brought one that looked somewhat like an apricot tree in full leaf. It was only slightly Christmasy even after we had dabbed it all over with tufts of absorbent cotton. There were no presents till late afternoon when our *lavandera* brought our washed and ironed fatigues and a baked chicken with head and claws still on. She tied a string around the claws and hung it on the tree. She had been tortured by Japanese soldiers; hanged by the wrists. When she raised her hands, brown scars were ridges in her brown wrists. We said, "Merry Christmas." She said, "*Mabuhay*." We would not see her again.

We began our celebration with chicken, and alcohol, and nostalgic songs, not any from the Army in World War II, but one that Paul Robeson had made popular, "The Peat-bog Soldier," a song from German concentration camps:

> Up and down the guards are pacing,
> No one, no one can go through;
> Flight would mean a sure death facing,
> Guns and barbed wire greet our view.

59

Several times we sang the refrain in German:

> Wir sind die Moorsoldaten,
> Wir ziehen mit dem Spaten
> In Moor.

The two or three among us who had worked on cases of Americans who had served in the Lincoln Brigade in the Spanish War felt the strength of the plea for Germany, "du mein Heimatland," to return to peace.

From that we went to a rollicking song we had learned from Aussie soldiers down under:

> I have sixpence, jolly, jolly sixpence,
> I have sixpence to last me all my life,
> I have sixpence to spend and sixpence to lend
> And sixpence to send home to my wife,
> Poor wife—

The bitter feelings of "I Wanted Wings," a Navy song out of the Pacific, were those we felt:

> I wanted wings till I got those goddamned things;
> Now I don't want them anymore.
> They taught me how to fly, then they sent me here to die,
> I've got a bellyful of war.
> Oh, I'd rather lay a woman than to fly a goddamned
>   Grumman.
> You can save those fucking Zeros for the other goddamned
>   heroes.
> I wanted wings till I got those goddamned things;
> Now I don't want them anymore.

We went to silent drinking and, when the alcohol was all gone, to singing Christmas carols off-key and drinking canteen cups of *tuba*. It was a sorry celebration after all, and when it was over some went to Mass. Others went across Dulag to *la plaza de las putas,* in search of what they had learned from New Guinea natives to call *pompom.* In a dozen or so coconut oil–lit huts women lived and worked, as they had under the Japanese, and at a price set by the *Kempei Tai*. In a nearby *barrio* young women, young girls, spoke to prowling GIs: "Ser. Good time, ser? You got cigarettes? Chocolate bar? You geeve me. Good time, ser."

On 26 December we gave up the house that had been our home for two months and, bitching at losing the little freedom we had, moved back to Corps headquarters. It was still in the swamp and our tent was set over a hole nearly waist deep. In the night a monsoon wind lifted a corner of our tent and rain beat in on us. We held on to the ropes till we could hold no longer and had to let the canvas flap. Water rose around our cots and floated anything light enough to float. In the dark and downpour I had to fish to my elbows for my wallet and credentials. In the morning, our gear wet, ourselves damp to the bone, we gratefully received orders to move on to the Sixth Army and higher ground.

All the way to Tanauan we saw ships that would be our convoy to Lingayen Gulf pulled up to the beach or anchored offshore. Loading was underway. So were briefings. Captain Frederick, now in command of the 306th Counter Intelligence Corps, the Sixth Army detachment, met me on my way to one. Saluting was not required in combat zones. We shook hands.

"I requested you by name," he said.

It did not seem right to tell him how glad I was. I did, for the first time, call him by his nickname. "Thank you, Fred."

The only one he had requested from XXIV Corps, the only agent who had worked so much with Filipinos, I was included in discussions of mistakes we had made. Leyte was prelude to Luzon, but it was provincial. Luzon was the center of government, a government fostered and controlled by the Japanese. All of us could see that better directives were needed.

29 December 1944. General MacArthur issued a general proclamation:

Whereas, evidence is before me that certain citizens of the Philippines voluntarily have given aid, comfort and sustenance to the enemy in violation of allegiance due the Governments of the United States and the Commonwealth of the Philippines and

Whereas, military necessity requires that such persons be removed from any opportunity to threaten the security of our military forces or the success of our military experience,

Now therefore I, Douglas MacArthur, General of the Army, United States Army, as Commander in Chief Southwest Pacific Area, hereby do publish and declare it to be my purpose to remove such persons, when apprehended, from any position of political and economic influence in the Philippines and to hold them in restraint for the duration of the war; whereafter I shall release them to the Philippine Government for its judgment upon their respective cases. . . .

Each CIC agent received a copy. Some, the eager and the disillusioned, the anti-Filipino and the anti-MacArthur, took it as a hunting license and the season wide open, with Luzon the hunting ground. Some saw it as too broad, too general, unspecific in defining "certain citizens" and "any position of political and economic influence." From what we had learned on Leyte, it would require us to put a large part of the population of Luzon in stockades. I could find little of what we had learned on Leyte in the proclamation.

31 December 1944. By mid-afternoon our New Year's celebration was underway and we were drinking alcohol cut with fruit juice, mixed canteen cupful at a time. After chow, as we lay in our bunks, trying to be oblivious to a noisy poker game, our talk turned to the invasion. Some of the combat troops would go in on the first wave. In a headquarters outfit, I would land three days later, 12 January 1945.

Rarely among soldiers I knew was there talk of death, of "getting it"—the way our agent friend Woody Hunter had gotten it, a Japanese bullet in the middle of the forehead in a landing—or, if the number was right, of not getting it.

"The way for me to go in," one agent said, "is to know I am not going to get it. The Japs ain't got a bullet with my name on it."

"Hell, yes," another agent said, "you've got to go in knowing you'll come out alive. You know somebody's going to get it, but not you. You don't, you might as well stand up and let 'em shoot you down." There was no general reliance on prayer—might as well trust in fate or luck.

A voice with the sound of conviction came from one of the cots. "If your time's up, it's up and you cain't do nothing about it. What is to be will be."

A quieter voice said, "If I make it I'll meet you at the Manila Hotel."

"It's a date."

Toward midnight a burst of rifle fire woke me. Instinctively I hit the dirt and hugged it. Japs? It had to be Japs. Infiltrators. The firing increased, and green and red tracer bullets whizzed low overhead. It was an outburst of our own, a game, a game that only the reckless would play—in this case headquarters troops who had carried guns three months without firing a shot. They had missed the sounds of combat. Now, letting off steam, not by any kind of plan, they were making the sounds of a fire fight, deadly weapons and live ammunition in their hands. "Stop it. Stop it." Yelling went through the tents, the voices hysterical. "Goddamn it, stop it. Stop wasting bullets." It did not stop. It spread. All up and down the area the rifle fire rattled. Configurations of red and green rose across the sky and men yipped and laughed and swore what we would do to the yellowbellies. It started without a signal, spontaneous, cock-like crowing. It ended without a signal, the passion spent.

In the silence that followed, a voice sounded through our tent: "Goddamn. Somebody coulda got kilt."

Another voice was louder: "Blow it out your barracks bag."

I loved not such a night as this.

THREE

1 JANUARY 1945. Captain Frederick took me to
a military briefing given by a Sixth Army colonel who had been
island-hopping for two years. It was a summary of where we had
been, where we were now, and where we were going. Things had
been bad but they were looking up. A new year. A new objective.
A new date, S-day, 9 January. Another calculated hop toward the
enemy homeland, following nearly three years of knocking out
one Japanese stronghold after another.

There was no boasting, but Allied troops had become increasingly confident, Japanese increasingly despondent, despairing.
From their diaries we knew how much. During a battle in the
jungles of New Guinea a Japanese soldier had written in his diary:
"Isn't God protecting the Imperial Army? Ah, how tragic is this
battlefield! Fellow comrades, are you going to let us die? Even the
spirits of invincible Japanese soldiers are despondent now. Please
God—" Their spirits may have been invincible; their materiel of
war was not. Their bicycles, useless in the jungle, had been discarded on the beach. They had left their cases of horseshoes behind and eaten their horses. Overwhelmed by the strength of Al-

lied men and materiel they wept in rage at "these *Keta*, these hairy white men," wrote poems on the beauty of cherry blossoms at Yasukuni Shrine, and, starving, distributed recipes for cooking human flesh so that it would taste like pork.

Their sense of defeat, apparent in New Guinea, deepened as the combat zone moved north. In less than three months Leyte had fallen, in a campaign that was devastating. Their land losses were great. The battle for Leyte Gulf had crippled their navy beyond recovery. Communication between Japan itself and their forces in the southern islands had been cut. So had their supply lines to oil and rubber in the Netherlands East Indies. Leyte lay athwart their route of retreat as well as of conquest. Regrouping from the south had become impossible.

Their dream of a Greater East Asia Co-Prosperity Sphere faded in the knowledge that the people they had schemed to liberate failed to welcome them and resented foraging soldiers who took their food and animals. Filipinos, co-Orientals, who had welcomed them with parades and Rising Sun flags, turned on them. In a *barrio* near Abuyog I saw two Filipino boys emerge from the jungle with the head of a Japanese swung on a pole between them. They had driven a bamboo pole through his ears, cut off his genitals, and sewed them to his nose. People on the road laughed and jeered; little boys ran after them. By any intelligence estimate Japan had lost the war but not the will to fight, nor the fanaticism that would imbue them till the last beachhead, in Japan itself, had been breached. War correspondents had called Leyte the graveyard of Japanese hopes. The appearance of the *Kamikaze* was taken as a sign, and a warning.

Since 13 December losses from suicide attacks had been heavy. On 28 December they had destroyed ships and lives near Mindoro, on the route the Luzon convoys had to take. Our main convoy for the Lingayen attack was on the way 5 January when it came under a major *Kamikaze* attack, this time with the best planes, the best-trained pilots—pilots fanatic, determined that our ships would not get through, pilots aware of naval defeats, of the fact that the navy, the Imperial forces, had to depend almost entirely on them. The attack was more lethal than Allied intelligence had anticipated. The battle for Lingayen Gulf would not be easy.

On 9 January our CIC detachment struggled to an LST drawn up to the beach near Tanauan looking about as military as so many yardbirds. Lieutenant John Platt, a serious young Ivy Leaguer from Pennsylvania, could not make us snap to. Neither could Mike Horowitz, our topkick, a lawyer from Baltimore. At last we would make the Nips pay for Bataan and Corregidor, but there was neither exulting nor boasting, only glum jostling as we stowed our gear on deck and found our bunks below.

Indian file, silent as Indians on the warpath, our convoy moved out of the Leyte Gulf and into the Surigao Strait. Since we were traveling in total blackout, I stayed on deck and watched as an occasional landmass stood out against a sky lit by the Southern Cross and other, unfamiliar heavenly bodies. Mindanao was on the left and then Negros on the right, sometimes close enough for us to see specks of light. There was little activity on deck, little talking, but there was a huddling together, shoulder to shoulder, hip to hip, bodies communicating the dark thoughts of the mind.

When day broke we were in the calm waters of the Sulu Sea, moving slowly, the convoy spread wide, the camouflaged hulls looking like parts of ships or no ships at all. It was 10 January. Lingayen landings had been underway for twenty hours, long enough for rumors to have spread from ship's crew to us. The landing had been easy; inland it was tough going. Intelligence, relying on guerrillas, had overestimated one, underestimated the other. Chances were we would not land under fire. My mind somewhat relieved, I stood at the rail, alternately reading *Swann's Way* and looking, pondering. I had never expected to pass this way. I would never pass this way again.

We skirted Mindoro Island, where action to divert the Japanese from the Luzon landing was well underway. Not much had been diverted. During the night we entered the South China Sea. From the bucking of the ship I thought we were in a typhoon that might be disastrous for landing, but when I went on deck the sky was clear, the sun bright. We were in one of the roughest stretches of water in the world, and it grew rougher as we moved north. The LST pitched and rolled. One minute, standing in the bow, I could look down the stern straight into the water. The next, I was looking almost straight up at the sky. Seasick soldiers lined the rails. Seasick sailors joined them. For a time it seemed that the divine wind, the *Kamikaze*, might again be intervening.

From a "Now hear this" we learned that we were passing the entrance to Manila Bay, too far out to see land, or the rock called Corregidor. When we were as far north as Subic Bay and Clark Field, there was another "Now hear this," for a general alert sounded. *Kamikazes* had been spotted. All Army personnel were ordered below. I had seen a *Kamikaze* attack, and knowing we could be boiled in oil like sardines in a can, I disobeyed the order. While Lieutenant Platt was trying to herd his men down the ladder I hid under a truck on deck.

Three planes did appear, thousands of feet up, silver in the late afternoon sunlight. Antiaircraft fire opened up from ships to the right and left of us, and it was like Fourth of July fireworks—explosions followed by balls of smoke bursting high in the sky, only the smoke was oily black, threatening. One plane was hit and went down toward the land, out of sight except for a trail of black smoke. One turned back. The third found a target—a Liberty ship—and came down in what seemed a slow-motion spiral. Shells burst around it but the pilot never wavered. I watched, numbed by the inevitability. With a roar and a crash the plane hit the superstructure and skidded into the sea. There was no eloquence among the men who rushed on deck, only low-voiced swearing: "Crazy sons-o'-bitches."

The Liberty shuddered, her course became erratic. We watched her fall behind, an easy prey for suicide pilots. Then reassuring messages came: damage was slight, casualties light. She would have to limp along but she would make it. So would two other Liberties, too far away for us to have seen the attacks. General alert was over. This time the *Kamikazes* had been little more than mosquitoes buzzing an elephant.

Quietly soldiers paced the deck. No one seemed to want to talk. When the sun was low enough not to seem like a spotlight on us the loudspeakers came on, not with the rasping "Now hear this" but with music, soft, soothing, familiar. The mood changed. It was "The Birmingham Jail," sung by a lonesome singer. In a longing for home, a longing to escape what we were in, we hummed, whistled, sang:

> Down in the valley,
> The valley so low-o-o-o,
> Late in the evening
> Heard a train blow;
> Heard a train blow, love,
> Heard a train blow-o-o-o,
> Late in the evening
> Heard a train blow.

The speakers silent, soldiers sat on the deck, almost touching, body to body, but detached, alone, some silent, some still humming the tune.

Dusk came and then the blessed cover of darkness. There was a respite from danger, and we were close to land, close enough to see lights in Filipino houses.

Our landing, scheduled for 1600 on 12 January 1945, was on time. Lingayen Gulf was serene, the waves gently rolling. Before us an uncluttered beach stretched for miles in either direction. Beyond the strip of beach the land was flat, green. Farther on, foothills rose, ridge on ridge, to mountain peaks. Because it was militarily, and propagandistically, strategic, we were landing where Filipino fifth columnists had waved their Rising Sun flags when the Japanese invaders had landed 21 December 1941. Our military objectives were the same: Baguio, the summer capital, was in the mountains to the northeast; Manila was down the Central Luzon plain to the southwest. We knew that General Tomoyuki Yamashita, Japanese commander in the Philippines, had evacuated to Baguio and taken José Laurel and his puppet government with him. Manila was left with caretakers for a government and strong Japanese forces to oversee the caretakers.

Our landing, like the others on either side of us, was quiet, orderly, almost by the numbers as we filed down the ramp and gathered on the sand. The Japanese troops had withdrawn to the hills, leaving only damaged houses and cheering Filipinos to greet us. We were guided past a tangle of tanks and trucks and supplies, past a lagoon to the north of San Fabian, to a place where the tide line ended in low banks. Here we would dig in for the night. Louis Duncan and I found a hole in a sandy bank, too small to be a cave but large enough for us to lie half stretched out, foot to head.

When darkness was full we saw a reddish flash on a mountain to the north and less than a minute later heard a shell cutting through the air, coming in our direction. We heard a faraway boom and then a nearby explosion that rocked the earth and sifted sand over us. On Leyte I had not heard a cannon so large, or felt a shell impact so powerful. Feeling safer outside, we sat on the bank watching flashes and waiting for explosions, each time trying to estimate by the whirr how close the shell would come, at what time we would know it was not a direct hit for us. In between, we said to each other, not eloquently but fervently, "God, I wish they'd stop."

In between, we scouted for rumors. From what we were told, the guns were our own 210s, captured at Corregidor and Subic Bay and now turned against us. The shelling could be a preattack softening-up. If so, we had little but the sea to back us up. Their forces were concentrated on the road between Damortis and Rosario, and in the mountains on a line between Rosario and Pozorrubio. We were in striking distance from either. Their shells kept exploding through the night; flares sent up by our frontline troops shone as signal lights. No kind of counterattack reached our area. When morning came, bright and peaceful, we saw shell craters in the sand, wide enough, deep enough, to bury a Sherman tank.

My direction was to be toward Manila. Captain Frederick had given me verbal orders: Sixth Army had selected an area near Calasiao for headquarters and would occupy it as soon as it was secure. My orders were to secure it. I would have with me Joe Sinay, a Filipino soldier who had been recruited in Manhattan. We were to work with guerrillas to capture or shoot Japanese infiltrators. I was to continue investigations of suspects arrested by the combat CIC unit as it passed through. A truck was loading for Dagupan. From there I would have to hike the remaining three or four miles.

Unshaved, unwashed, I climbed into a six-wheeler loaded with unshaved, unwashed soldiers, who had also been shaken by the night of shelling. We did not look or feel like returning conquerors. We traveled the same highway the Japanese had taken on their march to Manila, a highway described by a Japanese soldier: "The excellent roads of the Philippines which were administered by the world's richest Americans render much assistance to our automobile units."

They rendered little assistance to us. The bridges had been sabotaged by Japanese soldiers retreating to the north, or wrecked by American planes in a kind of overkill. The bridge over the Bued River was knocked out, and the driver turned off the highway near an American military cemetery, the crosses, no longer white, all that was left of the American defense of Lingayen Gulf. We came to a railroad crossing and he took it, straddling the narrow-gauge rails, the wheels bumping on the ends of ties. When we crossed the river I could see neither rails nor ties, only water deep enough to sink us if we went over. At a bombed-out railroad bridge the driver gave up and I had to strike out alone in territory where I knew neither friend nor enemy. A Japanese soldier traveling this way had written in his diary: "They only despise and underestimate us."

Another Japanese soldier traveling the same way had written: "They greeted us with Rising Sun flags and shouts of 'Banzai! Japon!'" I was determined not to be taken in too quickly by Filipinos waving hastily stitched Stars and Stripes or by little boys who yelled, "Hello, Joe. You geeve me cigarette, Joe."

Toward noon I came to Calasiao, three miles southeast of Dagupan, on the railroad that wound down through the Central Plain to Manila. There were people on the streets but the town was quiet. They had welcomed the American soldiers the day before. The most I got was "Mabuhay." In an area where there had been some fighting, Calasiao had escaped. Life went on as usual. Schools

71

were open. Masses were held regularly in the church. A bridal couple, the girl in a white *tierno,* the boy in a tuxedo, drove by in a *caratela* pulled by a Mongolian pony.

I asked for the captain of the guerrillas. He was Captain Guzman and I found him at his house near the church and school. He talked calmly, casually, as if the war had already passed Calasiao by. The Americans had returned. There was fighting, but it was far off. The people were glad. No longer would they have to fear *Kempei Tai* patrols. He had disbanded his soldiers but they could be called up again

I asked about a place to live, an office for the CIC.

"What is this CIC?"

I told him why I was there—why infiltrators and collaborators would be a threat to the Sixth Army.

"Ah," he said, "the CIC were here, but they made no arrests. You will find no collaborators in Calasiao."

Side by side we walked through the streets looking at houses. In the center of town, where two highways intersected at the crossroads of the area, we came to a two-story frame house. The location was good. So was the house. Captain Guzman called the owner to the street and talked with him, first in Pangasinan and then in English. Yes, he would be honored for the CIC to use his house. He had only to move to a smaller house in the back. There was no talk of rent or barter, and I could have the house at once.

I left my gear but not my guns and with Captain Guzman walked through the area that would be Sixth Army headquarters. The ground was high and sandy and there were wide openings among the trees. Perimeters could be easily established between it and Calasiao, between it and the highway. A small guard detail could patrol the area. My report would have been favorable but I had no way to make it.

Supper was at Captain Guzman's house, and the mayor made three at the table. The captain was an urbane man, probably in his late fifties, Spanish in features, military in bearing. The mayor, an older man, had the square face and brown skin of a Malayan. Both had been in schools taught by American teachers. Both spoke English with touches of an American accent. The captain also spoke

Spanish. They remembered living under Spanish rule; they remembered when the Americans took over from the Spanish. They were bitter about the Japanese occupation and repeated what I was to hear often: the Spaniards built churches, the Americans built roads and schools, the Japanese destroyed everything.

The latter was an obvious exaggeration, except as it applied to Japanese attempts to subvert the American-made Commonwealth and replace it with the Japanese-created Philippine Republic and to eradicate all evidences of Anglo-Saxon culture in the Philippines. In a propagandist statement close to a command, Filipinos were told that they were bound to shed the blood and sacrifice the lives of their people in one crucible with the lives of other East Asians. In this they had failed, partly because the Japanese considered themselves superior to other East Asians. Filipinos were ordered to bow to Japanese soldiers, an order that was enforced by the *Kempei Tai*. Now the time for bowing had passed. Japanese government officials had fled from Manila to Baguio in December. Filipino puppets had fled with them. The only government left in Manila was in the restraint of the people.

Captain Guzman opened a bamboo tube and took out an American flag. He had hid it away when the Japanese came. It was now mine because the Americans had returned. It was an emotional moment as we said good night.

Captain Guzman had said I could count on the loyalty of the people. By the time I had completed interrogations at the *municipio,* the church, and the school, I believed him. At each interrogation I asked the people to surrender their Japanese flags. They brought me prewar American flags. The Japanese flag? They would spit on the Japanese flag. What had the Japanese done for them? Taken their *palay* and starved them. Under the Japanese it was a time of fear. At the *municipio* they took me to a room where I waded ankle deep in Japanese invasion currency. Money no good. Take it, they told me.

I had messages to deliver. For six weeks I had lived at a station hospital out from Brisbane interrogating priests and nuns rescued from the Japanese at Hollandia. Theirs was a story of two years of

73

imprisonment, harsh treatment, atrocity, death. The priests were members of the Society of the Divine Word, the nuns from the Sister Servants of the Holy Ghost Order. When I left they had asked me, if I got to Luzon, to tell their story to the priests and nuns there, from whom they had not heard since Pearl Harbor.

I knew the sisters were in a convent in Manila. I was surprised to find that the priests were living in a monastery a few miles from Calasiao, close enough for me to send a Filipino messenger and for Mike Horowitz, my Jewish topkick, and me to go to supper that night.

When we arrived, the priests gathered around us, eager to hear what had happened to the missionaries and missions in New Guinea. I told them what it was like when I arrived at Camp Cable. The priests were pale, emaciated, the ragged clothes on their backs the only possessions left to them when they were captured. The sisters were in their hickory-stripe work habits, paler, weaker than the priests. The mission buildings and farms had been destroyed, the cows, pigs, and chickens killed and eaten. Theirs had been a two-year ordeal of starvation, flight from one part of the bush to another, kickings and beatings. For six weeks I had worked day and night to get their story down. I tried to summarize it for the priests now with a few cases.

Father William Hagan and Father Michael Clerkin were the Americans among them. One day Father Hagan watched Japanese soldiers bring an Allied pilot to camp and take him out again. He and some other priests went to a hillside to watch what they were doing. They soon knew what would happen. An officer gave the pilot a shovel. The pilot dug, and the hole took the shape of a grave. When it was ready, the pilot was forced to kneel beside it. The officer took his sword in two hands and with one blow cut off the pilot's head. The head fell into the grave, the body after it. When the grave was filled in, the soldiers went away singing. One of the soldiers recorded the scene in his diary. It was recovered from his body after a battle.

From the moment I had met the priests I sensed an uneasiness among them. I soon learned the reason. One of the priests had collaborated with the Japanese, spied for them against the Allies, turned in an Allied pilot who later disappeared and was presumably beheaded, and tattled on the other missionaries. He was at Camp Cable but they would not give me his name. My job was to interrogate him, force him to confess, and prepare the case against him. An American sister gave me his name. With Colonel Horton DuBard, commander of the hospital, listening in a cubicle on one side, and Captain Edward McLaughlin in a cubicle on the other, I questioned him, accused him, threatened him, and finally broke him down to weeping and telling his story. It was a strange story of disloyalty and deceit. He had been in charge of the mission sawmills and lumber business. He had worked for the Japanese in order to save them. I wrote his confession in the form of an affidavit. He signed it. MPs took him away handcuffed.

The Bishop Loerks story interested the missionaries most, but for it I had no ending. The Japanese had called Loerks "Mr. Bishop" and accused him of spying for the Allies. He probably had spied. As captain of his own boat he was able to go from one mission station to another on the islands of the New Guinea coast. On one of the islands the Japanese had arrested him, some Protestant missionaries, and civilians, including several children, and placed them on a warship. The missionaries had never learned their fate.*

---

*Following the war the story of Bishop Loerks and his colleagues was exposed during the war crimes hearings in Australia and reported by Father Ralph Wiltgen, SVD.

After Father Loerks, the other missionaries, and two Chinese children were put on board a warship, they were taken to Lorengau in the Admiralty Islands, under intimations that they would be taken from there to a mission station near Rabaul. At Lorengau other missionaries were brought aboard, including some Protestants, among them a couple with a child. There were now more than sixty on the ship. From there they were taken to Kavieng and then toward Rabaul, their disposition decided but not told to them.

Soon after they left Kavieng the Japanese rigged up a gallows in the

There were expressions of compassion, and then a moment of silence.

"Do you want to go back?"

"We want to go back."

The night before the Sixth Army headquarters moved in, Captain Guzman came to me at dusk. One of his guerrillas had reported that three Japanese soldiers had infiltrated the area—scouts on a reconnaissance patrol, he thought. They were in a schoolhouse three miles away. He would not call his guerrillas and alarm the people. He and I would kill them. We would surprise them in the darkness. He saw no trouble. I saw nothing but trouble, but I knew I had to go. I would have to report to Sixth Army the next morning.

An hour after dark I took my pistol and carbine and met Captain Guzman in the street near my house. We crossed the river on a railroad bridge and for a mile or so traveled almost silent on hard-packed road. Then for a time we crept over the dry patches and rough ridges of rice paddies. When we were less than half a mile from the school we picked up a trail between two rows of bamboo.

"You will lead," he whispered. "I will keep you covered."

Though my eyes had adjusted to the darkness, I felt rather than saw the trail. With one hand gripped on my carbine, the other reaching ahead, I kept as steady a pace as I could. When I thought we had to be near the school, there was a sound of footsteps, a

---

stern and shielded it from view with tarpaulins. The captain set the ship at top speed. One by one the missionaries were separated from the group and taken out through a tarpaulin tunnel. On the deck they, including the nuns, were forced to strip to their underwear. Then, with their hands tied, they were hoisted to the gallows beam. One by one Japanese servicemen shot them, cut them down, and let them drop into the sea. Because of the ship's speed there was little blood to be cleaned up.

The three children were left. Japanese sailors gave them bananas to eat and then tossed the children overboard.

strange sound of footsteps. Before I could stop, my hip and side brushed against something soft and warm and moving. I jumped back. Before I could hit the dirt Captain Guzman grabbed my arm. A voice, a Filipino voice, gave a low, startled cry. I was against the flank of a carabao, touching a rider astride, all of us at a stop.

Captain Guzman spoke softly in Pangasinan and then asked, "*Japones?*"

"No. No *Japones.*"

Captain Guzman had to see for himself. We went to the school, and after watching and listening and waiting, crept in, our guns at ready. There were no Japanese, and no signs that they had been there. We kept watch till midnight and went back to Calasiao.

Before I could make my report the next morning Captain Guzman was at my house. "The Japs were there—at another school, not far away. Seven of them." And then, "It was better so." That was his way of saying that with seven against us, we would have been dead. He had sent guerrillas after them, but they were too late. The Japs had escaped north to the mountains.

Sixth Army moved in and I made my report. My first nights at Calasiao I had heard Zeros flying low and seen flashes like lightning toward the mountains. Now there were no Zeros. There were Japanese stragglers but they were not a threat. Daily I watched the situation map at Army headquarters. Combat units, hard pressed at first, gathered speed as they overran Rosario, Pozorrubio, and towns as far east as Cabanatuan. Sometimes battle lines on the map had to be changed hourly. Casualties were staggering but enemy losses were greater. A special communiqué circulated through headquarters: the prisoner of war camp at Cabanatuan had been overrun and the American prisoners freed.

Captain Frederick came to me not with an order but with a quite unmilitary request. Colonel Elliott R. Thorpe, commanding officer of the Counter Intelligence Corps in the Southwest Pacific, had landed at Lingayen and would come the next day to inspect the Sixth Army CIC operations. We had to plan something to honor him. As a sergeant I had never expected to entertain a colonel at dinner, but that was what Captain Frederick was suggesting—a Filipino dinner, with Filipino food, a Filipina as hostess, young Filipinas to serve the table—with little more than twenty-four hours to get ready.

Joe Sinay insisted on a *lechon,* a roast pig, a celebration in true Filipino style. Though an Ilocano, he knew the Pangasinan language well enough to buy or barter for the pig, bananas, mangoes, and a chicken for a stew. The pig would be made into *barbacoa* in a pit dug in our backyard. It was good, he told the people, that the colonel was coming.

By dawn the next morning the pig was roasting and Filipino boys were cleaning and polishing our living room and setting up borrowed tables and chairs. Men and women brought gifts of *palay* and *muscovy* sugar and flowers, and loans of silver and china and an embroidered pina cloth and napkins, treasures brought out from hiding. Gently but firmly the women took charge. "It is for the colonel," they said. "It is an honor that he will come to Calasiao."

By mid-afternoon the room looked as if it was ready for a part in a *barrio* fiesta. Did the colonel like bourbon? I thought so. Someone brought Sinay a bottle labeled "bourbon type whiskey." It tasted somewhat like *sake* mixed with newly fermented fruit juice and brown sugar.

Before it was time for the colonel to arrive, the women came up the steps in a group—a hostess, several guests, several women to serve the table. All were dark-haired, dark-eyed, but in facial structure there were stamps of the many bloods that mingled in their veins—Malay, Spanish, Chinese, Anglo. All wore the traditional dress—the *tierno*—with long skirts and sleeves puffed high at the shoulders, a frame for throat and lower jaw. They also wore *bakia*—wooden sandals with native scenes carved and painted on the heels. At the sound of a jeep stopping outside, the women drew close together, holding their smiles as if they were waiting for a camera click.

Colonel Thorpe paused in the doorway long enough to take in the scene, and then entered. Captain Frederick and officers I did not know followed him. After brief introductions the hostess seated Colonel Thorpe at one end of the table, Captain Frederick at the other. *Mister* for the evening, I was given a place in the middle. After a speech welcoming the brave Americans, the hostess took her place next to Colonel Thorpe. For a moment everyone was quiet, in what looked like a carefully arranged tableau. We were five hundred miles or so from Leyte; the difference in absorption of the cultures of Spain and America was incalculable, absorption without obliteration of the Malayan.

There were attempts at lightheartedness, at making the evening seem like old times, but the fact of war kept the conversation subdued. Incidents of invasion and occupation kept intruding. Past this house in December 1941 Fil-American troops, a hastily combined Filipino and American Army, had retreated before the Japanese invaders.

"We pitied them," the hostess said.

The Japanese occupation followed.

"We hated them. The *Kempei Tai* came often. They were the worst."

Now they would never again patrol Calasiao. Calasiao was free. But not the Philippines. Manila was on our minds. We could only imagine how many Japanese had to be overcome between us and Manila.

After the *leche flan,* after the GI coffee, Colonel Thorpe rose and we rose with him. The dinner was over. Men shook hands, women curtsied. The colonel spoke his pleasure and went down to the jeep.

In the middle of an afternoon a truckload of Americans rescued at Cabanatuan stopped in front of my house. I knew that John Owens, my nephew, had been at Cabanatuan. I also knew that he had been on the Death March. I climbed up a side of the truck and came face to face with men who had been three years in prison. Their uniforms were new, their faces thin from starvation, or puffed with beriberi. They stared at me with eyes sunken and dulled with suffering and, I felt, reproach. They were the victims of Bataan and Corregidor. They were the ones who, when no help came, sang, "No mama, no papa, no Uncle Sam." They had a right to be bitter.

"Anyone know John Owens?" I asked.

They looked at each other silently and then a young soldier spoke. "You mean Peapicker? There was a Peapicker Owens at Cabanatuan last year."

"From Texas?"

"Yeah, from Texas. Tall guy from Texas."

"Yeah, old Peapicker. They took him to Japan last year. Last I heard, he was put on a ship in Manila Bay. Hope he made it. Some ships was sunk before they got out."

"Was he all right?"

"About like the rest of us."

The truck started moving. They were on their way home.

Late at night a Filipino came to our door, sent by the Sixth Army, he said. He was a guerrilla and had been to report to Sixth Army. He had to go back toward Manila. All he wanted from us was to sleep on our floor.

Sinay objected. "We'll get lice."

I thought of the man with leprosy. Better lice than leprosy. I let him stay.

He talked of his life as a guerrilla—always on the run from Japanese patrols, hiding in the mountains, striking when he could. Now he would have help from the Sixth Army. In front of our house he hitched a ride on an Army truck.

I believe his name was Ramón Magsaysay.* Magsaysay's guerrillas were recognized 1 February 1945 in the Zambales Mountains.

• • •

---

*Ramón Magsaysay (1907–57) became in the early fifties secretary of national defense; from 1953 to 1957 he was president of the Philippines.

80

The final Sixth Army briefing was a quiet, solemn, at times contemplative meeting with all the brass present except General Krueger. The meetings were held on the Calasiao side of headquarters, in a grove that shaded us from baking heat, away from the noises of kitchen and housekeeping and general camp life. Though no one wore insignia, I saw that I was the only enlisted man among thirty or more officers. I could only think that I was there at the recommendation of Captain Frederick, who had gone ahead with an advance unit. The briefings followed a pattern and language pounded into my head at Camp Ritchie: an operations officer reviewed the last day's progress, an intelligence officer listed estimated Japanese troop concentrations and possible problems with civilians, others talked of pontoon and Bailey bridges and the problems of transporting personnel and supply.

All the briefings were related to a situation map that showed a bulge down the Central Luzon Plain, with an arm reaching west across the Zambales Mountains toward Subic Bay. The operations summary was terse. On 29 January the Thirty-seventh Infantry Division had pushed down Highway Three and, after intensive fighting, had captured Clark Field and Fort Stotsenburg. While Japanese were still shelling from western perimeters General Krueger himself raised the Stars and Stripes at Stotsenburg. On the same day the Thirty-eighth Infantry Division had landed near Subic Bay, after a naval shelling so severe that for miles up the Zigzag Pass trees stood like bare poles, the limbs scattered like so many matchsticks. To the east, the Flying Columns of the First Cavalry Division, fresh from victory at Cabanatuan, were clearing resistance on Highway Five down as far as Plaridel, almost in striking distance of Manila itself. The Eleventh Airborne had landed and was approaching Manila from the south.

Place names as strange as Plaridel, names familiar to my eyes but not to my ears, showed large on the map: Arayat, Dinalupihan, Hagonoy, Calumpit. Calumpit was militarily the most important. Twenty-five miles south of Clark Field, the same distance north of Manila, it was at the only crossing of the Pampanga River from western Luzon to Manila. Here, on 1 February 1942, General

Jonathan Mayhew Wainright had held back the invading Japanese long enough to buy a little time. Now the Japanese could be expected to hold the highway and railroad bridges as long as they could before destroying them. The crossing had to be taken. The Candaba Swamp lay to the northeast; to the west, swamps and fish ponds and interlacing streams stretched to the shore of Manila Bay. Calumpit was at the little end of the funnel.

Intelligence briefings were given by Colonel Horton V. White, the Sixth Army G-2, the officer the Counter Intelligence Corps reported to, the officer who decided which of our reports should be marked for special attention at GHQ. A man strikingly tall, ruggedly broad in face and shoulders, he was easily visible on headquarters streets. I had not come face to face with him before. He spoke quietly of general civilian problems. For the first time the fighting would be in densely populated areas. If Manila had to be taken by force, protection of civilians would become crucial. In 1942 the Americans had elected not to defend Manila and had declared it an open city. It was hoped but not assumed that the Japanese would do the same. There was no reliable intelligence either way, no information on the number of Japanese troops in Manila, or their materiel and morale. Bottled up like rats, they might fight to the death of the last man.

White also briefed us on the Hukbalahap, the Communist movement in Central Luzon. Their guerrillas had helped free American prisoners at Cabanatuan, but in their zeal had come close to turning deliverance into disaster. The Army knew little more about them, and that not enough to take an official position regarding them. Colonel White's own concern was evident in his talk.

An officer whose first name was Joy explained how troops would be committed, and how reserves would be brought up to replace casualties. There was no elation in his face or in any of the other faces. For almost three years I had been absorbed in the burdens of the enlisted man. In sudden illumination I saw that officers also had their burdens, among them the burden of ordering men to battle, to certain death for an undetermined number of them. General Krueger himself had to share it. Not that day but the next and

82

the next, promises and decisions reached the scuttlebutt stage. General MacArthur had promised General Eichelberger that the Thirty-seventh Division would have the honor of entering Manila first. Then he promised the commanding officer of First Cavalry that his division would have that honor. Thus MacArthur set up a competition—a diabolical competition at least partially responsible for the needless loss of unnumbered lives and for the destruction of Manila, indeed the Pearl of the Orient.

There had been hope that the entrance into Manila would be made on General MacArthur's birthday, but that day had passed. On 30 January, General Krueger ordered the First Cavalry and the Thirty-seventh to drive on Manila. Now the competition was for the glory of the outfit. By the time they reached Calumpit, the troops had proved that an army bent on sudden conquest can be as disorganized as an army in retreat.

Without written orders, with nothing more than a verbal order from a commanding officer—a VOCO—to get ourselves to Manila any time, any way we could, the 306th CIC became a part of the disorderly dash. On 1 February, just at dusk, four of us were in a jeep headed south on Highway One, with Lieutenant Platt driving as if we had to overtake the Flying Columns. Tropical rain beat on the windshield and slashed in on us from the sides. A scattering of Filipinos in *caratelas* and carabao carts, some on foot, refugees from the fighting, appeared in the headlights, in lane, out of lane, crossing from one side to another almost too close for braking or swerving. It could only get worse the farther down we went.

At Camiling we came to Highway Three, the road to Manila. Sometime in the night we came to a jam-up at the Agno River crossing. The CIC insignia on the bumper of our jeep may have helped. We were moved forward past a number of vehicles and told to sweat it out. We were still sweating it out when dawn came and the sun lighted up the bombed-out bridge. Concrete spans stuck up at surrealistic angles, some half-submerged in water. American bombing? Japanese demolition? We never knew and never asked. The road was littered with the results of both. Engineers waved us on and we crossed on a swaying pontoon bridge.

We reached Tarlac, less than thirty miles from the Agno River, at 2100 the same day. Traffic at a standstill and not likely to move before daylight, we found the Thirty-seventh CIC headquarters and half a dozen agents, with a jail full of Filipinos they had arrested for suspected collaboration. Taking General MacArthur's order as specific instructions, worried because the mayor of Tarlac had just been murdered, surrounded by insurrection, they were doing what they could to keep civilian strife from interfering with military operations. We were in Huklandia.

"Fucking Huks. Fucking Commies. They think they won the war."

We listened, but we were moving on.

The next morning the dash toward Manila was still a barely moving caravan of military vehicles, traveling bumper to bumper, slowed at times by bomb craters, at times by Japanese wreckage that had to be pushed aside. We crawled past Clark Field, past Japanese planes destroyed on the ground, buildings crushed and burned, runways cratered from one end to the other—the whole a graveyard for Japanese men and machines. We cheered and jeered. The humiliation we had suffered at the fall of Clark Field and Fort Stotsenburg was lifted. The arrogance of pilots who believed themselves gods was being buried by bulldozers clearing strips for P-38s to land.

At noon we came to a halt in the middle of San Fernando de Pampanga, the capital of the province, a town that had escaped the destruction we had seen along the way. Crowds were on the streets, but they were not welcoming crowds. There were no American flags in sight, no cries of "*Mabuhay*, you come, Joe." These were not America-loving Filipinos.

People slowly drifted to the plaza between the church and the market. Among them husky young men carried hammer-and-sickle banners hung from bamboo poles. They passed under a banner hung between two buildings: HUKBU NING BALEN GNG HAPONES. "People's Army Fighting against the Japanese," a young Filipino, with no friendliness in his eyes or voice, told me. There were other signs, hand-printed, the hammer and sickle crudely sketched: "Join the United Front," "Liquidate the Puppets," "*Mabuhay* Juan de la Cruz."

Feeling alien, I walked through the market and among people gathered in front of the church for a mass meeting. My inclination still was to be friendly and to learn what I could. Their responses were either sullen or belligerent. In a mixture of Pampanga for the people, English for Americans, speakers called for revolution—against Japanese, collaborators, puppets, USAFFE guerrillas, Americans who had taken sides against the Huk. One claim was constant: the Huk had liberated the people from the Japanese. It was the Huks who had struck the enemy from Mount Arayat and the Candaba Swamp. The Huks had saved the people. Now the people would join them. Those who opposed them would face Huk justice.

"They will be liquidated," a man with a Japanese rifle told me. "It is the way of the Huk."

Shaken by the potential for violence and revolution I had seen, I went back to our place in a line that was beginning to move. Out on the highway again, we could see Mount Arayat rising out of the plain to our left, as we had seen it since mid-morning, serene, commanding, protective—a haven for Aguinaldo's Insurrectos, fleeing Japanese soldiers, revolutionaries, bandits. By their own claim the Huks had appropriated the caves on the slopes as hideouts, the whole mountain as their symbol of strength.

Late in the afternoon we were in a crush of vehicles trying to cross the Pampanga River. On the other side lay Calumpit. In between were the broken concrete spans of the highway bridge, the twisted steel that had been the railroad bridge. From our side, engineers worked and sweated and swore over a pontoon bridge with shifting ramps and without even a rope for a banister. The sun went down, the night turned black. More waiting, and then we were on planks that rose and dipped as weight shifted from one line of drums to another.

Across the bridge, still on the slope that was the riverbank, we

85

again came to a halt, to wait for a line of northbound traffic to pass. The vehicles were traveling blackout. Pinpoints of blue light passed, followed by other pinpoints of blue. A jeep stopped beside us, almost close enough for me to touch. There was enough natural light for me to see the silhouette of a man on the back seat. For an instant there was a sweep of light from an engineer's flashlight, long enough for me to see the cap with the scrambled-eggs visor, the shape of the head, the set of the jaw, the slant of the corncob pipe. The general, or a caricature of the general. Whichever, I hated his guts. His jeep moved on. So did ours.

Simply by passing through he set rumors flying, some based on fact, some created in the minds of GIs glad for a chance to add to the myth of "Dugout Doug." The facts, as they came out, were almost as bizarre as the fiction. He had thought Krueger too cautious, the planned blitzkrieg too slow, and had come down from the heights of Tabacalera to jack Krueger up. First Cav had entered Manila and he had delivered his "I have returned" speech. He was working on plans for his triumphant march through the streets of Manila. His place in history had to be orchestrated and secured before the tragedy—not his—could be played out.

We sweated out the traffic six miles or so to Malolos, where it was confirmed that the First Cavalry had entered Manila in the late afternoon. The race was over. The honor belonged to First Cavalry. But intelligence was ominous. Japanese forces were not withdrawing. They were digging in for a siege. Government buildings, churches, and Intramuros, the ancient walled city built by the Spaniards, had been heavily fortified. Thousands of civilians, including many *Maka-Japon,* Japanese sympathizers, had taken refuge in the same part of the city the Japanese were defending. They might be starved out. The cost of digging them out was beyond comprehending, yet the orders were to press on.

We were tied up in traffic at the edge of Malolos, bumper to bumper, unable to move. Orders came for us to dig in wherever we could. We hiked into the *población,* where we found a place to sleep on the floor of a stone building, the capitol building of Bulacan Province.

In the darkness, amid the quiet sounds of men sleeping, I had a feeling of having come face to face with history. Here General Aguinaldo had convened the congress that declared the Philippines a free republic and elected Aguinaldo the first president. Here the Insurgents framed the Malolos Constitution. From here the Insurgents carried on a campaign against the Americans that was not ended till February 1899. Not far from here, in the mountains, Aguinaldo was tricked, deceived, and forced to surrender. With a choice of swearing allegiance to the United States or spending his life in prison, he took the oath of allegiance. His capture ended the Insurrection but left seeds of discontent.

The quiet of night was broken by the sound of firing and the splat of bullets on our outside walls, and then of firing along the walls. Unwittingly we were caught in a war of Filipino against Filipino, of USAFFE guerrillas against Hukbalahap guerrillas, with no protection but thick stone walls, no action possible but to hug the floor and wait for dawn. USAFFEs held the town, Huks the outskirts. USAFFEs shot randomly into the country, Huks just as randomly into the town. What burned our asses was that they would not let us sleep.

Morning came, Sunday morning, quiet, the traffic still not moving. Radio units passed along fragments of communiqués from Manila. At 1900 the Flying Squadrons had freed civilian prisoners at Santo Tomás University and the military prisoners at Bilibid Prison. Resistance being lighter than they had expected, they had penetrated as far as Malacañan Palace. Thirty-seventh Division soldiers, led by guerrillas, had also entered Manila. They had encountered sniper fire but little more. Taking Manila suddenly looked like a picnic. MacArthur would have his triumphant parade.

With nothing to do but wait, three of us walked through the market and past stores open for business. Men and women smiled at us; little boys yelled "Hello, Joe." A Chinese buy-and-sell man asked us to come inside his storefront and see the souvenirs he would sell us for victory prices. We did not need money. He would take cigarettes, chocolate bars, anything we had to trade. When we held back he showed us his USAFFE guerrilla identification and told us a convincing story of how he had worked in the underground for the Americans. When he found out we were from the CIC he invited us to his house to meet his wife and daughters and have dinner with them. We would be safe. The Huks had stopped shooting before daylight. Now they would be in the *barrios*.

"They are cowards. They only fight at night."

He feared the Huks. They kidnapped and killed. He had to keep armed guards at his house day and night.

We went with him to a frame and concrete house that was large and somewhat Chinese in trim. His Filipina wife and *mestiza* daughters greeted us in a living room decorated with Chinese porcelains and Filipino weavings of grass and bamboo. His wife was a Tagalog from Bulacan, the child of a Filipino landowner. The daughters, with their brown skin and straight black hair, had the Malayan look of their mother except for the slight slant of their eyes. Eager to please to the point of fawning, they gave us nipa palm wine and a dinner of vegetables and rice with pork, chicken, and fish for viands—all bartered, he explained, from people he knew in the *barrios*. Japanese soldiers had raided the *bodegas*. People in the *población* were starving.

They wanted to talk about America and the Americans. I wanted to talk about them. First was the question of anti-Chinese feeling. On Leyte I had heard Chinese called the Jews of the Orient. Did he feel the prejudice? He treated the question lightly. Did he not have a Filipina wife? On the question of collaboration he was evasive. He had been in the buy-and-sell all through the occupation but never with the Japanese. There might be collaborators in Malolos but he did not know who they were. On the question of Huks he was vehement. "They have liquidated so many in Bulacan."

Before we left the table, shooting started again—a fire fight in broad daylight, not far from us. "Huks," our host said. "Only they shoot into town. The USAFFEs will fight back."

Nervously we gave them chocolate bars and cigarettes and told them good-bye. He sent four bodyguards armed with Japanese rifles to guide us through protected streets, where we could walk close to walls, sheltered from bullets.

"These Huks," a guard said, "they call us *Tulisaffe*. Robbers. They would kill us." He was walking beside me. "Only yesterday we were with the American soldiers and Huks shot at us. We shot back. We buried two Huks in a rice paddy."

When we were near our jeep a fire fight opened up behind us.

"Let's get the hell out of here," one agent said.

"If the Nips don't get you, the Flips will," another said grimly.

With the race to Manila over, the snarl of vehicles changed to an orderly flow of traffic, to orderly waiting at streams for fords to be tested or temporary bridges to be built. We crept along in line until about 1600, when we were halted near the village of Coloo-can, just short of the entrance to the Balintawak Brewery.

"Fall out!"

Cheers rose from vehicle to vehicle. We would be there for a long break, a lot longer than a piss break, or any other usual break. We saw soldiers running into the brewery and out again, carrying their helmets like buckets. Beer vats were open, unguarded. Japanese guards had been evacuated, Filipino workers had fled. *Beer.* I ran with soldiers all around me, past dozens stopped in their tracks, drinking, their faces hidden in their helmets. I pushed my way to a vat and dipped my helmet in—the same in which I washed my socks and underwear—and got pushed back along the highway with only a part of the beer down my gullet.

"Battle stations!"

The command was an electric shock, repeated down the line of vehicles. An officer jumped up on the hood of a jeep yelling. "Helmets! Put on your goddamned helmets! Get ready to fire!"

With a trickle of beer down my back I headed for a telephone pole at the edge of the road bank and made the last few feet creeping and crawling. I raised my head and saw a column of Japanese soldiers coming from the southwest, marching at something like double time, traveling not in formation but in a shifting huddle. They were not in rifle range, but if they held their course they would pass north of the brewery and cross the road about where I was lying. We would have to fight. It was like a movie scene played in jerky motions with the outcome inevitable. Inevitably they would charge. Inevitably I would have to pull the trigger, if I could force myself to. What a time for recalling Corporal Gaydon leading a dry-run charge yelling "Kill, kill, kill!" And, surrealistically, Matthew Arnold's words, "where ignorant armies clash by night."

For the first time I leveled my gun at a human being—not at a single one but at a drab mass of moving humanity. Suddenly the mass broke and men scattered like quail before the hunter, away from us, toward patches of jungle growth. To the south I saw what they had seen, an American infantry outfit bearing down on them. When both chased and chasers were out of sight I took my finger off the trigger and locked the bolt.

Two soldiers crept out of a marshy place behind me. One, in a voice that might have come from Tennessee or Arkansas or Oklahoma, was saying, "I laid there in the grass shakin' like a dog shittin' peach seed." The other one said, "Man, you said it." The alert over, they took off their helmets and headed for the beer vats.

Another order. The brewery would be our bivouac for the night. I went to the building assigned to the CIC, a residential building, the house that had been occupied by the Japanese overseer. He and his family had left in a hurry, so recently that Japanese flower arrangements in Japanese vases were still fresh.

In the last minutes of a red-and-purple sunset I spread my blanket on the bare, polished floor of what had been a luxurious bedroom on the second floor. Duval Edwards, somehow separated from his own outfit, came in. He had no blanket to spread. Typical of him, he had given it to a soldier who needed it more than he did. We had soldiered together off and on for two years, each trying to shape himself into the kind of soldier that would fit the image of the CIC, each sharing with the other thoughts that to the brass would be disaffected. He could share my blanket. Stretched out in our sweaty fatigues and combat boots, two soldiers on one GI blanket, we talked as we had talked at Camp Ritchie and after Hollandia, each still worrying about performing the ultimate in soldiering—shedding the blood of the enemy.

He had a new experience to add. Hiding in tall grass on a patrol, he had watched a Japanese soldier coming toward him, his rifle at ready, a look of fear in his face. Duval had taken aim with his carbine and, unable to pull the trigger, waited. The Japanese soldier, exploring close but not seeing him, turned away and was soon hidden in tall grass.

As darkness deepened, sounds of explosions increased. Duval and I stood at a south window and watched columns of flame-lighted smoke boiling and rising. The Japanese had made their decision known. Manila would be destroyed. Soldiers crowded at the windows and grieved. We would get to Manila, but the city would be gone. There was angry bitching. A senseless race had been won, a city lost. The gods of war had prevailed. There was a kind of ironic retribution. General MacArthur's triumphant entry would never take place. As he had before, Dugout Doug would have to settle for less.

•   •   •

Our rendezvous point was Bilibid Prison, our VOCO to get there any way we could. We were on our own and mostly on foot. Directions were sketchy: eight or ten miles down the highway we would come to the northern section of Manila; there we would hit Rizal Avenue and stay on it till we came to a big square building that looked like what it was—a prison. We started in the blue sky and bright light of beginning sunrise. Ahead, the brightness was lost in heavy clouds of black smoke. The intermittent roar of distant explosions warned us that we were heading toward a holocaust and the holocaust was spreading. Farther on, I could see flames rising under the pall of smoke, orange-red mingled with black. Through the night, destruction of buildings and bridges had been going on—by the Japanese. Only limited American forces had penetrated the city, and they had been ordered to use only limited artillery. The general still wanted to save the city.

A few miles farther on I was walking in the reality of total war. Soldiers and their vehicles filled the road and spilled over the sides. Filipino refugees fleeing north took to the shoulders and ditches. In hasty flight, many were barefoot, many scantily clothed, some smeared with dried blood. The strong carried their sick, their wounded, their dead. A young woman walked straight ahead wailing softly over the dead child in her arms. Of men who slowed to catch their breath I asked if there was any part of the city left. Some stared at me, dumb; others wept and wailed and picked up their pace. Around me, ahead of me, I saw what Clausewitz's total war meant—people uprooted and made destitute by battle, people terrified in the omnipresence of violent death.

And not Filipinos alone. American casualties too became a part of the traffic. Soon after the highway became a street I met a jeep moving as slowly as a hearse, headed north. One boy lieutenant was driving, another sat beside him. Wrapped in a blanket, strapped on the hood, was a body turned stiff, the boots sticking straight out. The driver pulled up beside me. "Graves registration?"

I did not know.

"Americans?" I asked.

I knew already from the tautness in their faces, the grief in their eyes. "Our captain. Snipers got him." Killed in the street, instantly, they said. They had to keep going till they found a place for him, no matter how long it took. He was their captain, their friend. They could not leave him lying in the street.

"I am sorry," I said.

They nodded and drove on.

Every step forward was a step into battle and the litter of battle. Smoke covered the whole of the sky and the sun was visible only as a blood-red glow, the shape of a circle barely discernible. I came to a street sign: Rizal Avenue, in name another perpetuation of José Rizal. Almost at the other end I would find Bilibid Prison. I came to the Bonifacio monument and rested at the foot, feeling strangely alone, as alone as the statue in the swirling movement of soldiers and refugees. A moment to catch my breath and I had to move on—down a street of storefronts bashed in, houses deserted and open, people cringing as they took cover from wall to wall. And over all, the sickening smells of a city burning in the madness of war. Feeling something of the madness in me, I quickened my pace.

It was late afternoon when I came to an outer wall of the square that was Bilibid Prison. The battle had raged around it and moved on, enveloping in smoke and flame streets toward the Pasig River, and toward the port area. Walls at the northwest corner of Bilibid were slowly burning, and no one tried to check the flames. Japanese soldiers lay dead in the streets, caught by bullets while fleeing for sanctuary, some toward the white concrete walls of Far Eastern University, some toward a formidable roadblock they had set up on Quezon Avenue. Wrecked vehicles stood where they had been hit. Beyond, toward the end of Rizal Avenue, there was a steady rattle of machine gun fire.

Captain Frederick and Duval Edwards were at the gate, checking in agents as they appeared. They quickly showed me the wheel-like construction of the inner building. The administration offices were the hub. Cell wings extended from it like spokes on a wheel. We came to the wing that had been occupied by the *Kempei Tai*. Their departure had been sudden. They had left pieces of uniforms, half-empty footlockers, soap and towels around the concrete tubs they had installed for their hot baths. We liberated a footlocker apiece. Not much there for spoils of war.

With deserted cell after deserted cell for our choosing, we moved into what might have been a *Kempei Tai* dormitory. The floor was bare and polished. It was furnished with a sunken toilet in a corner. From my window, across what might have been a recreation area, I could see the wall burning, the flames low, not leaping. The sight created among us not a sense of panic but a kind of enduring inevitability. "If it's gonna go, it's gonna go. All we've got to do is git up and git."

In a courtyard near another entrance we came upon American prisoners of war the Japs had left behind, hundreds of them, in what seemed to be fixed attitudes of waiting. Three years they had been there, and their prewar fatigues hung on them ragged and faded. They surrounded us, clung to us, and in a sort of broken chorus told us the story of their rescue. Saturday morning was not like other mornings. There were no guards around, no orders, nothing but silence. After a time the prisoners knew something strange was happening and left their cells. There were no guards to stop them. Starving—for three years they had been starving—they began hunting for food. All they found were some bags of shelled corn. They ate it raw. Afraid to go out, they waited and hoped, and prayed. At nightfall they heard the roar of tanks outside the walls and were terrified that the Japs had returned. Then they heard voices—American voices. They were free, thank God. Free at last. And sick. Too much raw corn.

I went from one to another. "You know Peapicker Owens?"

Some did. He had been in Bilibid for a time. Some remembered him from the Death March.

"Where is he?"

No one knew. Some prisoners had been shipped to Formosa. He might have been among them. He might be dead. This set them to telling stories of Japanese cruelty on the Death March. Theirs were wounds that would never heal.

A boy with an East Texas accent, a farm boy no more than twenty-one, pulled me aside. His face and belly and ankles were swollen from beriberi, his only clothing a pair of ragged shorts and a blue jumper faded almost white. When he learned I was from Texas he edged me around a wall, away from the others, and after I had promised not to tell on him, showed me an old fatigue jacket he had hidden under his jumper. "I took it this morning," he said. "Nobody seen me and I took it." There was cunning in his face as he hid it again. I understood. He was not begging; it was that war had reduced him to thieving. I did what he did not expect. I opened my infantry pack and gave him my khaki uniform, jungle boots, and underwear. He held my hand and wept; he wept as he covered his nakedness. I last saw him carrying his ragged jackets and shorts under his arm, holding them tight, unable, because of nakedness and starvation, to comprehend what had happened to him. War had done more than change the shape of his face and ankles.

In the night I climbed a lookout tower and gazed across a city lighted by flames, rocked by explosions, undergoing a wrath unceasing, from an enemy cornered like rats in ratholes, from friends driven by rage to revenge. By then we knew that our intelligence had again been faulty. Manila was being defended not by the Japanese army but by the navy. The army might have withdrawn. The navy, with the *Kamikaze* spirit, would fight to the end with a fanaticism that would leave not one defender alive.

It was the night of 5 February 1945. Manila had been under siege forty-eight hours.

Battle at night was the worst, when the overstrained nerves and overwrought mind created phantasms that mingled the reality of exploding shells with the illusions of the enemy, ghost-like, running, running, with bayonets fixed, with terrifying cries of *"Banzai! Banzai!"* Battle by day, when light finally came, was not much better. Shelling was sporadic but unceasing. We could see wreckage where shells had exploded on a roof or on a prison wall. We could see the white ashes and blackened concrete where the fire had burned itself out and left a breach in the wall. Gray-faced in the gray light at the windows, we talked of finding a safer place, knowing there was none. The shells were coming from across the Pasig, from guns zeroed in on any place we might go.

At 0700 I met Captain Frederick at the gate on the side toward the Far Eastern University. Fighting in the streets had moved on, but the debris of battle remained, charred and twisted reminders. A dozen or so men, soldiers and rescued soldiers, stood with the captain, in the attitude of viewers who had come into the open to measure the wrath of a storm, a storm threatening to circle back. In the lightning flashes, the thunder of explosions, the storm seemed to hover over the Pasig River, in a sky dark-clouded by smoke. The enemy had chosen the Pasig as a major line of defense.

When Captain Frederick spoke of the day ahead there was frustration in his voice—the frustration of knowing what jobs we had to do, of not knowing where to begin, in a city largely held by the enemy, with the government buildings in the hands of the enemy. Days might pass before we could cross the Pasig. There might be little we could use when we did get across. There were three thousand or more civilian internees and rescued soldiers to interrogate and document for subversion, collaboration, enemy atrocities.

My assignment, the first he gave out, was to write a general report on the civilian internees at Santo Tomás University. First, at my request, I would deliver messages from the Sister Servants of the Holy Ghost from New Guinea to their sisters in the convent in Manila, not too far from Bilibid.

In the heat of an early sun I walked through the stench of burning buildings and rotting flesh. Japanese soldiers still lay where they had fallen. Flies blackened their faces and the ooze that wet the pavement around them. I had never seen a dead American soldier without feeling tears. I went past the Japanese dead feeling neither curiosity nor compassion.

The sister who answered my knock called the Mother Superior, and within two minutes I was sitting in a comfortable chair in the parlor telling her why I had come. Within five minutes another sister brought a glass pitcher of beer and set it on the top of an upright piano. The Mother Superior was remarkably calm. Would I have some beer? It was early in the morning but she had no coffee to offer. I would. She poured it and began asking questions about the missionaries in New Guinea. It was the same story of privation, sickness, and death I had told the priests, but worse because of the Japanese attitude toward women. They had been worked harder and denied more. And the Mother Superior? she asked. "Sister Frances, an American. A Japanese officer kicked the other Mother Superior to death just before they were rescued at Hollandia."

"Why?"

"He had killed and cooked a pigeon for himself. She asked for

96

the broth for a sick sister. He went into a rage. 'You're always begging,' he said, and began kicking her. There was no way to stop him till she was dead."

I told her about Sister Ottonio, the other American sister in the group, who had been a missionary to lepers. She and her own sister, Ann, had been on a Japanese gunboat when it was strafed by Allied planes. Ann was struck in the leg and died from infection.

"She is a strong woman."

I told her a story the sisters had told me. When Japanese soldiers invaded their mission, the commanding officer took over the priests' house. One morning he came to the sisters' kitchen with a chamber pot in his outstretched hand. "Fill with soup," he ordered. Gleefully they obliged him.

Another story I did not tell her. When the sisters were living in the bush at Hollandia they had no latrines. Each morning and evening Japanese soldiers would march the sisters and make them squat in a line. Then they would command *sssssss* and *sssssht*. The slow ones got knocked over with a rifle butt.

Things were better for them in Australia, I told her, where Allied ships had taken them. General MacArthur himself had ordered blue wool and white linen for them to make new habits for themselves. When the time was right, they would be returned to New Guinea.

"What happened to the Bishop?"

I did not know what had happened to the bishop.

At Santo Tomás Internment Camp—STIC to the internees—I entered through heavy iron gates that had been battered and bent by American tanks. Inside, in what had once been a well-ordered university campus, gaunt men in worn and faded clothes, with the restlessness of ants in an ant bed, walked and talked and shook hands with me and with anyone else in uniform who had come to see and hear what had happened to them. I listened to as many repetitions of the story as I could. For three years, stone walls and armed guards had indeed a prison made, a prison with the population of a town cramped into the confines of a university—a population made up of Americans, British, Dutch, Russian, almost anyone not a citizen of the Axis—and a prison where respected women of means fought over space large enough to lay a single-bed mattress, where prostitutes bitched noisely at each other over prices they charged their customers, where Japanese guards answered pleas for help with a giggle, where the prison command greeted a person bereft by death with no compassion beyond a "So solly."

Three Americans, when they heard why I was there, took me to see where they lived and how they lived. We went through academic halls that had been turned into dormitories for women and children, along an outer wall past shacks that prisoners, mostly women, had built for themselves and called *cabanas,* to an area of bamboo and thatch huts that men had built for themselves and called shanties. All the people I talked to were waiting for the Army to move them out and on, but as they waited they followed routines that had been their lives for three years. Women washed clothes in tubs set in a sink outside; men policed up.

On a bench in their shanty I listened again to the rescue story. For days they had seen enough American bombers over Manila to know the Japanese were losing. The question was, How soon? They had seen their daily rations, never adequate, drop to starvation level for the strong, below survival level for the sick and weak. Hope glowed and rumors flew with each sighting of an American plane.

About 1930 Saturday night they had heard tanks rolling through the streets. Japanese, they had thought at first. Then they heard American voices and saw Japanese guards firing toward the gates. There was a crush as tanks pushed down the gates and fighting began around some of the buildings. Hardly before the prisoners realized what was happening, the Japanese had fled. The prisoners were surrounded by American soldiers piling out of tanks. They had been saved and not too soon.

My notebook became a collection of fragments from many interrogations. There were many complaints about Jo-Jo, their name for the Japanese commander, and his guards, for whom the Geneva Convention did not exist. I had names slipped to me of internees who had gotten special favors by working for the Japanese. All spoke gratefully of Filipinos who for three years had smuggled food in and messages out, and of the guerrillas who had guided the Flying Columns through the streets of Manila. Subversion among Filipinos? They rejected the idea.

Toward noon there was an assembly at the entrance to the main building. General Carlos Romulo was to make his own "I have returned" speech. Like released springs, those who could bounded forward. The weaker were slower but they came. Those on the ground stretched their arms up toward the building; those crowding windows and balconies reached down toward them, in a moment that brightened gaunt faces, hollow eyes. Then, cheering and waving, they cleared the way for Romulo. Stocky but jaunty in his American Army uniform, he waved back and shouted "*Mabuhay!*" Then he talked of the long ordeal they had shared and the victory to come. He had been a part of it, all the way from the flight from Corregidor to that moment in Manila. He had left with the general and returned with the general. It was more than a return to Manila. The puppet government was gone. Old plans would come into being again. Americans and Filipinos would work together toward 4 July 1946, when the Philippines would at last be an independent nation.

"They'll never be ready in a year," the old Philippine hands said.

Ready or not, all of us knew that independence would be given. Anything else would be political disaster.

The speech over, the crowd moved toward the dining hall. I watched an American soldier walking hand in hand with two little girls. In the dining hall I tasted the gelatinous bean curd mixture left by the Japanese. A taste was enough. I watched them eat and wondered not that so many looked like living skeletons but that they had survived at all.

The meal was ended abruptly by the sound of sirens and orders to take cover. Some of the internees refused to hit the dirt one more time, even though they knew artillery shells were coming. Some stood up and shouted their defiance. Some, with the actions of the mentally deranged, wandered in and out of buildings, as if oblivious to the attack. I found room for my head and shoulders in a Japanese pillbox and crouched there till the barrage stopped.

The shelling over, I went out to the main walk. The soldier I had seen lay there, decapitated, a piece of broken shell near him. The little girls had escaped. I went back to see the men I had talked with in the shanty. They had refused to budge. Their shanty had been blown away, and they with it. There was grief, anger, bitterness at the kind of enemy that would shell a civilian compound. The attack had to have been deliberate, for revenge.

I had to add the atrocity to my report—one more crime against humanity, no matter with whom it had originated: Hirohito, Yamashita, the naval commander holed up in the walled city.

When I got back to Bilibid, Captain Frederick was just inside the entrance. For the moment his bearing was less military. His face was flushed, his voice trembled. "They nearly got me."

"When?"

"Right after you left."

He had been on his way inside when a shell had hit with such force that he was knocked against a wall. He ran back outside and found nine men, who had been standing with him, dead. Some of them were prisoners of war, freed, waiting to go home.

"Poor bastards. A hell of a note."

Instinctively I put out my hand. He grasped it with a hard grip. We said no more. No more was needed.

• • •

"We got Aguinaldo."

Captain Frederick spoke quietly to Louis Duncan and me. Emilio Aguinaldo. Arrested and in Bilibid Prison. The most famous Filipino the CIC had arrested so far. We were there because Duncan would prepare the case against him; I would be a part of the initial interrogation.

The agents who had arrested him did not know who he was but had taken the word of Filipinos that he was a collaborator. When they had entered his house they found what they considered conclusive evidence: he had hanging in his living room a Japanese flag big enough to cover a wall. In the dossier we had already started on him there was more damaging evidence. He had made propaganda broadcasts for the Japanese in support of their scheme for a Greater East Asia Co-Prosperity Sphere. In speeches and writings he had endorsed their slogan, the Orient for Orientals. Guilty as hell, we prejudged him. Nevertheless, Captain Frederick wanted us to be diplomatic in our interrogation.

When I got to Aguinaldo he was in solitary confinement in a cell with no furnishings but a straw mat to sit or sleep on, a small washbasin, and a toilet bowl sunk in the floor so that he had to squat over it, peasant fashion. Barefoot, stripped down to *barong Tagalog* shirt and shorts, he looked more like a *tao*, a peasant, than like the dynamic revolutionary leader I had expected, but he was the real Emilio Aguinaldo, not the paper man I had created from reading books. He was old, seventy-five or so, but nimble as he rose from his haunches and came toward us.

I approached him with curiosity and considerable awe. American propaganda had pictured him as ambitious and brutal. According to Spanish, Filipino, and American records he was ambitious and brutal. He was a self-appointed revolutionary, a self-appointed general, a self-appointed shaper, with Apolinario Mahini, of the Malolos Constitution. When Andres Bonifacio, his comrade in revolution against Spain, had become his rival for leadership, Aguinaldo had had him arrested and shot. His election as president of the Philippine Republic that he had helped proclaim followed without opposition. I remembered reading about another side of him, the side imbued by the spirit of José Rizal, a revolutionary with such courage and conviction that when he was executed by the Spaniards, he faced the firing squad and shouted his last words, "*Viva España!*"

The difference with Aguinaldo, as it came out in the interrogation, was that he wanted not loyalty to the Spaniards but freedom from them. At the age of twenty-eight he had left teaching and become the military leader of the Insurgents in their fight to enforce the rights of the *bolo* against the Spaniards, a fight that won from the Spaniards the promise of such reforms as freedom of the press, freedom of assembly, and expulsion of Spanish religious orders. In turn, Aguinaldo had accepted a settlement of money for himself and agreed to self-exile in Hong Kong. That agreement was broken within months by what Americans call the Spanish-American War.

As I watched him and listened to him I could not think of him as a prisoner. Yet he was there, a prisoner of the Americans, small, frail, but unyielding. When I asked him about his defection to the Japanese he retreated to a corner. When I went close to him again I could see contempt in the set of his lips, and anger in his eyes.

We were instructed to interrogate him not on his past—that was fully documented—but to build the case against him for collaboration, subversion, sedition during the Japanese occupation. We began with the flag taken from his home. He treasured it. Why? The Japanese had honored him by giving it to him. "The Japanese are my friends. They never betrayed me." His voice trembled. "It was only the Americans who betrayed me."

"That was a long time ago."

And better forgotten, but he insisted that if we were to continue, the past must precede the present. The past, as he limited it, began when Commodore George Dewey sank the Spanish fleet in Manila Harbor. As Aguinaldo saw it, that was the beginning of American duplicity in the Philippines, the beginning of promises made to him and the Filipino people, the beginning of promises broken. In May 1898 he had returned from Hong Kong to Manila on a United States ship, coming, as he believed, to lead the Filipino people to the freedom they assumed was theirs. Dewey himself had promised that he could take all the weapons he needed from the captured Spanish arsenal. When for the second time Aguinaldo declared himself president of the Philippines, Dewey broke his promise.

When the Americans could have helped the Filipinos to freedom, he complained sadly, they reneged on any promises they had made. By then, they had seen how much wealth there was to be exploited, looted, and they had become landgrabbers as greedy as any Spanish *haciendero* or religious order. They declared the Philippines their own, and thus initiated the first Filipino-American confrontation. Aguinaldo became the leader of the Insurrection. Against at least seventy-five thousand American soldiers, he led a guerrilla army that had the support of the people and that killed thousands of Americans. They were unable to defeat him; only through bribery and duplicity were they able to capture him. They forced him to sign an oath of allegiance to the United States, but he had never ceased to be a burden on the American conscience.

He talked of the present in a voice low, impassioned.

"They made us their colony. They made their puppets to help them run it. Look at Quezon. Look at Osmeña. Puppets. Traitors to their people. When the Americans were losing they did not stay with their people. They escaped to Washington and safety."

If he was a traitor to the Americans it was only because of his loyalty to the Philippines. It was not sedition, as his enemies claimed, when he had fought for independence. He was neither anti-American nor anti-Filipino when he had argued against the establishment of the Commonwealth Government. If he was pro-Japanese it was because they had given independence to the Philippine Republic. "They made us free."

It was the propaganda of his broadcasts. Was he free when he made them?

"I spoke for them but I was free."

The Americans had had him jailed. They would do with him as they had done before, as they wished. Since his youth, he had spoken for the political conscience of Filipinos. That conscience dictated that they be granted independence. The Japanese had given it. The Americans would take it away.

"It will be only a year."

He was pessimistic. "American business will force a delay."

When it was time to go I shook his hand. He let me take his hand, but he bowed in the Japanese manner. Made uneasy by his insistence on American wrong not righted in nearly fifty years, I began a report full of contradictions, just as American-Filipino relations appeared to be. I had to charge him with collaboration, but I tried to soften it by saying that his passion for Philippine independence, not on American terms but his own, had clouded his perception. What appeared to be fifth-column activities could be the restiveness of many Filipinos who resisted any foreign domination—Spanish, American, or Japanese.

103

On one point I believed him unequivocally. Filipinos had not asked Americans to come in, as I had been taught to believe. In view of his eloquence, the argument that only through American intervention would democracy be developed seemed flimsy indeed. Through his eyes I saw that the conquest of the Philippines was but an extension of manifest destiny, transformed into neo-colonialism and maintained outwardly as a kind of missionary endeavor in which religion and commerce worked hand in hand. How noble was our experiment in behalf of our little brown brothers?

My day with Aguinaldo was baffling, the next more so. Captain Frederick named me agent-in-charge of investigating the puppet Philippine Republic government and its high officials for evidence of collaboration, subversion, and treason. I did not know enough to do the job passably and said so. Neither did any of the five or six agents who would work with me. Again the Army had provided too little too late. The progress up from the South Pacific had taken three years—ample time for training CIC agents in Philippines affairs, ample time for study of the impact of American flight and Japanese occupation on the civilian population. The same three years might have been used for compiling dossiers on possible defectors and setting policies for dealing with seventeen million Filipinos. An incomplete name file got left behind in Brisbane.

Two directives, issued toward the end of the Leyte campaign, were conflicting. On 23 November 1944 President Osmeña defined three kinds of collaborators: those prompted by desire to protect the people, those afraid of enemy reprisals, and those motivated by disloyalty. On 29 December 1944 General MacArthur stated that those citizens of the Philippines who had given aid, comfort, and sustenance to the enemy should be apprehended and held in restraint for the duration of the war. Each CIC agent, by combining the two, could justify any arrest he made.

In our own kind of blitzkrieg we had descended on Manila, outrunning expectation, outrunning planning. Half a dozen or more CIC units were operating in the Manila area with little or no coordination. Earnest and eager, agents filled municipal jails and Army stockades with suspects, high government officials and little buy-and-sell men thrown in together on the single charge of collaboration. At least in Bilibid we had a little more to go on.

We knew that when General MacArthur and President Quezon were planning their escape from Corregidor they had named certain persons as caretakers of the Commonwealth Government. We knew some of the names, but not all. We knew also that in the intervening years some of these became outright collaborators, or took on the coloration of collaborators. A roster of officials in the Japanese-created Philippine Republic read like a roster of the Commonwealth Government shuffled and reshuffled. The roster was also remarkably like the *ilustrado,* the social elite of Manila. At the moment, the officials were out of reach. In turn leaving affairs in the hands of caretakers, they had fled with the Japanese to Baguio, the summer capital, on 21 December 1944.

In the Bilibid office we had files of the Manila *Tribune,* the semi-official voice of the Japanese government in Manila, and the Manila *Times*. From these, in one day, we would be able to compile our own list of collaborators and charges against them. Captain Frederick agreed to the idea, over the objections of agents who wanted to go out on their own hunting expeditions. Evidence of collaboration and of treason was staggering. José Laurel headed our list. An agent read a quotation from him aloud: "My prayers are that the Americans don't come back." At another time he stated that he wanted an authoritarian government, a constitutional dictatorship. At another, he swore to liquidate all guerrillas.

Manuel Roxas was second, and the most puzzling. He had long been close to General MacArthur. At the flight from Corregidor he had been left as chief caretaker. Aloof from the Japanese at first, he later became close enough to play golf with them, and to prepare, write, and sign the puppet constitution. We felt contempt for Laurel. For Roxas, we felt anger that spilled over on the general.

Day after day the papers printed Japanese propaganda. The "Asia for Asians" slogan became standard in quotations from officials, whether Japanese or Filipino. Typical was one from General

Takaji Wachi, military commander in Manila. "You are Filipinos and belong to the Oriental race. No matter how hard you try you cannot become white people."

Ironically, the names of Filipinos who repeated this propaganda were Spanish, Caucasian, white, or white with an admixture of Chinese or Malayan: José Laurel, Manuel Roxas, Benigno Aquino, Teofilo Sison, Claro M. Recto, Jorge Vargas, José Yulo, and Camilio Osias. Osias, Minister of Education in the Laurel cabinet, had ordered that the bow replace the handshake in all schools and colleges.

In the middle of the afternoon I took the list of names and charges and wrote a memorandum for Captain Frederick. I ended it with an opinion that we had no directive that could be applied to Roxas, or to Jorge Vargas, who had stated soon after the Japanese took over, "We have absolute trust in the Japanese forces." In less than a month Vargas had flip-flopped from pro-American to pro-Japanese. So had most of the others prominent in the Commonwealth government. I panicked. The general and his old hands in the Philippines had prewar political connections with most of these men that we had been ordered to jail. Without more specific instructions, the job was too complex for any one agent or even for the whole CIC.

"We've got to have help," I told Captain Frederick.

He read the memorandum and read it again. The problem was there, but he had no solution.

"Somebody's got to."

I expected him to take it higher up. He wanted to hold off a few days, let things work themselves out. He was my commanding officer but I had to go against him. "If you won't, I will."

"You're on your own, but you goddamned well better go through CIC channels."

I got only as high up as a major. His answer was uncomplicated: only the general knew how he wanted to deal with men who had been his comrades and friends, and the general had not spoken.

Frustrated, angry, knowing that a sergeant does not make demands of a general, especially if the general is Douglas MacArthur, knowing at the same time that I had to live with myself, I put a blue memorandum sheet in a typewriter and addressed it to General Douglas MacArthur. I stated the problem and made my demand: that we be given a directive for handling such sensitive political cases. I signed it both as Special Agent 2142 and Technical Sergeant 18106462, and I demanded that it be forwarded at once to the general's headquarters at Tabacalera, near Tarlac. It might come back with a directive, a reprimand, or not at all. Nothing came back. My memorandum did not get through.

In the meantime, with Bilibid overflowing with people arrested by the CIC, and with charges circulating that some guerrilla leaders were collaborationists, Captain Frederick asked for a background summary.

Shrewd Filipinos had learned that the best protection against the CIC was a commission in a guerrilla outfit or an ID card bearing the name of a recognized guerrilla. Forged signatures served as well as the genuine. The rush to become guerrillas was overwhelming. Conflict between the puppet elite and the guerrillas had been growing for some time. Now, as the puppets lost power, a new elite based on real or figmented guerrilla activities came into being. In the provinces, a little-known *cacique* could propel himself into prominence by appointing himself an officer and recruiting soldiers. CIC cynics said that anyone who could buy or beg an Army shirt automatically became a captain. If he also had shoes he became a major. From what we could see, a straight-faced Army gave approval to most outfits that applied, and names like Ferdinand Marcos with his Markings and Ramón Magsaysay became prominent. Recognition became expensive for American taxpayers. In Luzon alone some sixty thousand guerrillas were recognized and awarded pay—some retroactive to the beginning of the war—and full veterans' benefits for themselves and their families to some indefinite future. At the same time, many guerrillas earned everything they got.

Critics of Franklin D. Roosevelt traced many of the irregularities among Filipinos to his decision to emphasize the European Theater at the expense of others, especially those in the Pacific. Fil-Americans—Filipino and American soldiers, hastily regrouped into a single army—had reason for complaint. Military defenses had been consistently inadequate. Heavy losses in ships and planes at Pearl Harbor and immediately following had rendered them more so. Furthermore, Americans were not candid with Filipinos on how devastating the attacks had been. Filipinos were not prepared for the speed of the Japanese drive down from Lingayen Gulf, or for the disorganized retreat of the Fil-American forces to Bataan and Corregidor, or for the declaration of Manila as an open city, or for the vacuum left on 1 January 1942 when Quezon and Osmeña fled with MacArthur to Australia. Like the American soldiers who were singing "No mama, no papa, no Uncle Sam," they felt deserted, defenseless. Filipino soldiers bottled up on Bataan deserted across Manila Bay, some to become guerrillas, some to lie low till the war was over. Filipino civilians did what they had to do to survive.

Triumphant, arrogant, merciless, the Japanese moved into the vacuum and rapidly assumed political as well as military dominance. Instructions that MacArthur and Quezon had left to Manuel Roxas and other caretakers were hasty, oral, and subject to various interpretations. On 2 January 1942 the Japanese occupied Manila and immediately pressured officials to cooperate. Pressures were accompanied by threats. The effect was confusion and chaos. Adjustments, personal and political, had to be made.

On 5 January 1942 José Yulo, ex-speaker of the Assembly, called government officials to his home to discuss ways of dealing with the emergency. A consensus reached, they asked Japanese occupation officials to continue the Commonwealth Government as an instrument for stability. The Japanese refused. They saw in such a move a continuation of white power and rule. On 8 January 1942 they ordered Jorge Vargas, mayor of Manila, to convene all the former officials and reorganize the government, with Vargas as chairman of an executive commission. The question of Philippine independence was a bargaining point for the Filipinos, a propaganda windfall for the Japanese. Americans had 4 July 1946 as the date. On the twenty-second of January Premier Hideki Tojo promised independence at an earlier date.

Fifth-column Filipinos strutted. On 6 February General Aguinaldo exacted some pay for what he felt the Americans owed him. He broadcast a strong anti-American statement and an impassioned appeal for support of the Japanese. Yielding to what seemed inevitable, Manileños waved paper Japanese flags in street parades and shouted their enthusiasm for the Greater East Asia Co-Prosperity Sphere. Social and cultural life, for forty years dominated by Americans, was now dominated by Japanese. People studied *Nippongo* and struggled with Japanese street names that had been substituted for Anglo. Resistance was reduced to scattered guerrilla units who had to take to the mountains.

Puppet independence was more than a year in coming, partly because of stringent Japanese terms, partly because the more astute Filipinos feared losing their bargaining power. Both sides knew that for propaganda at home and abroad, independence had to come. In May 1943 Tojo made a triumphal visit to Manila, where he was greeted by streets lined with people waving flags and with puppet officials bowing lower and lower to show their will to please. Independence was set for 14 October 1943. The date was kept and José Laurel realized his ambition to be president of the Philippine Republic. Overt resistance subsided for a time. Allied advances, however, gave new hope to those weary of the occupation, and guerrilla ambushes became a daily threat, especially in Central Luzon. Japanese peace and pacification campaigns ended in failure. By 1 September 1944, such incidents had increased to the extent that Laurel declared martial law. On the twenty-second, a month before the Leyte landing, the Japanese pressured Laurel into declaring war against the United States and Great Britain.

Before Captain Frederick could approve my report and start it up through channels, Colonel White ordered him to San Fernando, Pampanga Province, where Sixth Army had set up headquarters for the duration of the Luzon campaign. I, with my batch of notes, was sent to Malacañan, a mile or so from Bilibid, to be in charge of the palace guard. My orders were to prevent looting, especially of government files, and to keep the palace in readiness for President Osmeña's return. As the only American there, I would be completely in command, completely responsible. The Filipino major in charge of the guard was expecting me and I would have a jeep of my own.

At about 1300 on a bright hot day I parked my jeep on the palace grounds. Before me stood the stately mansion—the White House of the Philippines—that had been home to Spanish and American governors-general, to Manuel Quezon and José Laurel. All around were signs of war—shell holes in the lawn, grass littered by American soldiers who had rushed on with no time to police up—and the sounds of war—machine gun fire near the river, artillery from the enemy emplacements across the river.

A Filipino in uniform with the gold leaf of a major on his collar tab came to the jeep, and gave a kind of mixed bow and salute. "Major Jesus Vargas, sir."

I wore no insignia but I showed him the CIC badge pinned under my lapel. "Owens."

"Ah, Colonel Owens. We were expecting you."

His report was brief. His seventy-five men were well deployed. There had been no serious incidents since the American command post had crossed the Pasig upriver from the palace.

The major took me to a government building at one end of the palace grounds to meet Nicanor Roxas, who had been executive secretary to José Laurel. Roxas took me to the palace to meet Mrs. Geronima T. Pecson, President Laurel's secretary.

Mrs. Pecson was waiting at the foot of the great staircase.

"Colonel Owens," Nicanor Roxas said.

With the graciousness of a First Lady she shook my hand and welcomed me to the palace, apologizing because I would not find everything in order. Only that morning the last of the wounded American soldiers had been evacuated to hospitals. "Would you like to see the palace?"

She led the way up the stairs. Nicanor followed me. At the top we looked down and I saw that she had waited on the spot where anyone coming to see the president had to wait. Suddenly I realized that these three were the caretakers not only of the palace but of any vestiges of the Laurel puppet government in Manila, and that she was chief caretaker. As we went through the presidential offices she was called Imay, the nickname for Geronima, by some of the people we met. To others she was Mammy, or Mummy.

How long had she been at Malacañan? Since the beginning of the Japanese occupation. She had been a teacher. Her husband was a judge. She had pretended to be the palace cook, then the housekeeper, and then the nurse. She had become private secretary to Jorge Vargas and José Laurel. Had I followed General MacArthur's directive I would have arrested her. But she was too useful.

They did not show me the twenty-four rooms of the palace, but they did show me the splendor of the palace proper—the great ballroom, the state dining room, the library. In the state dining room there had been looting: Japanese had taken away one of the three crystal chandeliers.

"What a pity," Mrs. Pecson said. "Those awful Americans." She recovered herself quickly. "Those awful Japanese."

The presidential suite, elegantly designed, elegantly furnished, was on the second floor with windows that opened onto the Pasig River and the Malacañan Botanical Gardens on the other side. From the windows, or the holes where windows had been shattered, I had another view of Manila burning.

In the center of a parlor was a glass case with one side broken. In it, on a stand, was a gold and jeweled sword, a souvenir hunter's dream. "The Emperor's gift to President Laurel," Roxas said.

I studied it but did not touch it. I could see it only as another evidence of Laurel's perfidy.

For a moment the three of us looked out the windows. All of us feared that the Palace would be destroyed. Mrs. Pecson was bitter. "They know it is the presidential palace. President Laurel wanted to declare Manila an open city but the Japanese would not let him. If they only had."

The presidential bed and bath were mine if I wanted them. I did not. The room had been bombed once. Chances were it would be bombed again. Instead I chose the bed and bath of a rather ordinary suite on the floor below, directly beneath it. She did not show me the suites that had been occupied by General Wachi and Hisamichi Kano, a Harvard graduate and the civilian liaison officer between Manila and Tokyo. She did bring me General Wachi's alligator briefcase for my papers and Kano's Remington portable for typing reports. Both men had fled.

Alone at the windows in the presidential suite, I spotted what buildings I could across the Pasig, all of them south or southwest of the palace, all of them ones the Japanese had elected to defend, the Americans to take. The five main bridges across the Pasig had been demolished. Engineers had channeled the river between walls too steep for scaling. The crossing from the palace boat landing and through the Botanical Gardens had been relatively easy, the casualties relatively light. The prize now for the Americans would be the power plant on Provisor Island, City Hall and the Legislative Building, built to withstand earthquakes, and Intramuros, the Spanish bastion with stone walls up to forty feet high and fifteen feet thick.

Colonel White had prepared an intelligence report calculating the costs in casualties. GHQ overrode it. General Krueger was reluctant to push. Push was a part of General MacArthur's timetable. Those who had argued that the Japanese could be starved out and Manila saved, a minority at any time, had lost. The battle in all its fury was on.

I thought the palace might go any minute. It almost did that same afternoon. I was opening up files in the presidential office when a single shell hit the wall on the river side. It was like the tremor of an earthquake. A barrage of smaller shells followed, hitting palace walls and digging craters in the palace lawns and gardens. My jeep was down there. I ran like a turkey, through the hall, down the stairs, and out to my jeep, knowing only that I had to get out of there. By the time I got to Bilibid I was telling myself and others that I had had to run to save the jeep, though I knew I had run to save my own hide. Later, when the shelling was over, I had to go back to the palace and face Mrs. Pecson. I was embarrassed. She spoke the plight of thousands of Filipinos: "I had no place to go."

In a quiet room, inside layers of stone walls, I sat at table with Mrs. Pecson and Nicanor. She apologized that there was not much food. She had been giving it out to refugees, but she did have a bottle of wine from the presidential cellar. Other arrangements had been made. Major Jesus Vargas would be my bodyguard. Chingi, who had been valet to Quezon and Laurel, as well as to Wachi and Kano, would be my valet. Mrs. Pecson did all this for me, she said, in appreciation for the things Americans had done for her, even when she was a child. In 1901, when she was five years old, she had met American teachers, called Thomasites because the first arrived on the transport *Thomas*. They were dedicated teachers. She had tried to be like them.

Later, when we were in total blackout, I read by black-shrouded candlelight in my room. As much as possible had been done for me. Major Vargas sat outside my door with his carbine on his knees; Chingi sat across from him with a chamber pot ready should I call. Reading and writing about the Japanese takeover of the Philippines became an emotional binge. They had set out to humiliate Americans. They had done so at Pearl Harbor and on the Death March. Every step in the formation of the puppet government, every proclamation by a Filipino quisling, carried on this humiliation. So did their attempts to obliterate everything Anglo-Saxon and substitute things Japanese. Detectable, after the Leyte landing, was the Japanese will that what they could not have they would destroy. Shelling the palace had only one purpose—to destroy.

José Laurel, exposed fully in his papers, was their chief tool. They had chosen wisely and with considerable foreknowledge, if not actual coaching. He had lived in Japan and was a student of Japanese politics and culture. In his files were treasonous letters dated as early as 1934. His ambition was to be president of the Philippines. The war opened the way. After the American defeat, he courted Japanese occupiers and pushed himself forward at every turn. His fawning proved profitable. On 14 October 1943 he became president.

He was president, but neither he nor the Japanese *Kempei Tai* could put out the fire of rebellion that flamed in many islands, and especially in Central Luzon, where their own reports showed they could not control the Hukbalahap. Japanese intelligence reports passed on to Laurel named Kasutoro Arehandrino, Rui Tarokku, and Hose Banaru as the military and political leaders of the Huks, and noted that these leaders' beliefs and organizations were strictly Communist. Their objective was to establish a Democratic National Socialism with help from America. Hose Banaru was using guerrilla units to carry out a revolution and form a Communist nation.

There were file folders full of reports of Japanese soldiers and Filipino civilians murdered, of landlords and priests kidnapped, of towns left in fear, of people fleeing from the provinces to Manila. Japanese soldiers patrolled the *barrios* but could not find the Huks. Neither could the less than half-hearted Philippine Constabulary. It was too easy for the Huks to hide in mountains or swamps. Instead of helping the situation, Laurel's declaration of war against America only increased the number of outbreaks. These reports alerted CIC to serious Huk trouble in Central Luzon.

Chingi did more for me than hold a chamber pot. I was not allowed to unbutton a shirt or unlace a boot, to slip off my pants or underpants. He bathed, massaged, dressed me, always without a word unless I forced it out of him. He was doing for me what he had always done for President Laurel.

One morning before Chingi could get me shaved and buttoned up, Nicanor Roxas came to my room. Kano had just telephoned Mrs. Pecson. He was hiding in the home of Filipino friends and wanted to surrender, but not to American soldiers. Would I go? Yes. Nicanor drove a presidential limousine. It would appear official to Filipinos and would reassure Kano.

Traveling inside American lines, we were stopped at checkpoint after checkpoint, each time with a warning to watch for dugup places in the road, where mines had been placed. Engineers had cleared a track in the middle of the road. We had to stay in the track or risk being blown up. Cautiously we followed the track. Nervously we passed jeeps and trucks that had been blown apart. We could have turned back but I was too eager to capture Kano.

We turned off a winding driveway and came to a house, a mansion, still untouched by war. A woman met us, took us to a small sitting room, and gave us coffee. In a lace *tierno* with high puffed and embroidered sleeves she might have been receiving for a formal occasion. It was, she explained, that she wanted to honor the American colonel. I wanted to know about Kano. Halfway through coffee she said quietly that Kano was no longer there. American soldiers had come and he had run away. He feared they would kill him. If only I had come earlier.

I did not believe her and asked to search the house. She consented graciously but turned my search into a guided tour. We followed her through a parlor lavish with a collection of Oriental art objects, and through bedrooms with silk canopied beds. Toward noon, still with the feeling that Kano and others could be hiding in parts of the house we never saw, I gave up and went with Roxas back to Malacañan.

"Colonel Owens?"

It was morning again and Nicanor was waiting. In the night there had been another call from Kano. He wanted to surrender to the American officer. He was in Pasig, across the river from the Wac Wac Country Club, alone and unarmed. It was a pity for him.

"Will you go?" Nicanor asked.

"Yes. We could use him."

We went in the jeep, working our way slowly past checkpoints, shell holes, broken-down barricades, among tanks and trucks going the same way. Toward the middle of the afternoon we passed the clubhouse on our left and stopped at the edge of a brushy growth. We left the jeep and started toward the river. Roxas pointed to a group of houses half-hidden by trees. "There. We must go there."

I worried. Was he worth it? Front lines could not be far ahead of us. There were fresh tank treadmarks and shell-shredded trees. When we had gone no more than a hundred yards a soldier in leaf-and-twig camouflage stopped us. Two others came out of the underbrush and held their guns on us. If we were not spies what were we doing there? Who was the Flip?

Explanations futile, I demanded the name of their outfit.

"First Cav."

I had been attached to First Cavalry on Los Negros.

"Who is your intelligence officer?"

They did not know. I asked to be taken to him.

They marched us like prisoners to the clubhouse and kept custody of Roxas while I went in. I followed a sergeant to a room where a young officer was leaning over a desk.

"Sir—"

The officer looked puzzled for a moment and then burst out, "W'y, Prof, what in hell are you doing here?"

Jimmie Cokinos. An Aggie from Beaumont. I had flunked him in sophomore English. He gave my hand an Aggie grip—not quite bone-cracking.

Quickly I told him why I was there and where Kano was hiding. As the highest-ranking Japanese official in the Philippines, we had to get him. He would be useful to us all the way to Tokyo.

Jimmie looked at his watch and then showed me the situation map. We were on the north side of the river, the Japs on the south. I was too late. A new push was starting.

"W'y, Prof, I cain't let you go out there. You'd get killed."

In minutes artillery would lay down a barrage along the river. I could get caught in it and end up dead. So could Kano. He was not about to let me go.

At Malacañan Mrs. Pecson said, "I pity him," and waited for more messages. No more came.

Outward show of loyalties was a problem for Filipinos who had been in and out of Malacañan under the Spaniards, the Americans, the Japanese, and now the Americans again. I was not certain of any of them, even Mrs. Pecson and Nicanor Roxas, or whether their loyalties would be switched again if the Japs came back. I reserved judgment because I had to use them. I had no choice. They both insisted on their loyalty to the Americans and their friendship to me. So did the men and women they let in to see me, among them refugees who stayed in the palace because they had no other place to go. Among these was Meding Laurel, President Laurel's daughter-in-law, the wife of José Laurel, Jr.

Each had some proof of loyalty, no matter how flimsy. Some brought me gifts to prove their loyalty. Some invited me to their homes. Some who had husbands at Baguio cried and prayed that they would soon be rescued by the Americans. Remnants of the Manila *ilustrado* found their way to the palace. Their latest change in loyalty was not always complete. Like Mrs. Pecson, they sometimes said "Those awful Americans" when they meant to say "Those awful Japanese." To me the question of collaboration became increasingly complex, the tangled skein impossible to untangle, except where there was unimpeachable evidence.

First Cav crossed the Pasig and began an encirclement of the city from the east. Infantry soldiers captured Provisor Island and the power plant south of the palace and were now fighting street by street in residential areas. Farther down, from the Ayala Bridge to the port area, the Japanese held out, aided by two advantages. First, the river was walled in—riflemen had to cross in small boats and scale a wall under enemy fire. Second, still attempting to save some of the city, General MacArthur continued his restriction on artillery support. Casualties were so high that, according to a rumor later substantiated, one general refused to commit more riflemen. When restrictions were lifted, the hell that was to be the destruction of the center of Manila began.

From palace windows, aided by Filipinos, I could figure out plans of action—first on the north bank and then on the south as the drive turned toward the government buildings. Farther away, to the east, flame and smoke marked the battle lines of the First Cavalry. To the south, in the area of Nichols Field, the Eleventh Airborne was moving up. For the Japanese the last escape route had been cut off. It was surrender or die. There was no surrender.

A Filipino in American uniform came to the palace with a message from Bilibid. José Laurel's home had been captured. I was to go at once and rescue documents useful to the CIC. The house was on Peñafrancia Street, in Paco. The driver knew the way.

We crossed on a temporary bridge north of the palace and took a street through Pandacan, directly into the range of Japanese artillery. By the time we got to Paco, in some streets whole blocks of houses were burning on either side. Smoke burned our eyes and we could feel the heat of flames. The smell of burning flesh was sickening. Refugees stumbling through rubble held out their hands for help we could not give them.

The driver was silent all the way to Peñafrancia Street. He stopped at a house that had been shelled but not demolished. "This is it, sir."

A young lieutenant, the only guard, came to the steps. I showed him my badge.

"Good thing you got here," he said. From the door he looked back over the burning city. "God, this is awful." His language was inadequate.

He took me to what might have been a sitting room—office. One corner was an open shell hole. A safe stood at one side with the door blown open. It would not swing to.

"Impact from a shell," he said. "It was this way when I got here." He lifted a chest from the safe. "Look."

The top was open. Jewelry—gold, diamonds, rubies—spilled over the sides. Laurel's jewelry. I lifted up my two hands full. On the bottom were layers of Spanish gold coins.

What to do with it, the lieutenant worried. Left, it would be looted. Taken, the taker could be court-martialed. Whoever had been in the house was no longer there. They might be among the dead in the street. I thought of Meding, Laurel's daughter-in-law, at Malacañan. The lieutenant was glad for me to take them to her. Anything to get them off his hands.

There were documents, mostly family documents. I left them. In the files at Malacañan was enough evidence of José Laurel's treason to hang him, if we had the will or the guts. I doubted we had either.

I sat in the back seat of the jeep, braced, and the lieutenant put the chest in my arms. The fighting had passed on, in the direction of Intramuros.

In my room at Malacañan, with doors closed and bolted, with Mrs. Pecson, Meding, and Nicanor watching, I emptied the chest on my bed. Meding touched pieces lovingly. Mrs. Pecson and Nicanor made an inventory of necklaces and rings, brooches and bracelets, and gold coins old as Spanish conquests.

"The family will be so grateful," Meding said.

I turned in a signed inventory and receipt. In my report I was noncommittal, but not to myself.

Day by day the drive toward Intramuros became more savage, with fighting street by street, building by building, room by room. Japanese in their suicidal fury, knowing there was no escape, raped and tortured and butchered Filipinos and destroyed anything they could that came to hand. More on all sides died, fewer escaped.

Elpidio Quirino fled from his home in Ermita and made his way to Malacañan, exhausted, distraught. He slumped into a chair and sat with his fists under his chin. We gathered around him and listened to one horror after another until our comprehension was no longer qualitative, only quantitative. Nine members of his household had been brutally murdered by Japanese soldiers gone berserk, driven to take as many lives as they could before giving up their own. He talked himself out, and we had few words to comfort him. Almost ritualistically we touched his arms and hands.

My tenth day in Malacañan and preparations were underway for President Osmeña's return. It would be a sad homecoming. The palace was waiting for him, but the buildings that would have housed his government had been destroyed, in a fury not yet over. The final destruction of Intramuros was not yet over.

My last visitors at Malacañan were Major Labatt and Colonel White himself. I met them at the foot of the great staircase. Before I could explain anything, Mrs. Pecson and Nicanor joined us, to show us through the palace. They apologized that it was not what it had been before the war. They lamented the missing chandelier and the damage to the presidential suite. They were grateful that I had been allowed to stay with them. They would have offered wine but Japanese bombs had destroyed the wine cellar.

In the halls Filipino guards saluted. To me they said, "Good morning, Colonel," and "Would you go this way, Colonel?" I cringed. Impersonating an officer? They could throw the book at me. I felt the sharpness of our visitors' glances.

At the foot of the staircase they thanked Mrs. Pecson and Nicanor. To me they said, "Come with us." Looking straight ahead they preceded me out the walk and through the palace grounds. Not far from their jeep they stopped abruptly and turned toward me, but not on me. Both were laughing. Colonel White spoke, only one sentence: "If he ever gets to be an officer he will know how to act like one."

We shook hands and they let me go.

• • •

Ordered by VOCO back to Bilibid, by the time I returned all of us knew we were in a no-win situation—that the final push into the Walled City would cost too much in lives of Americans, Filipinos, Japanese. Any American victory now would be a defeat for all mankind, Americans included. The sacking of the city, the release of the deadliest of weapons, including hunger, had been underway for days. Relentlessly it went on. We knew that the Japanese command had broken apart, and that Japanese troops, out of control, had turned their fury on Filipinos, in a confrontation of Oriental against Oriental, in an orgy of revenge for rejection. We knew but did not let up. Publicly, we were saving Filipino lives. Privately, American soldiers spoke of the will of the general not to be thwarted.

17 February. The drive to end enemy resistance in Manila began, but not with cries of "Remember Bataan," "Remember Corregidor." These battles had been overshadowed by the cumulative memory of Guadalcanal, Kwajalein, New Guinea, Leyte—by all the sights of water and sand washing over American soldiers dead on lonely atolls, all the searing by napalm and flamethrowers, all the days and months and years of futile lives.

This was the unknown I had enlisted for—unknown, unthinkable, in spite of all the Army had done to turn me from what I had been—a humanist—into a killer. As I watched the drama of men and machines moving forward almost as if by the numbers I gave way to the morbid feeling, the morbid curiosity to see all there was to see. In the open space of a prison courtyard I huddled with other soldiers. I felt a comradeship of horror—a horror that expressed itself not so much in words but in faces pale under Atabrine yellow, in eyes Atabrine yellow staring into eyes that looked the same. Safe from the fury, we could rejoice in what we were seeing, or regret that a better way had not been chosen. I hated everything I was seeing.

I went to another part of Bilibid, to the section reserved for Filipinos arrested by the CIC. They did not want to talk; they were watching us, as I had been watching. At the gates distraught men and women waited, hoping for word from inside of relatives whose escape was into prison. They watched and listened, their eyes focused on the layers of black smoke dotted with the white of phosphorous shells, their ears throbbing from the cacophony of battle. They held my hands and talked to me. Quietly they mourned the loss of their dead, the destruction of their city. In their voices I heard the hollowness of deep regret, tinctured by anger just as deep.

On 19 February, driven to see all that I could see, I climbed the tower of a six-story building near the Escolta, on the American-held side of the Pasig—not a building really, only a blackened frame of steel and concrete. Soldiers were climbing ahead of me, lining up behind me, risking their lives for sights they would describe to their children and grandchildren. As I climbed I met soldiers carrying a dead soldier. How did he get it? The question met them at every step. Sniper's bullet. At the top. I could have turned back but I did not. With no more than a low "Goddamn it," we met and passed on.

Through a jagged hole I could see the stone walls and concrete blocks guarding the gates to Intramuros, the rectangles and squares inside that were college and university buildings, and farther away the tower of San Augustin Church. Lower and to my right were the walls of Fort Santiago, the ancient Spanish fortress where Rizal had awaited his execution, where Japanese had interned and beheaded Filipino dissidents. The whole was medieval, except that the moats had been filled in and made into green parks, now fields of Japanese bunkers. Builders of these fortresses had built well. Days of shelling had marred but not destroyed. Only obliterating bombardment could breach such walls. Only hand-to-hand fighting could destroy the enemy within. The final orgy, the final passion, had begun and no training film had been like it. It was kill, kill, kill for soldier and civilian alike, and no way to save treasures that could have belonged to the ages.

23 February, 0730. The final assault began. I was watching from a courtyard in Bilibid. Shells went over on a low trajectory, hurtling like lightning bolts from the hands of an angry god—low enough for me to follow even the smaller ones from the time they came into view until they dropped out of sight in fire and smoke. In an hour ten thousand shells fell on the Walled City alone. A succession of dive bombers, swinging low, untouched by antiaircraft, dropped bombs with explosions that made the earth tremble as far as Bilibid. Hell on earth? That and a thousand times more.

Mid-morning, when the bombardment lessened, I went back to interrogating Filipino prisoners. Their temper had changed and they wanted no questions from me. Neither did the people outside the gates. They had watched their city, the brightest pearl in their string of pearls, being not blemished but pulverized. For some, tears were not enough. They cursed the Japanese, the Americans, all invaders.

By the twenty-fourth, Intramuros was in American hands. So was the Philippines General Hospital, which, in spite of the Red Cross on flagpole and roof, the Japanese had fortified and defended room to room, with nothing but anger for the patients or for civilians who had taken refuge there. So was the General Post Office by the Pasig and the Manila Hotel by Manila Bay. A temporary calm lay over the city, but it was only temporary. The Japanese still held the Legislative Building. The battle would not be over till the last building had been taken and every gun had been silenced.

25 February. Time for our ritualistic lifting of a canteen cup at the Manila Hotel. With three other agents in a jeep I crossed the Pasig on a Bailey, temporary for the Ayala Bridge. Like sightseers in the wake of a tornado we circled the government buildings at a safe distance, out to the apartment buildings on Taft Avenue, and

through rubble to the edge of Burnham Green and the Old Luneta. We were then three or four hundred yards from the Manila Hotel and not far from where Rizal had been executed.

A few soldiers, none of them our friends, waited in jeeps or gathered in small groups talking and laughing, daring each other to a game only the reckless would play. We had won the hotel but the prize hardly looked worth the taking. MacArthur's prewar penthouse had been blown off. Finding a place to raise a toast seemed unlikely. We wanted to take a closer look, but there was occasional rifle fire from bunkers farther down the green—Japanese snipers still holed in.

"Hell, I'm going to make a dash for it," a sergeant said. "Any takers? I got plenty o' room."

There were none. He swung his jeep around and floorboarding, zigzagging, drove hell-bent for the nearest wall. Before he had gone halfway, rifle fire sounded from a bunker. On he went.

"Damned fool."

The words came from behind me. Then there was cheering all around me. He was almost there, and then he was there, striding up to the entrance.

"By God, he made it."

Some followed. Others drifted away. I went back to Bilibid and read General MacArthur's latest proclamation:

On behalf of my Government I now solemnly declare, Mr. President, the full powers and responsibilities under the Constitution restored to the Commonwealth whose seat is here re-established as provided by the law.

Your country thus is again at liberty to pursue its destiny to an honored position in the family of nations. Your capital city, cruelly punished though it be, has regained its rightful place—Citadel of Democracy in the East.

Meant to lift up, to give comfort, his words were less flamboyant, his tone more subdued than usual. No matter what he said or how he said it, though, there was no concealing from those who had been there the fact that the Four Horsemen had been through Manila, and there was little doubting who had held their reins.

A VOCO from Captain Frederick was waiting for me at Bilibid. Hukbalahap trouble had broken out at San Fernando, and the Sixth Army area was threatened. He had Colonel White's approval for me to report immediately.

By 1600 I was out of the rubble and stench of Manila on my way north up Highway Three. It was still clogged, mile after mile, with people fleeing the fighting, plodding along, heads down, not stopping to look back, not asking if it was safe to turn back.

FOUR

BY THE TIME I PASSED Malolos there were only a few refugees on the road. After Calumpit and across the Pampanga River, the people I saw belonged to the scattered houses and clustered *barrios*. Fighting had come near and then passed them by, leaving only a bomb crater here and there to remind them. It was a beautiful land, with the emerald of rice growing to the gold of rice ripening, a quiet land that seemed to belong to the long ago. Women with faces brown as nipa thatch watched from windows and doors. Men as brown walked in the fields, some in pairs, *compadres,* holding hands. A boy astride a carabao turned the animal away from a wallow and, with a kick of bare heels, sent him lumbering along a ridge between paddies.

Ahead and to the right I could see Mount Arayat, first a dark blue shadow in the late afternoon haze, and then a yellow-tipped cone in the blue-sky sunset. Out of the plains and swamps it rose, distant but dominant, raised there by volcanic flow in some unremembered past. To me it spoke of peace. It also spoke of conflict. As I watched, three red tracer bullets rose from the base, so synchronized, so directed from the left that they had to form some signal, in its redness a signal sinister.

There was an afterglow of sunset when I came to San Fernando, to the old Spanish church, a pile of gray stone with a cross on top, and the *convento* beside it. Windows and doors of church and *convento* were shut. A priest in a white cassock was outside scrubbing a heavy, varnished door, washing off a red hammer and sickle—the sign of the Huk. On the other side of the road three Filipinos squatted in a doorway, watching the priest, watching me as I slowed to read a faded sign: LAND FOR THE LANDLESS.

I turned left at the church and went west, past stone warehouses that had been taken over by the Sixth Army for headquarters, and past rows of pyramidal tents set up for headquarters soldiers. From there I could see the house I was looking for—a large frame house, once grander than the houses around it but now run down, the paint streaked and faded to an ugly yellow, the balcony railing sagging under a tree that bore strange fruit, the leaves the color of limes, the fruit the shape of cotton buds just before opening.

A black-on-white CIC sign hung on a stone post at the entrance to a graveled lot; below it was another sign: MILITARY ONLY. I parked against a palm in a row of palms—areca, the betel palm. I dropped a chain around the gearshift lever and locked it to the steering post; too many stolen jeeps had been taken over by the "jeepney" taxi trade.

Through a narrow entrance I went into what had been a parlor flanked on one side by a sitting room. Both had been turned into Army offices. Field tables, chairs, and typewriters crowded the inner wall. A sliding window opened on one southside wall. Through it I could see the areca palms and my jeep. A Filipino crossed the yard, his wooden *bakya* grinding in the gravel. He picked up several nuts—enough for a good long binge. He was Pabling—our boy. Agents were sleeping in a large room on the first floor back. I gave Pabling my gear.

Alone still, I studied some of the Huk signs piled on a desk. They carried the same argument I had first heard and rejected at John Reed meetings ten years earlier in Chicago. Only the names, only the scene had changed. The same argument had been labeled Russian and "Red" and dangerous in training session after training

126

session in Army schools. The Army assumed that we were equipped to handle cases of Communist subversion. Russia was now our ally but not to be trusted.

Captain Frederick came down the stairs carrying a hand-sketched map. The sitting room was his office and he spread the map out on his desk. "Welcome to Huklandia," he said, with a sweep of his hand over the map. "Take a look."

A large area, larger than our training had prepared us for, it included most of the rich plains of Central Luzon—the provinces of Pampanga, Tarlac, Nueva Ecija, Bulacan—the rice paddies, the sugar plantations. San Fernando, the capital of Pampanga, was close enough to the geographic center to have been the capital of Huklandia, but the political and emotional center lay somewhere in the vicinity of Mount Arayat, at the edge of the Candaba swamps. The captain moved his finger down the Pampanga River from the *población* of Arayat to San Luis. "That's where we raided last night. MPs got a tip. It was their headquarters. You'll see what we dragged in."

He sat at a desk spread with hand-printed signs and purple-dittoed propaganda sheets, some on Japanese rice paper. I sat across from him and took notes. It had been a surprise raid, about midnight, on a schoolhouse at San Juan, a *barrio* of San Luis, which had been turned into a Huk command post and barracks. CIC had arrested two leaders and about twenty-five followers, some of them women, and had confiscated enough propaganda to stick them.

"MPs locked them up." He handed me a list of names compiled by agents: Juan de la Cruz, Guan Yek, also G-Y, FDR, Scarlett O'Hara.

I studied the list. "Aliases?"

"All aliases as far as we can tell. Their Huk names—their underground names—they call them."

The CIC job was to get their real names, addresses, and political or military titles and ranks. He made it sound like a Huk order of battle. At first, Sixth Army thought we had come up on a local fight between Huk and USAFFE guerrillas. But it was more than that. The USAFFEs were fighting to reestablish the past, with Nacionalista Party control. The Huks were fighting to establish a Communist government under a United Front.

My assignment, already approved by Colonel White, sounded very much like a Japanese peace and pacification campaign. Captain Frederick called it restoring law and order. Whatever it was called, the Japs had failed at it and our prospects did not look good. I had a free hand to interrogate, investigate, make recommendations, jail and hold suspects as long as I wanted to. I would work in the open myself, but I could create my own underground.

He talked more about the raid. "I went along to keep an eye on the MPs. Everything went right till we got to the *barrio* and surrounded the schoolhouse. As we closed in, the MPs lost their heads and started shooting. People inside scattered. We grabbed as many as we could. No telling how many got away. Enough to make plenty of trouble."

He looked at the list again. "Damnedest thing. An old man and his son came to the jail this morning. They were not captured in the raid but they wanted to be put in jail with their comrades. He was serious. The MPs jailed them."

He added names to the list: Bernardo and Tomás Poblete. "The old man has two aliases that we know. El Mundo and José Banal."

José Banal? Japanese *Kempei Tai* had a report on Hose Banaru. "Huk military commander in Pampanga Province?" I asked.

"Yes."

"He is a self-avowed Communist."

"I am not surprised. Commie bastard."

He handed me a mimeographed order signed "Juan de la Cruz, Commander-in-Chief, HUKBALAHAP." "Start with him."

Upstairs, in the light of a gasoline lantern, I went through the documents, first the map and then pages and pages of half-misquoted, badly understood Marxist doctrine. There were also sketchy accounts of how the Hukbalahap had developed as a semi-political, semimilitary, openly violent arm of the United Front, itself made up of loosely organized groups. The leaders, prewar radicals, were using the war and the vacuum created by the war to promote Marxist control of government in Central Luzon.

From Malacañan records I knew how the Huks had outfought and outthought the *Kempei Tai* and the provincial governments. Their manifesto was to the point: success depended on coercion of the masses, liquidation of the opposition, and intimidation of all through secret warfare and terrorizing raids.

The Japanese stance had been to treat them like enemies. The American tactic was not too different, especially at Sixth Army headquarters, where reports of Huk sabotage and Huk liquidations were brought in daily. Captain Frederick thought we should be tough on them. He could count on me.

Bored by repetitions in their propaganda, I stood on the balcony, in darkness made luminous by the green-white glow of fireflies. I listened for the soft, quiet voices of Filipinos, but the people had left the street, afraid. An MP jeep patrolled back and forth, the bluish glow of blackout lights like a pair of unwinking fireflies. An MP guard in combat boots walked a post beneath the balcony. Another irony of war: Japanese lines were miles away, our only enemy was our own people.

In the blackness of night Lieutenant Ripley, the executive officer, pushed back the mosquito netting on my cot and leaned over me. In lantern light his suntan took on a yellow glow. Atabrine yellow tinged the pink of his cheeks and showed in the whites of his eyes. His voice was a cautious whisper. "Keep quiet. Can't tell when the gooks are listening."

A sealed message had come from a man who said he was a USAFFE guerrilla and before the war had been a Philippine scout. He had information about the Huks but was afraid to come to the CIC—he and his family would be liquidated. He would meet us only on a lonely road in the dark.

Driving blackout, we went through San Fernando and south on the highway toward Manila. A few miles out, in sight of the Philippine Constabular, we turned to the left. When we had passed the buildings we stopped and locked the jeep. By then I was beginning to feel that the whole trip was a cloak-and-dagger affair.

We found a carabao trail and followed it at a slow, cautious pace, our only sound the scuffing of boots on dry earth. Half a mile or so in, where another trail branched off, we stopped in the shadow of a clump of bamboo.

Suddenly we heard the sound of bare feet slapping hard ground.

"Lieutenant Ripley?"

A small man, slight as a boy, came out of the bamboos. He had come barefoot, like a *tao*. He talked hurriedly, in a voice low, intense, of the revolt among his people and of the Huks leading it. "You must know what the Huks do. They go with their guns and bolos to the people who own land and have stores of what we call *palay*—the rice. They confiscate in the name of the Hukbalahap. Anyone refuses, he is foxholed. These are Huk words—*confiscate, foxhole*. Their leaders in jail have sent out orders. They will take revenge. They will liquidate Americans who try to stop them, the way they liquidate Filipinos, the ones they call puppet. We must all be afraid."

He took my arm and I could feel trembling in his hand. "You will investigate the Huk?"

How in hell did he know? Gooks listening? "Yes."

"You will make this Juan de la Cruz tell what he has done to the people?"

"Do you know his real name?"

"I know. Luis Taruc."

Taruc. To the Japanese, Tarokku.

"It is the way of the Huks. They use Huk names to hide what they do, but the people know their real names."

"Guan Yek?"

"Casto Alejandrino. He looks Chinese."

Taruc, Alejandrino, Poblete. These were the main Huk leaders, and we had them all in jail. I asked for names of non-Huks.

"You will talk with Don Pablo. Don Pablo Angeles David. His house is in Bacolor. Huk squadrons have threatened to kidnap and liquidate him for robbing the people when he was governor of Pampanga. He has to keep guards. He will tell you what the Huks do."

"I will see him. Anyone else?"

"The priest in San Fernando. He read from the pulpit, making it a sin to join the Huk. Now they have a price on his head. He has guards and does not leave the church and *convento*."

It was time for him to go. He shook hands but did not give his name or where we might find him. "It is dangerous for me to meet you. They say I am a spy for the CIC. Our names will be on their liquidation list. When I know something, I can find you."

He disappeared among the bamboos. Nervously, Ripley and I went back to the jeep.

Liquidation list? Christ. We were in a bolo war as brutal as the one that had driven the Spaniards out, and as hard to squelch as Aguinaldo's Insurrection. But with their three leaders in jail we might be gaining.

I parked in front of the yellow concrete jail and went to a small room that was both guard post and office. An MP studied my badge and credentials and opened the heavy door to the inner court. He held up a ring of keys. "Nip or Flip?"

I had a quick glimpse of rows of bars with arms reaching out, faces pressed between, of iron-grilled cells set in a square around a sun-dried court. Every cell looked out on the court. Every prisoner could see us as we stepped inside.

"Filipino. Juan de la Cruz."

"Oh, him. He's expecting somebody. I thought it was gooks, his wife bringing him some clothes."

He took me past a cell where eight Japanese prisoners of war sat naked and silent over cans of cold C rations. They were young, their bodies strong, well fed. One stroked his crotch with one hand and ate with the other.

"Always got ahold o' his dog, the son-of-a-bitch," the MP said, his voice softened by a Southern slurring. His voice had the same contempt it had for the Flips. "Soldier gods, hell. They used to be guards here, doing the same thing I'm doing. They cain't say nothing in English but you ought to hear them when they get going for the Emperor. Sunup every morning."

He went to a corner of the court where the sun had not reached and unlocked a cell. I started in, toward a man squatting in a dark corner, but stepped back, sickened by the smell of vomit. The man stood up and came toward me, holding a tin bucket from an Army kitchen. "This is what they gave me," he said, with no other greeting. "I was sick and they brought me this. They do not take it away."

The guard let him set the bucket outside, but the stench still hung heavy in the dead air of the cell. I was there to interrogate the man who called himself *Supremo* of the Hukbalahap, but the stench was more than I could stand. When I complained to the MP he sent a Filipino with soap and water and a rush mop.

While I waited for him to wash himself and for the floor to be scrubbed I walked around the cell blocks, looking at the prisoners but not talking to them. Most of them were young, country looking, fresh from the *barrios,* the boys in shirts and *abaca* shorts, the girls in Army fatigue uniforms—the boys Huk soldiers, the girls propaganda leaders. Some looked sullen, some angry. One old man, twice the age of the others, squatted inside the bars but did not look up. A young man, hardly more than a boy, squatted beside him. Bernardo Poblete and his son Tomás, I was sure. I made the full round of the cells and came back to Juan de la Cruz.

The sweet smell of coconut-oil soap freshened the air. He was waiting for me, small, thin, wiry, brown with a wetness of water and coconut oil. His hair was black and slicked back. His eyes, darker than the brown of his skin, were sunk under a high, wide forehead—sunken and defiant. He was wearing not the uniform that would suggest the *Supremo* but the *abaca* shirt and shorts, the dress of the *tao,* the peasant.

"Juan de la Cruz?"

He answered me with a question. "You will investigate me?"

I took out my notebook and heard the hardness in my voice. "I want your real name."

"Luis Taruc. I do not hide it."

"Then why do you call yourself John of the Cross?"

"It is the name given to the *taos,* the poor masses. I am one of them and they are glad for what I do. To honor me they call me Juan de la Cruz—like John Doe."

Not the same, I thought, but did not dispute him. "Birth date?"

"June 21, 1913."

"Birthplace?"

"*Barrio* Santa Monica, in the town of San Luis, Pampanga."

"Parents?"

"Nicanor and Ruperta Taruc, also Pampangans."

"Their occupation?"

"Peasant farmers." He paused in search of a comparable term. "Sharecroppers."

"Now back to you. Education?"

Emotionless, almost detached, he told the story of a boy who, determined not to spend his life as a tenant farmer, walked miles barefoot to elementary school, left home and went to Tarlac, where he could work his way through high school, and took up tailoring to support himself through college and law school in Manila. He mixed his story of how he lived and worked and studied with the story of the agrarian revolt that was growing in Central Luzon and how he had become a part of it. He described the revolt as radical but nonviolent. His voice became emotional as he talked of the poverty and oppression in his own family, of his father's bitterness at harvest time when he had to give more than half of his *palay* to the landlord.

Quietly I asked him about the rise of the Hukbalahap. He evaded the question. "I will tell you the story of the Filipino people—"

I demanded history, not the propaganda I could quote to him. Reluctantly and then shrewdly, as if seeking a convert, he began at the beginning.

The war had brought dissident groups together, to form guerrilla groups to fight the Japanese and the Filipinos who collaborated with the Japanese, and to form united political resistance. In March 1942 their leaders met between Cabiao and Arayat, where the provinces of Pampanga, Nueva Ecija, and Tarlac come together, close enough to Mount Arayat and the Candaba Swamp to go into hiding if Japanese patrols came near. After days of debate they organized the Huk and developed a slogan: "Drive out the Japanese bandits! Death to puppets and collaborators!" In the latter they carried over prewar hatreds that were anti-landlord, anti-clerical, and anti-Jesuit, the biggest landlord of all. The leaders vowed no allegiance to Japan, to America, only to the Filipino people in a Philippines freed by them as they took over and ran the government. They elected a military committee: Luis Taruc, Casto Alejandrino, Bernardo Poblete, and Dayang-Dayang, a woman squadron leader.

"Where is Dayang-Dayang?"

"Dead. Dead because she was betrayed."

"Who betrayed her?"

"A spy for the Nipponese. He is now foxholed."

I asked for Alejandrino to be brought in. For a moment the two faced each other, not speaking, not saying to each other what they must have wanted to say, of three years as comrades at arms, less than two days as fellow prisoners. The jailed silent because of the jailor.

"Casto Alejandrino?"

"Yes."

"Alias Guan Yek?"

"Yes."

"Also alias G-Y?"

He nodded and added, "For the underground."

During my interrogation of Alejandrino the two squatted facing each other—Taruc, Pampangan with a Malayan look; Alejandrino, Pampangan with Spanish blood from the shape of his head, Chinese from the slant of his eyes.

Alejandrino was different in another, more significant way. He was the son of a landowner, a *cacique*, a part of the feudal land system inherited from the Spaniards. He had become a radical not from disadvantage but from conviction. Prewar, campaigning against the Nacionalistas, he was elected mayor of Arayat. To show his solidarity with the leftist radicals he was sworn in with a clenched fist. He and his wife were proud to be organizers of the Huk. He was proud to bear the name Guan Yek; she was proud of the Huk name she had chosen for herself, Scarlett O'Hara. She had been arrested with the others but not jailed. She would come with clothes for him when the Americans let her.

Alejandrino was well educated, articulate, well grounded in

134

revolutionary rhetoric, but where Taruc was straightforward, Alejandrino was evasive, less convincing. Yet they stood together question after question. In their struggle for the cause, neither had yielded on principle or tactic, they assured me, nor would they yield, no matter what the Americans did to them. Even in prison? Prison, they warned me, was a physical restraint but no more. Even in solitary, they could send messages out, have information sent in. Defiantly but not arrogantly they said the Huk would go on.

At what cost? This was part of the report I had to write. Taruc and Alejandrino claimed the Huks had killed ten thousand Japanese and Filipino collaborators. They claimed as many Huk soldiers in squadrons roaming Central Luzon, taking military, political, economic control as they went. They defended confiscation of rice and extortion of money as necessary to support their revolution.

My report delivered, I went over Luis Taruc's story and in it saw a part of my own. A sharecropper in Pampanga was different from a sharecropper in the Red River Valley only in the size of the landlord's share: in Pampanga he took half the rice, in East Texas a third of the corn and a fourth of the cotton. In both cases was a peonage of debt. Bondage by credit in the company store was the same one place or the other. Allegiance to *cacique* or landlord— allegiance to and reliance on—was a bond feudal in concept, demeaning in application. I understood the injustice Taruc felt. Though he swore he was not a Communist, he had turned to Communism for a way out. That I could not understand. For that he was an enemy.

When I came to Captain Frederick's office again I heard a woman's voice, loud, angry, American with a New York accent, demanding that the Huks be freed at once. He called me and I went in. He was at his desk. An angular, hardfaced woman was pacing the floor, berating him, berating the Army for the raid, the arrests, the deaths of Huks she claimed American soldiers had killed in Malolos. As an American she demanded the release of Taruc and Alejandrino.

His face was red, his voice controlled. "I can do nothing for you, Mrs. Lava." To me he said, "Will you interview her?"

He did not say interrogate. She started berating him again and he walked out on her.

She would answer only a few of my questions. Yes, she was an American. She was Ruth Propper from Brooklyn. Yes, she was Vicente Lava's wife. Files in Malacañan Palace identified Vicente Lava from Malolos as a Communist propagandist and courier, and both he and his brother Jesus as political advisers to the Huks.

"Are you also a propagandist and courier?"

Instead of answering, she accused me of trying to get information to use against her and her husband.

"Are you a Huk?" I demanded.

No answer.

"Member of the Communist Party?"

Still no answer.

"What is your work for the Huk?"

No answer, only another tirade against Americans who would jail Filipinos who had killed so many Japs. She demanded to see Taruc and Alejandrino. She demanded a pass to the jail. I endured her anger but did not yield.

Her daughter came for her and they went toward the church. I followed them past it and into the market. People ran after her and she stopped to talk with them. Then she went behind a blind in a stall where a red-lipped, black-toothed woman sold her wares: lime, areca palm nuts, and green betel leaves. I waited but I did not see her leave.

In our files someone had entered two notes: she claimed to be a graduate of Barnard College; Vicente Lava had a Ph.D. in chemistry from Columbia University and in his research was to rice in the Philippines what George Washington Carver was to peanuts in the American South.

The next morning, before I could go to the jail, Captain Frederick called me to his office. Don Pablo had sent a demand for help. The treasurer of Bacolor had been kidnapped and the money left in his care was missing. It was the Huks. They would take the money and liquidate him. Only the Americans could save him. Captain Frederick ordered me to go. Don Pablo was important to the Army. So was the treasurer. Elected before the war, he had served throughout the Japanese occupation. He was the kind of continuity the Army and the Nacionalista Party needed.

The sun was coming up when I headed west on the route of the Death March. In rice fields on either side of the road men worked with nets swung on bamboo poles, catching insects that looked like grasshoppers, running across paddies with the nets before them, hardly turning their heads at the caravans of tanks and trucks roaring past. For them, food mattered, not the war. What there was to eat had to come from the land, and there was not enough. Their catch would be fried in coconut oil and eaten as a viand with rice, if they could get the rice.

For generations, conquering soldiers had passed along this same road, laying claim to the land, subduing the people who worked the land. Invading master after invading master had come and gone, the changes one to the other marked only by the color of their skin, by their uniforms and machinery of war. I drove slowly, watching the workers. Their faces remained intent on grasshoppers; their bare feet kept nimbly to ridges between rice paddies. These were the *taos*. These were the ones the Huks were stirring up with promises of land and a bigger share of the crop.

At the edge of Bacolor I came to Don Pablo's house—a house of wood, broad and square, a feudal castle built with wide verandahs to shelter it from sun and typhoon. Palm trees shaded it on either side. Rows of tall thin areca palms separated a winding driveway from nipa huts—quarters for the retainers.

I turned into the driveway and stopped, startled by the sight of a machine gun mounted on a tripod and manned by Filipino soldiers in American Army uniforms. One came toward me and saluted. "You have the badge, ser?"

I lifted the flap on my shirt pocket. The guard examined it and saluted again. "Don Pablo expects the CIC. Will you not go with me to Don Pablo?"

We walked the length of a broad walk and entered a door that opened into a large office. Several men waited, one seated at a desk, the others standing or squatting around him—all dressed in embroidered *barong Tagalogs* that hung hip-length over pants of white sharkskin or American khaki. The man at the desk rose.

137

"Don Pablo?"

He took my hand. "We are glad you have come. We fear for the mayor. It is the Huks."

He was short, stocky, with a broad brown face under close-cut white hair. He looked what he was—a *cacique* of *caciques*. He might have restrained the fear that animated his voice, but he was a former governor, a wealthy man, a large landholder, a man in danger of being kidnapped, robbed, killed. Once before he had been kidnapped but he had escaped. They would come again, and this he feared. So did the men around him. They could be next.

"Has this been reported to the police?"

Don Pablo was their spokesman. "There are no police. They have gone with the Huk, after the Americans returned. Before this, the Huk held the country, we held the town. Now they are taking the town."

"What about the soldiers outside?"

"Ah, they belong to the USAFFE. They are only a few, and under orders from the American Army. I asked the general for protection and they are here. They must stay."

"I've got to have help. I don't know where to start."

"Ah, we have help for you. Come with me."

He took me through a large darkened room, preceded by the skittering of bare feet as women of the household scattered before us. At the end of a hall we came to a smaller room, a family worship room, with a red-and-gold altar and silver crucifix at one end and a row of dark chairs along a dark wall. A young boy knelt at the altar.

"The son of the treasurer," Don Pablo said. "He will tell you."

Don Pablo left me standing near the altar. When the boy did not move or speak I knelt beside him. He gave me a quick glance and turned his eyes again to the crucifix. Just when I thought he would not speak, he leaned toward me.

"I will tell you. We were sleeping at home—all of us in one room because of the Huk. Late at night we heard them calling my father's name. When he did not answer they said they would shoot. He begged them not to shoot and went out. I pitied my father. They called him *tulisan* and took him away. Till now we have not heard from him."

"Who were they?"

He was afraid to talk. I asked him to go with me to his house. He was afraid to be seen with the CIC. Don Pablo came and said that he had to go. He went with me to the *municipio* and through a street of wooden houses. He lived in one of these, but we went only to the front.

"Can you think of anyone?"

There was one, an American mestizo called Georgie Morrison. He had gone with a Huk squadron.

"Where can I find him?"

He lived with his mother in the *barrio,* in a house the boy knew, but he would not go with me. I went to the *barrio* alone and asked at the house for Georgie Morrison. He was there with two others, easily recognized by the blond cast of his hair and cheeks. The others were brown-skinned, black-haired, Malayan. All three were young swaggerers. All three were defiant till I drew my pistol. Then they went with me meekly to Don Pablo's.

Don Pablo gave me a room on the ground floor and sent men from his office to interpret when the language was Pampangan. One by one I asked the suspects, "Do you belong to the Huks?" One by one the answer was "No, ser." They did not know the treasurer. They did not know there had been a kidnapping. My voice got louder and more accusing. They refused to look at me. I sent two out and kept Georgie Morrison.

I tried being friendly. "I need help. Can you tell me anything about the kidnapping?"

"No, ser."

This did not please Don Pablo's men. "Ser," one of them said, "if you will only beat him he will talk."

I objected. Threaten him, yes; beat him, no. I sent Don Pablo's men from the room. Then I threatened him with everything I could think of, including torture in the way of the Japanese—bamboo splinters driven under his fingernails. I went to the door and asked for a piece of bamboo. When I turned back he was crying. He grabbed my hand.

"The treasurer is dead, ser. I myself have killed him."

"Who ordered you to?"

139

"I do not know, ser. It was a command, ser."

"Why?"

"He took money from the people. It was only that we wanted to take back from him what he had taken from the people."

"Where is he?"

"Ser, if you will only go with me."

Leaving the other two with Don Pablo's men, I walked with him on a railroad track half a mile or so toward *barrio* Vicente. Suddenly he stopped and squatted on the roadbed, beside freshly dug earth.

"It is here, ser."

As if compelled to show me, he scratched away some dirt and exposed a bare leg. "It is the one, ser."

I made him cover up the leg and marched him back to Don Pablo's. Don Pablo and his men gathered in the room with us. They listened to me and responded in a manner that seemed fatalistic: a friend is dead, so a friend is dead. I wrote out a confession and Georgie Morrison signed. The other two also signed but only as accomplices.

"Why did you do it?" I asked them.

"It was for the Huk, ser."

When we were on the railroad track, away from Don Pablo and his men, they added, "He was the enemy." For the first time Georgie Morrison showed remorse. "Now I am ashamed."

The sun was hot on the diggers. The body, bared, was beginning to bloat. Burial had to be at once. Don Pablo had sent a railroad cart and two men to push it. Calmly the killers lifted the body out and on the cart. In handcuffs they walked with me ahead of the cart.

In Bacolor I went to tell his wife, not knowing he also had a concubine. She already knew and stood before her door wailing. The priest? she asked. I had to tell the priest. I went to the church. The priest knew. He also knew about the concubine. His decision was abrupt. He could be buried in the churchyard but not by the Church. It was permitted for him to be buried in his mother's grave.

With the handcuffed killers behind me I stood outside the

churchyard wall and watched two groups gather—from the town, family and friends of the dead man, but not Don Pablo; from the *barrios,* Huks and friends of Huks—each group enemy to the other. A man with hammer and chisel chipped away cement and lifted out the stone door to the vault. With his hands, he pulled out old bones and tossed them at a basket. At last he brought out a skull and dandled it one hand to the other. The mourners wailed; others laughed. The body on a stretcher was slid inside.

I took the young men to the jail in San Fernando and went back to a gratefully friendly Don Pablo. He had a meal lavish enough for a *merienda* waiting for me: viands from Army supply, rice and vegetables and fruit from his own acres. I wrote notes for my report in his office, and his hand might have guided mine: the notes were strongly pro-Nacionalista, pro-USAFFE guerrilla, anti-Huk. For the first time I recommended that if the Huks were not stopped, Central Luzon would have to be put under martial law.

I ended my report with an appreciation to Don Pablo.

Before daylight the next morning Captain Frederick shook me awake. There had been another kidnapping, the Commonwealth mayor of Guagua was missing. It looked like a Huk offensive. Squadrons were scouring the countryside, plundering where there was anything to plunder, recruiting young men and women to carry the banner and bolo.

"You'd better get going. Report in when you can."

I went west on Highway Seven, the road toward Dinalupihan and Olongapo on Subic Bay. When I arrived at the *municipio* Huk soldiers were still asleep in the halls. The Huk mayor, who was also a squadron leader, was opening his office on the first floor. The prewar mayor had been forced to move to the second floor. It was like other towns in central Luzon—two mayors, both claiming to be the choice of the people, one by the Nacionalistas, the other by the United Front—two mayors battling over the right to govern. In Guagua the battle appeared to be over and I was confronting the winner. I asked about the other mayor. He directed me toward a vacant office on the second floor. "Have you seen him?" I asked.

He did not answer my question. He had to tell me why he was

141

elected mayor. It was the power of the Huks. They had driven out the Japanese. Next the Americans and Filipino imperialists would have to go. Only then would Filipinos have true independence. I could have recited his speech.

I left him talking and searched all of the second floor, only to find it empty, deserted. I did not find the priest at the church. A caretaker told me the Huks had found him guilty of charging excessive fees for the sacraments. He might be in Manila. I did find the mayor's house, also deserted, and then his *compadre,* his son's godfather. There were enemies of the mayor. The *compadre* knew their names and where they lived, but he would not go with me.

"It is sad for the mayor," he said. "Sad for all of us."

An hour later I had a signed confession from a young man who seemed too gentle to be a murderer, and too ready to confess, as if he gloried in the crime.

"Where did you kill him?"

"At the river."

"Did you bury him there?"

"Jes, ser."

Abruptly he named friends who were with him, but I would not see them. They were hiding with a squadron in the *barrios.* Their order had been to take the mayor from his house in the dark. They took him to where the river runs through *cogon* grass. They beat him with a bamboo till he confessed that he had taken money that belonged to the people, a crime for which Huks made foxholing the penalty. In the dark they made him dig his grave. When light was in the sky they put him in the grave and began shoveling dirt over him.

He grabbed my wrists.

"Ser, I have the heart of a woman. I could not see a man buried alive. I cut his neck with a hoe."

Feeling sympathy for his youth, but revolted by his crime, I took him with me in the jeep, through town, past young men and women with Huk banners. At the edge of town the road narrowed to tracks made by the wide tires of carabao carts and, a few kilometers on, ended at a wall of gray-green *cogon.* The blades were serrated like a knife. I made him walk ahead and part a path for me.

We came to the riverbed, a stretch of dry sand hot in the sun, and turned upstream. A few hundred yards of plowing through the sand and he stopped to study some trees on a bluff.

"It is here."

That part of the riverbed looked like any other part.

"How do you know?"

"I will show you."

On his knees he began scooping out sand with his hands but it rolled back faster than he could scoop it. He looked up.

"I will only get a shovel."

I followed him out of the riverbed and toward a nipa hut set alone in the fields. A man and woman in brown rain hats were picking melons the size of coconuts. We asked for a shovel and the man brought it.

"You will eat the melon?" he asked me.

The woman sliced one with her bolo. She gave each of us a half, and from her look, I knew how grudgingly.

Again the boy dug. There was a whetting sound of sand on metal, and then the shovel struck the bamboo club. He lifted it out, a sandy, bloody piece of evidence. Again the sound of sand on metal, and then a solid thump. Another stroke cut away hair and scalp and bared a bloody skull.

"It is as I told you," the boy said calmly.

Feeling watched, I looked up. The man and woman had come to the edge of the bank and were looking down into the grave. They stared a long time and without a word went back across the fields.

We pushed sand lightly over the mayor and left him in his grave. I set the bamboo club in the sand to mark the spot and leaned the shovel against it.

Back in the jeep I asked the boy how he felt about what he had done. His voice was flat, emotionless. "It is not for me to feel. That is the discipline of the Huk."

Near the *municipio,* the mayor's *compadre* spoke to me furtively. "You have found him?"

"Yes."

"It is known that you have found him. The Huks know. The order has gone out to a squadron. They will not let you take the

143

body." He put his hand on mine. "It is a sadness for the people."

To me it was a threat the Army could not stand for. We had yielded too much already. Back in San Fernando, Captain Frederick listened to my account and agreed. He went to Colonel White and within an hour returned with a weapons carrier and a squad of soldiers eager to get at the Huks.

In Guagua I went to the Huk mayor. I wanted to tell him why I was there but he knew. I told him we would fire if we were fired on. He looked at the weapons carrier and soldiers but there was no sign that he would call the confrontation off. When I demanded help for removing the body he arranged for a bamboo stretcher and two Filipino bearers. We took them.

Before we came to the *cogon* grass we could see men in rain hats crossing fields toward the river. We could see bolos and clubs but no rifles. We left the weapons carrier at the edge of the *cogon* grass and, with tommy guns at ready, worked our way zigzag to the river bed. Beyond where the body lay, the men in rain hats had lined up on the bank, motionless, watching. The sergeant placed his men between them and the grave with guns trained on them, also waiting. A bearer took up the shovel. Nothing happened.

When we knew it was a standoff, the bearers lifted the body out on a straw mat and placed it on the stretcher. With the soldiers guarding our rear, we went slowly to the weapons carrier.

The best we could do for the mayor was to leave him at the churchyard with his *compadre.*

The show of force had worked. Sixth Army was ready to show more of it.

There was a message at the office from Don Pablo. A man in a *barrio* south of Bacolor was known to be the squadron leader who had ordered the foxholing of the treasurer. He had to be arrested and his gun confiscated. Reading the message as a command, I went to the *barrio,* a crowding of nipa huts along a creek bank. I had seen crowding and poverty in *barrios* on Leyte, and had smelled the foulness of sores left by the yaws. I had seen the same in Manila, in parts of Tondo, crowded by Filipinos and Chinese— streets of buy-and-sell, of open sewers, of disease and death. I had heard the pimping of an adolescent boy: "My sister, ser. She is djung. Two pesos only, ser."

In a *barrio* just as poor, as crowded, I found the house and climbed the bamboo-pole ladder. There was only a woman surrounded by half-naked children. She spoke Pampangan. I had no interpreter. She understood *esposo* and shook her head. I searched for the gun. Nothing.

Frustrated, I went to Don Pablo, who greeted me with praise and blame: praise for standing my ground in Guagua, blame for not capturing the man and his gun. He already knew what had happened. The man had gone out the back door when he saw my jeep. I did not find the gun. It was hidden in the thatch above my head. I should know more about Filipinos.

Any empathy I had with Luis Taruc, any tolerance for the Huk cause, had been shattered by the time I got to the jail the next morning. In non-Huk as well as Huk parts of Pampanga, the night had been a long living in terror, with armed Huk squadrons patrolling roads toward Angeles, Arayat, Malolos, Dinalupihan, with reports of kidnappings and liquidations, with skirmishes between Huks and USAFFEs breaking silences with sounds of rifle fire. Through the day before, propaganda units had put up posters faster than CIC agents and MPs could take them down. "Free the Huks," "Death to All Traitors," "*Mabuhay* Juan de la Cruz." Other posters called the people to a mass meeting in front of the church in San Fernando.

Huk leaders boasted that seethings in the *barrios* would come to a bloody boil at a site they had chosen: in front of the church, the enemy, only a few hundred feet from Sixth Army, also the enemy. It would be a Huk challenge to President Osmeña and to General MacArthur himself. As if his return was also a full restoration, MacArthur had decreed that the Commonwealth Government would be reformed as it was on Pearl Harbor Day. Officials, with the exception of those under investigation for collaboration, would resume their duties. He did not allow for the political unrest in Central Luzon, or for the local government under Huk officials elected by Huk voters, or for the will of the Huks to use the gun and bolo. Because the general thought martial law politically damaging, the Sixth Army had to be the peacekeeper.

As I entered the jail I heard the sound of saws and hammers. The frame of a structure was rising in the courtyard. I stopped, hardly believing what I was seeing. Only a gallows could take that shape. Only someone with a sick mind could order it built there, in full sight of every cell. No prisoner could look through his bars without seeing the shape. I went closer. Army carpenters were working from printed instructions, and literally by the numbers. The floor at the trapdoor level was in place. They were cutting and nailing the steps the condemned would take. *Sixteen treads. Seventeen risers.* The men read and sawed and counted.

"How are the prisoners taking it?" I asked the guard.

"Not good. Scared."

I saw for myself. As I walked past cells, prisoners stretched hands between bars and cried, "Please, ser, if you will only pity me." "If you will only save me." José Banal stared at me but said nothing.

When I came to Taruc's cell he gripped the bars and said angrily, "You see what they build. It is said they will hang us." He put his face between two bars. "This is how we will die." His tone softened. "I am glad you have come. I have things to say."

He squatted near the bars. I sat on the floor across from him. Neither of us could keep from looking out as carpenters fitted member after member and hammered. I could not tell him for whom the gallows was being built. I could suspect who would be the first to swing from it, but I had not been told.

Taruc had not finished talking of what it was like to be poor in Pampanga. "You have been on the road by the Pampanga River?"

I had. He had been a child in a *barrio* on the Pampanga River. His life was like theirs. He knew what it was like to be hungry. He knew what it was to be a boy with nothing to wear but a knit shirt that did not come down to the navel. He knew the humiliations. It was to help people like them that he had gone to school. It was to help them that the Huk had come into being.

Pfc William A. Owens in Houston, Texas, 23 June 1942.

Segments of the Death March, which followed Bataan's surrender on 9 April 1942. As many as one hundred people might be buried in a single grave on the March.

えんえんと続いてゆく捕虜の列。一糸乱れざる米軍の統制でもある。

Japanese on a Corregidor street exulting over their victory. Filipinos and American soldiers departed from here for the Death March.

Triumphant Japanese soldiers wave their Rising Sun flag in front of an American building, once a prize of Corregidor.

In front of the demolished church at Dulag, Generals Douglas Mac-Arthur and Walter Krueger celebrate the victorious American landing.

Troops of the Twenty-fourth Division waiting for enemy mortar and machine fire to be cleared before moving inland from Red Beach on A-day. Landings had to go around and through the palms.

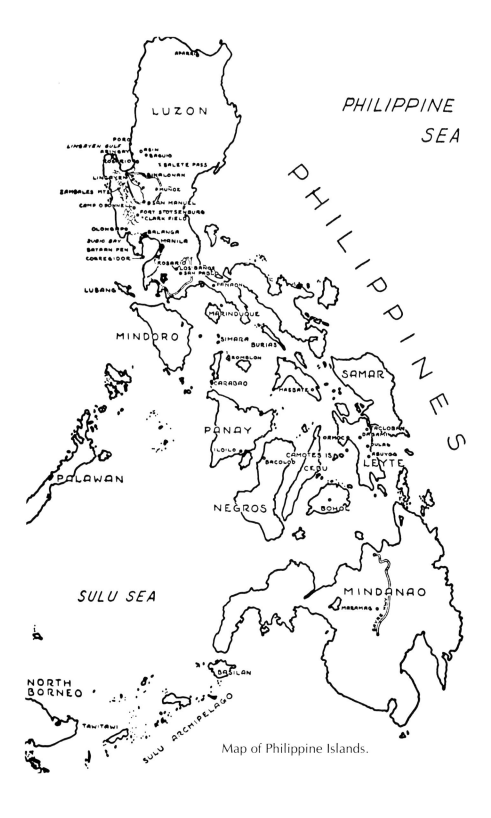

Map of Philippine Islands.

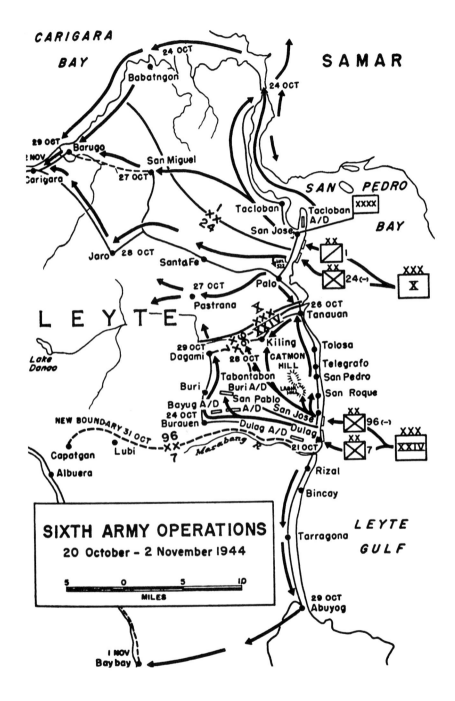

CARIGARA
BAY

SAMAR

Babatngon

24 OCT

24 OCT

29 OCT
! NOV
Barugo

Carigara

San Miguel

27 OCT

SAN PEDRO
XXXX

Tacloban
A/D

Tacloban
San Jose

BAY

LUNETA

XX
I

Jaro   28 OCT

SantaFe

XX
24 (–)

XXX
X

Palo

L E Y T E

27 OCT
Pastrana

26 OCT
Tanauan

X
X
XXX XXIV
X
X

Tolosa

Lake
Danao

29 OCT
Dagami

28 OCT

Kiling

CATMON
HILL

LABIRI
HILL

Telegrafo
San Pedro
San Roque

Buri

Tabontabon
Buri A/D

Bayug A/D
24 OCT
Burauen

San Pablo
A/D
San Jose

Dulag A/D

Dulag

XX
96 (–)

XX
7

XXX
XXIV

NEW BOUNDARY 31 OCT

96
XX
7

Lubi

Marabang

21 OCT

Capatgan
Albuera

Rizal

Bincay

SIXTH ARMY OPERATIONS
20 October – 2 November 1944

LEYTE
GULF

Tarragona

5   0   5   10
MILES

29 OCT
Abuyog

I NOV
Baybay

Sixth Army Operations Map.

Sixth Army Plan. 1 November 1944.

The legislative building in Manila, a crumbling piece of ruins from which the enemy had to be pried in order to save Malacañan. Day and night, bombs blasted the buildings and craters pocked the palace grounds.

For **PECSON**

SENATOR

Mrs. Geronima T. Pecson, keeper of the Malacañan palace during the Japanese raids and later the first woman senator of the Philippines.

25 October 1944. A direct hit on an ammunitions dump by a Japanese bomber—some three hundred men died.

Staff of the Hukbalahap Regiment: Lieutenant Owens, at right; Major Frederick, second from right; Colonel Bernard Poblete, alias José Banal, at center rear; Poblete's son Tomás, to his right.

Hukbalahap Regiment, Minalin, Pampanga, May 1945. Major Harold F. Frederick, right, and Lieutenant William A. Owens, second from right, inspect camp.

The *luneta* of Minalin, Pampanga, 22 May 1945. Lieutenant Owens inspects arms and inducts recruits into the Hukbalahap Regiment.

Major Frederick supervising soldiers of Hukbalahap Regiment, who are preparing for combat.

Major Frederick and Lieutenant Owens inspecting Hukbalahap bivouac.

The Hukbalahap Regiment in last salute to Lieutenant Owens, left, and Major Frederick, right, May 1945.

After the Hukbalahap Regiment's departure for combat, the mayor of Minalin, Pampanga, "crowned" Lieutenant Owens with a Filipino rain hat, naming him an honorary *tao,* or peasant.

As he talked I watched the workmen raise a beam and then a crossbeam. I watched them lower a rope with a hangman's knot. I watched as they tested the trapdoor. There was no way not to watch, no way not to listen to him, or to the jumbled pleadings of prisoners who did not want to die.

"We had to have the Huk."

"Do you have to kill to get what you want?"

"There are some. The Japanese, and now the *tulisaffes*."

I asked about the treasurer and the mayor, killed by boys too young to know what the Huk had asked of them. He could see them, or boys like them, watching the gallows going up. There was no softening, no attempt at justification. "In a revolution like ours, mistakes will be made."

I showed him a mass meeting poster. "Will you stop it?"

"It is too late. The people will come. It is the will of the people and they will come."

I left him and drove through *barrios* where Huk squadrons roamed with their hammer-and-sickle banners. From their hemp sacks and Army musette bags I knew they were taking forced contributions of food but I did not stop them. They could be armed. *Kempei Tai* had discouraged carrying concealed weapons by requiring men to tuck their *barong Tagalogs* in their pants. These men wore theirs outside.

Later I went to Don Pablo. He took me to a verandah and we sat in wicker chairs overlooking a garden. He knew why I had come but I told him the places I had been and the kinds of trouble I had to predict if the mass meeting should go on.

"Americans are too easy on the Huks," he said. "That is known."

He had more to say. It was the way of Americans to compromise. There could be no compromise with traitors. Taruc was a traitor. So was Alejandrino. Bernardo Poblete was a murderer. It was he who had murdered a manager at the Pasudeco sugar central. He had said this to General MacArthur, his friend.

On a stair landing, after I had left him, I heard the sound of beating and a man screaming. I ran to a guard room. USAFFE soldiers had stripped a man to his *abaca* shorts and had forced him to kneel. With bamboo rods they had beaten him across the back and shoulders till welts rose.

The man saw me and stretched out his hands. "Please, ser, help me. I have done nothing."

The beating stopped. A soldier faced me. "He is a Huk. We will make him confess."

"By beating him?"

"Jes, ser."

"Don Pablo's orders?"

The soldier evaded. "You are the CIC?"

I showed him my badge and ordered the man to put on his shirt and come with me.

"You will investigate him?"

"Yes, in the protection of the jail."

For his own safety he had to be in protective custody. I put him under arrest and he went with me willingly. On the way to San Fernando he said he was not sure but he thought that some of the USAFFE soldiers had been members of the *Makapili*—Filipino soldiers organized by the Japanese to fight Americans. At Don Pablo's he had seen soldiers who were *Makapili* before they became USAFFEs. At San Fernando he held onto my hand. He was glad I had come, glad that he would be safe in jail.

I had not left enough time to go again to Don Pablo's.

When I arrived at his office, Captain Frederick was at the church, the cathedral, talking with the priests. The market was beginning to fill up with people arriving for the mass meeting and the priests were afraid. The Huks were anticleric. At least one priest had been liquidated. Others had left their parishes and fled to Manila. The priests were asking Captain Frederick to order American soldiers to guard the church. There was a room upstairs in the *convento* where he could watch and see what the Huks did.

I had to patrol the road from Guagua and Betis to see how many people were coming in from the *barrios*. There were people on the road—I could not tell how many. Night, impenetrably black, came down on me west of Bacolor. Afraid to use full lights, I traveled blackout. All along the way shadowy figures showed for a moment and then leapt into darkness.

When I returned, Captain Frederick was in his office, going over crowd control plans he had received from the Army. Soldiers were coming, a detachment with enough tanks and firepower to fight the whole Huk army. Soldiers would patrol the streets that night. So would CIC agents. The priests were our friends. We had to prove we were theirs.

When I went near the church the streets were dark but not silent. There was a hum of voices from people packed close together along church walls and a clack of wooden sandals from people crowding in. Sharp above these sounds came the booted tread of soldiers patroling the streets, squad after squad, shoulder to shoulder.

When morning light flowed in at the windows, I went to the balcony to watch. An old woman was stooping around the areca palms, picking up nuts, undisturbed by Huks with banners taking a shortcut across our parking lot. A tank crawled past, headed toward the jail. Soldiers in green helmets and green fatigues sat on the hatches, not moving, looking as if they had been pressed in the same mould that had shaped the contours of the tank.

Filipinos walking toward the jail opened a way for the tank in the center of the concrete slab. They kept their bare feet and wooden sandals to well-worn paths on either side. Some carried red banners; some carried food wrapped in banana palm leaves. Some shouted "Free the Huks!" to others going toward the church. Whatever the direction of their feet, their faces were the same: weary, sullen, angry. The ones who went to the jail pressed together and stared across an open space at the blockaded entrance. Four heavy tanks stood between. All was silent except for a faraway tapping of bamboo on bamboo.

At the church were more tanks, but the soldiers let the people gather, their faces directed toward a platform, cannon muzzles at their backs. Huk squadrons grouped near the tanks and on the edges of the crowd. A dangerous confrontation was in the making. It might have been stopped earlier, but not now. Neither side would be turned back.

149

I showed my badge at the *convento* door and was ushered to an upstairs room where I could see, but not be seen. A young priest waited in a chair by mine to interpret for me. Only a few years out of Spain, he had become fluent in Capampangan, the language of the province.

A noise from the crowd made us turn to the window. A man in white pants and red-embroidered shirt leapt to the center of the stage.

"We know him," the priest whispered. "He was a priest of the Church, but he is Filipino and would not follow the discipline. Now he is a Huk and speaking for the Huk."

Silently the crowd listened to him welcome them in the language Americans had shortened in name to Pampangan; silently they watched when he left the stage and stood among them, waiting. For what? My interpreter did not know.

A woman in a bright red *tierno* stepped from behind a bamboo screen and bowed to the shouts of Filipinos, the whistles of American soldiers. She waited a moment and went to the center of the stage, where she stood with her eyes steady on a tank and the mouth of a cannon.

"Scarlett O'Hara."

"Alejandrino's wife?"

The priest did not know.

She raised her hand in a clenched-fist salute and held it. There was a murmur and a shifting forward of people returning her salute. When they were quiet she lowered her hand and began speaking.

Again the priest whispered.

"She is commander of propaganda and entertainment for the Huk. She is announcing a pantomine she herself has written. She herself will play the spirit of the true Filipino. It is called *The Sorrows of the Philippines*."

With a toss of her head she began a gay dance, a happy dance, without music or castanets, the rhythm of the dance the clack of her *bakya* on the wooden floor. The brown of her skin was touched with gold in the sun; the red of her dress flashed and burned.

She stopped and reached her arms toward the sun. Six men came leaping through the crowd, their Spanish helmets flashing silver, their wooden broadswords raised for combat. She fled before them, and the stage was filled with leaping bodies, stamping feet. On and on she ran, her black hair flying loose in the wind, till she could run no more.

At the center of the stage the men closed around her, with their sword points touching her. When she saw there was no escape she sank to her knees and leaned her head forward so that her hair covered her face. The crowd stared, silent. The only sound was again the faraway tap-tapping of bamboo on bamboo, a message. In a whirling dance one of the men transformed himself into a priest in a white cassock and a Spanish friar's hat. He stopped with his hands raised as if to bless her and dropped an iron chain around her shoulders.

While the priest stood with his hands raised, six men dressed like American soldiers, with rifles and campaign hats of the Spanish-American War, came to the stage and pointed bayonets at her. As she lay prostrate on the floor, six Americans fought five Spaniards, while the priest stood to one side, his arms folded. In an orgy of bayoneting the Americans won and tossed the Spaniards from the stage.

The tap of bamboo came again, sharper, faster. She raised herself slowly to her knees and stretched her hands out to the Americans. As if hardly seeing her they danced past her, and the priest danced with them, around and around at a treadmill pace, to the steady tap of bamboo.

The pattern was broken by five men in the peaked caps of Japanese soldiers. Shouting "Banzai!" and swinging their Samurai swords they ran through the crowd and onto the stage. At the moment of encounter, the Americans threw their guns down and ran.

Again the priest stood aside. With folded arms he looked on while Japanese soldiers threw her to the floor.

Their dance was arrogant but brief, broken by six Filipinos coming to save her. They wore white barong Tagalogs and brandished Moro krises, except for one, the leader. He wore the brown abaca shirt and shorts of the tao, the symbol of the Huk. Slashing and stabbing, they drove the Japanese from the stage and threw the priest to the floor. The leader lifted the woman to her feet. Again she whirled in a lively dance and he whirled with her.

Again there was a tapping of bamboo. Silently the dancers left the stage. Silently the people waited, and as silently the American soldiers. The bamboo tapping for sending messages I knew—Filipinos called it the jungle telegraph. I understood the patient waiting of the people for the speeches that would come. I did not understand the priest's bitter comment: "Lies. All lies. And the people believe them."

With the first propaganda harangue over and the likelihood of nothing different to follow it, Captain Frederick and I went to lunch with the priests in the refectory. Still engrossed in dance rituals that indeed showed the sorrows of a people, I asked the priest why there was no truth in them. He talked about the traditional rituals of the Church, kept by Spanish priests as well as they could keep them among people converted from paganism. The problem for the Church was that pagan rituals were deeply ingrained and there were never enough priests to keep them from creeping into traditional worship. A folk Catholicism had developed, with beliefs and rituals the church could not accept. I admired *The Sorrows of the Philippines*. He condemned it. He rejected the use of anything religious for political purposes.

The last speech ended, I walked among the crowds in the market. There had been neither violence nor disturbance. The tanks and soldiers had withdrawn. I went to the jail. The carpenters, their work finished, had gone away, leaving their structure like a bent elbow against the sky, with the rope hanging from the beam, the hangman's noose motionless in the still air.

• • •

San Fernando was quiet the next morning. Troops and tanks had moved toward front lines farther north, where Japanese resistance was strong and American progress was slow. Other places in Pampanga were not so quiet. The show of troops and tanks at the mass meeting had left the Huks hostile. My informers came in the night to tell me how hostile. So did the Huk mayor of San Fernando. Overnight the Huks had many spokesmen and a sheaf of posted threats: more kidnappings and killings as long as their leaders were in jail; more liquidation and foxholing of landlords and priests, and then of Americans. I believed them. So did landlords in their *calesas* and *caratelas,* fleeing, taking their families to safety in Manila. So did CIC agents, bringing in first a report of a Chinese squadron in Floridablanca largely supported by Chinese Communists on the mainland, and then a report of the arrest of two Moros from Mindanao, there to study Huk revolutionary tactics.

In the night, a Huk squadron had bribed or threatened Filipino guards at an Army ammunition dump near Bacolor to let them take enough cases of guns and ammunition to arm several squadrons. In my investigation of the guards all I could get them to say was "I am ashamed, ser."

Orders, we knew, were coming from San Fernando jail, but we were powerless to stop them. We moved Alejandrino to Taruc's cell and isolated them as well as we could, but we could not shut out the jungle telegraph of bamboo tapping, or the message conveyed by the way a jail visitor had his hair combed or his rain hat tipped. Harassed by Huk lawlessness and by landlords begging for protection, General MacArthur's headquarters wavered between hard lines and soft lines, afraid to appear as harsh as the Japanese, afraid to damage our Oriental example of American democracy.

Sixth Army requested limited martial law. GHQ, tacitly admitting that we had failed to restore law and order, was willing to compromise with the extremists, even in questionable ways.

"Why not use the Lavas?"

The question had come through channels from GHQ down to Captain Frederick. Now he was asking me.

"Risky."

"Why?"

We both knew. So did Sixth Army. It was a compromise and the Lavas could take advantage of it. The problem handed to us, we went over their files. Vicente Lava had been head of the Communist Party in the Philippines and a friend of such radical social reformers as Juan Feleo and Pedro Abad Santos, the former elected Huk governor of Nueva Ecija Province, the latter martyred by the

Japanese. Ruth Propper, according to informers, had been a Communist courier between the United States and the Philippines. As intellectuals the two were widely recognized. He was a member of the American Academy of Science and highly respected for his research in sugarcane. GHQ hoped the Lavas were humanitarian enough to be repelled by senseless violence and reasonable enough to understand that Huk disruptions could only hinder preparations for Philippine independence. Nothing in their files supported that hope.

Captain Frederick's order was terse. "Bring them in."

I brought them from their home in Malolos not with a command but with a request, not with a plea but with a promise that there would be a fair review of both sides. Our only expectation was that they would help reduce violence and bloodshed. They made no promises.

Less reluctant than her husband to go, Ruth Propper sat on the front seat with me, making me captive to her bombardment of Huk complaints. The main one was the Malolos massacre, in which American soldiers had disarmed a Huk squadron and let the USAFFEs murder as many as twenty of them. I argued that our records showed different circumstances, and only two Huks killed. Her answer was that Huks would not forget the Malolos massacre. Her husband, the scholar turned social reformer, remained quiet, reserved. He was no longer scholar or scientist or academic. Under the Japanese he had left his laboratory to become, with his brother Jesus, counselor to the Hukbalahap. He listened to her condemn the CIC, and nodded gloomily.

At the office Captain Frederick explained what was being asked of them. The time was right, he told them, to show the people that there was a nonviolent way. Fighting was moving farther away—to the north in Luzon, to the south in Zamboanga—and would soon be over. In a little over a year the Philippines would be free and democratic. Differences could be settled at the ballot box. They were polite but skeptical. After many questions, they agreed to work with us, but in a manner that made me question their commitment.

"You will give the orders?" Vicente asked.

Captain Frederick gave the orders. We would go to towns and *barrios* and talk peace to mayors and *barrio tenientes*. He thought we should start with the larger towns in Pampanga.

"You do not know Pampanga," Vicente said. "There are many USAFFEs."

They were afraid of the USAFFEs. They would meet with Huk mayors but not with Commonwealth mayors. They would travel with me all day but at night they would go back to Malolos. It was safer for them at Malolos. Vicente did not want an interpreter. He was Tagalog but he knew Capampangan well enough to interpret.

Ruth Propper almost stopped us before we got started. She became emotional about the Huks in jail. If only the Army would release Taruc and Alejandrino the people's trust would be restored and there would be no need for us to go. Captain Frederick was firm. Once the violence had stopped their release would be considered.

She was persistent.

"The Army pays USAFFEs to fight Huks. Why won't the Army pay Huks for the thousands of Japanese they killed?"

Captain Frederick had no answer. He knew that guerrilla leaders were building political power with Army dollars and benefits. Ramón Magsaysay had increased his unit from under a hundred to several hundred. Ferdinand Marcos had enlisted many more in his Markings.

Suddenly she changed her tone. "We will go."

An ill-assorted trio, we went south on the Manila highway, turned off on a dry-weather road, crossed a railroad and a creek bridge rickety under a jeep, and passed through the *población* of Macabebe on a road that would end at Masantol. For reasons they did not explain they wanted to start at Masantol. On either side of the road we saw men and women harvesting rice in a way that might have come out of Biblical times. Men and women cut stalks with their bolos and gathered them in bundles in their arms. Women and children trampled the stalks on bamboo mats. Women with split bamboo trays winnowed the grain in the wind. Outside nipa huts women hulled rice, pounding, pounding with wooden mortar, wooden pestle. I asked why they still did it this way. Lava, the

155

scientist, had no answer other than that they had always done it this way. It pleased the people.

"See how peaceful it is," the Lavas said.

I saw but was skeptical.

"What percentage will the Huk take?"

"Not so much as the landlord. Only enough for the squadrons. The people are glad to give to the brave men who saved them from the Japanese."

I did not argue.

Masantol was at the edge of a low swamp and close to Manila Bay, with rice paddies on one side, fish ponds on the other. The Huk mayor met us at the jeep and welcomed us. When we told him the Lavas would speak he sent runners to call the people to the *municipio*. He asked me if I knew José Banal and I suspected this was why they had wanted to start at Masantol.

While the people were gathering, the mayor took us to see *barrio* Esteban, where Banal and his squadrons had fought a company of Japanese soldiers. The Japanese had more men and better weapons. Banal had only the weapons he had picked up after the defeat at Bataan. With these and not enough bullets he had held the Japanese off for two days.

"We honor El Mundo," the mayor said. "It is a pity that he is in the San Fernando jail."

I let the remark pass. I still had not interrogated José Banal.

People gathered at the entrance to the *municipio*. Some shook my hand. Some knelt before Vicente Lava and kissed his hand. I was the CIC, the mayor told them, and he asked me to speak. Speaking for the Army, I talked only about the need for a government without violence, and about the Army order against carrying weapons. Vicente talked to them much longer and in Capampangan. I felt that he was saying the same thing and I did not ask for interpretation. When he finished, the mayor announced that the order against carrying weapons would be enforced in Masantol. I believed him.

When the crowd began to drift away we went back to Macabebe and had a coconut drink with the Huk mayor in his thatch house. He took us to *barrio* Alasas, where José Banal also had fought Japanese soldiers. He had held out against them as long as he could and at night had had to withdraw and hide in the Candaba swamps. Japanese soldiers never again came to Masantol and Macabebe.

"He is a great fighter, this José Banal," the mayor told me. "Many Macabebe scouts fought with him. You have heard of the Macabebe scouts?"

I had heard of them as mercenaries who fought fiercely and changed sides when reward outbalanced loyalty. I had also heard of how they pretended to be soldiers for Aguinaldo but only long enough to betray him to the American Army. The mayor was eager to tell us more. He took us past stone fortifications built by the Spaniards when Macabebe was one of their centers. The work had been done by Indians brought from Mexico. These Indians never went home. They stayed in the Philippines and married and had families. Blood of people the Spaniards called *Indio* in Mexico flowed in the veins of people in the Philippines, also called *Indio* by the Spaniards. He told the story as certainty. He wanted us to know why the Macabebe scout was a fighter, how the scout had the warrior strain.

He had more to tell me. Twice in the early days of Spanish rule, Macabebe soldiers had taken part in the massacre of Chinese in and around Manila. Loyal to the Spanish in their fight against Aguinaldo, the scouts had fought a detachment of his rebels on Mount Arayat. A year or so later, now on Aguinaldo's side, they had helped to capture Macabebe, San Fernando, and Bacolor, and eventually to drive the Spaniards out. The Spaniards gone, they fought with Aguinaldo against the Americans. Still nimble-footed in their loyalties, they fought with the Americans against Aguinaldo and forty years later against the Japanese. I thought then why he was recalling so much. Pampangans would fight Americans to gain independence.

I could detect no feeling of animosity or threat, but strong pride in the fighting men of Macabebe. The mayor was affable in meetings on the street and in a larger meeting at the *municipio*. He was less so when I asked about Huk squadrons in Macabebe. They had none, but others did pass through, hunting Japanese stragglers. The mayor talked to the Lavas in Capampangan and they went to eat with friends in a *barrio*.

He took me to a Victorian house not far from the Spanish fortifications. Our host was a landowner, and before the war one of the elite in Pampanga. I was not the first American he had entertained in his home, and there had been guests as well who were members of the *ilustrado* in Manila. During the Japanese occupation he had become a supporter of the Huks and a contributor to their squadrons.

"You like the *pancit?*" he asked. "It is the bread of Pampanga."

I knew it only as strips of rice noodles drying in the sun. I said yes and he led us to a dining room that might have been American. Over our noodles and vegetables he talked about changes under the Japanese. For centuries under the Spaniards and then the Americans the Pampangans had maintained a two-class society: landlords and tenants. In the unrest before Bataan and Corregidor the movement had been toward one class. Fearing the Japanese, many landlords had gone to Manila, and the people had had to depend on the Hukbalahap to defend them. Whether he completely agreed with the Huks I could not tell. He had been allowed to keep his land. In return, he contributed *palay* from his crops, without counting *pavanes* or complaining.

When we were with the Lavas again the landowner assured me that the Army would have no trouble in Macabebe, but there should be no attempt to disarm or disband the squadrons.

"Is it not so?" he asked the Lavas.

They agreed.

In two more days we had worked our way up the Pampanga River through the towns of Apalit, San Simon, San Miguel, Candaba, San Luis, and across to Arayat, through scenes of hopeless poverty, through the seeding ground of some of the most violent rebellions in the Philippines. The Lavas had me stop in the poorest *barrios*. They showed me where dissident groups had had their beginnings. Most had failed but new ones kept rising. Among them were the Santa Iglesias, a strongly anti-Catholic movement that preached not the promise of heaven but the promise of land on earth when the hold of church and *cacique* could be broken. All this in Pampanga Province, which the church had regarded the most Christian of the provinces.

By the time we reached Candaba, I thought our campaign was going well, but I found myself excluded from community discussions because the Lavas used little English and failed to interpret for me. My informer from San Miguel told me that though they were speaking to the people in favor of law and order they were also advising squadron leaders to take their soldiers and weapons and go into hiding—in the Candaba swamps, where there were boa constrictors. Americans would not follow them there. When I challenged the Lavas, they had the arrogance of righteousness. What they did they did for the people.

I took them to Malolos. Our parting was full of anger. They had betrayed me and broken their promises to the Army. To them I was the deceiver. I had feigned friendship, friendship and an open mind, only to use them. Law and order? That would have to come out of disorder, as the Huks gained strength.

• • •

Not the silence of peace but the sounds of violence followed. Day and night reports of trouble came in, reports of fire fights and kidnappings in towns and *barrios* Huks had not claimed before. In darkness they surrounded a *barrio* and fired into it, not with a salvo but with a slow, random pattern that left people sleepless and afraid. In daylight they entered the *barrio* and after a propaganda rally asked for volunteers and donations of *palay*. The ones too frightened to resist shared what they had and let their names be put down as Huks. The ones who resisted had their goods confiscated, were tortured into swearing Huk allegiance, and in countless cases faced death in a foxhole.

Some squadrons turned destructively anti-American. They raided arsenals and supply dumps. From ambushes they sniped at Army vehicles. The gasoline pipeline from Lingayen Gulf to Clark Field became a target for sabotage. Filipinos, Huks or not, cut holes in the line, filled whatever vessels they had, and left the gasoline spilling on the ground. The line was cut faster than engi-

159

neers could repair it. Some days all planes at Clark Field had to be grounded. Attacks on Formosa and targets closer to Japan had to be delayed.

Inevitably, I felt, their anger turned toward me. First there were rumors, and then captured evidence. Huks had put a price on my head—ten thousand pesos dead or alive. I worried and Captain Frederick worried with me, but I had to keep working. He did limit my travel to daylight hours and to frequently traveled roads. Roads north, east, and west were almost deserted by civilian traffic, but not the road south toward Manila. It was still the escape route for families in *caratelas* drawn by Mongolian ponies.

Our informers reported that Huk squadrons were massing, some at the caves on the side of Mount Arayat that they called their Flying Fortress, some deep in the Candaba swamps. From either place they could attack and retreat. In either place they could hold out indefinitely, even against the American Army. These reports repeated a message that never changed: the longer we kept Taruc and Alejandrino in jail, the more violent the attacks would be; the more civilians killed, the more vicious the retaliations against the USAFFE. Request for martial law still denied, Sixth Army turned again to compromise, this time with Taruc and Alejandrino. It was a compromise that would embarrass the CIC but we had no alternative. The orders from Colonel White were to begin negotiations.

The timing, we all knew, could be defeating. The first execution at San Fernando was scheduled. Mendoza, the first Filipino to receive the death penalty for spying for the Japanese, would be hanged. Requested but not ordered to be an official witness of the execution, I chose not to but to work my time around it.

I entered the courtyard a little before sunrise. The hangman and a doctor were at the gallows. Mendoza stood inside the gate, his only companion a young priest. He was a condemned spy. For him there would be no ceremony, no band playing the dead march, no detail of soldiers drawn up to watch.

Just as sun glow touched the western wall of the courtyard, an MP gave a command. Mendoza hesitated. The priest began a prayer and they moved slowly toward the gallows. Startling handclaps echoed through the courtyard. The Japanese soldiers were

160

summoning their gods for morning worship. They were standing in their cell, facing outward, and there was a subdued "*Tenno Heika. Banzai!*" Some were crying. Some glanced furtively at the gallows.

"A hell of a way for East to meet West," I said to an MP as I left.

When I went in again, the body was wrapped in an Army blanket. The Japanese prisoners were silent. So were the Filipinos. They squatted with their eyes cast down, as if they had seen more than they could bear. My throat tight for them, I passed close to their cells. Some reached their hands out to me but said nothing.

Taruc and Alejandrino were squatting at the back of their cell, their rice untouched in cans beside the door.

"You came too late," Taruc said bitterly. "You would have seen Army justice. You did not see what we saw. You only saw them take the body away."

He talked angrily against an Army that, with twenty-four hours a day for hanging, hanged at the time of Japanese morning worship. It was a tradition to hang at sunrise, he knew, but the Army could have waited—for the Japanese if not for the Filipinos who had to live the day in such a knowledge of death, a fear they might be next.

I gripped his hand for a moment. He returned the grip. "You do not come so often," he said quietly.

"I went other places."

"We know. You went with the Lavas. My friends tell me you went many places with the Lavas." His tone became accusing. "You go with them but not with me. The people want to see me. They want to see me in the *barrios*. I thought hard of you because you took them when the people wanted me. They do not do what you want and you have come to me?"

"Yes."

"Why?"

I was looking into the eyes of a man who had ordered the deaths of hundreds, perhaps thousands, but I could not see in them the eyes of a killer, only eyes that had looked on death. "We need your help."

"You had the Lavas."

"They are propagandists. You are the *Supremo*."

He was essential. He could command; Huk soldiers would obey. He had to know that people could no longer tell the difference between a Huk squadron and bandits robbing in the name of the Huk.

"You can help."

"In jail?"

It would be a way of working toward their release, I suggested. They were not willing to agree without immediate release. They would go as free men or not at all.

When I knew that arguing was futile I went to José Banal, who had lived nearly twice the years of Taruc, who had served as soldier for both the Americans and the Huks. In loyalty to one he had surrendered as prisoner to the other, and for both he had suffered. After so many days in jail he looked older, weaker, but there was no anger in his talk with me, only a sadness that Americans after so many years did not know his people. If I could only see how they lived I would know that by nature they were not violent—wars and oppression had made them so. They wanted to be led in the ways of peace and justice. He knew a *barrio* on Manila Bay called San Juan. If I would only go to San Juan I would understand better. He made it imperative that I go.

Most of the way I was on the route of the Death March. Slowly I drove past rice paddies where families were at harvest. They might have been a thousand miles from the sounds of war; they might have belonged to a past a thousand years old. They looked not up but down, at the land, the rice. These were the essentials, the things that mattered, these and the rituals of seasons. The dry season was about to be over, the rainy season about to begin. They worked to keep the rhythm.

The scene changed briefly as I went through one *población* after another: Bacolor, Betis, Sexmoan, Lubao. After I turned southward at Lubao I saw only the *taos* José Banal had wanted me to see, and I understood a little of what he had meant when he sent me. The way of the *tao* was the way of semiprimitive man. The people in their wide rain hats and rough *abaca* garments must have looked the same when the first Spaniards came, the first Americans, the first Japanese. Whatever change in thought had reached them, whatever awakening they were going through, the land was the same, and the seasons, and the planting and harvesting had to go on. The people belonged to the land, no matter who held the title.

The concrete slab road ended in a dirt road rough even for a jeep, but I kept on and on, through *barrios* Santo Tomas, San Nicolas, Primero. At last I came to San Juan, where the land ends in swamps and a network of rivers and fish ponds at the edge of Manila Bay.

It was the quiet time of sunset. The men had tied up their boats and hung their nets to dry in loops of web on tall bamboo poles. They were now in their homes—bamboo and grass huts built high on stilts that were ringed with the records of many tides. Smoke seeped through thatched roofs. I paused and caught the mingled smell of cooking fires, and fish and *palay* in cooking pots. The motor off, I could hear the muted sounds of many voices, and then the louder voices of people who had come to doors and windows.

I turned back where the land ended, and through each *barrio* the sound of the jeep brought people out to stand and look as I passed by. Seeing them, so many of them, all expressionless, like masked faces in a mass meeting, I knew a little of what José Banal had wanted me to comprehend. In such places was the reservoir of revolution, waiting only to be stirred by a leader. In places like this the Huks would win. Enough *barrios* won and there would be no turning them back. If not the Huks, some other self-proclaimed messiah would come, and with him less of peace, more of the sword.

In Lubao, on my way back, I picked up an order signed by a USAFFE commander. It was brief: "Shoot Huks on sight." I went at once to the *municipio* to see Major José Lingad, officer in charge of the USAFFE in Lubao. He was courteous to me but firm in his conviction that shooting Huks was the only way to stop them. There was new trouble from the Chinese squadron in Florida-

blanca. But the USAFFE would stop them. With their United States
uniforms, weapons, and pay they would recruit an anti-Huk army.
That was their mission. They had killed many already.

"How many?"

He ignored the question. Instead he took me to the drill field
and barracks. He had the soldiers and equipment of an army the
size of a company.

Late at night on 14 March 1945 I gave Captain Frederick a report on what was an open declaration of war between USAFFEs
and Huks. I saw no way to secure the law and order of our mission. Neither did he. On that day he had received word that General MacArthur had for the third time turned down a request for the
use of troops in Central Luzon. In another of his inconsistencies,
the general had given the reason that he knew Pampanga and was
sympathetic with the Huks. Agents, disillusioned, disaffected,
gathered in the office and bitched. The general was playing politics. All Filipinos were his little brown brothers. To us it seemed
that the Commonwealth Government had a long way to go before
it could deal with disaffection, let alone with insurrection.

With one statement MacArthur had destroyed much of the ini-
tiative in our outfit to arrest, investigate, prepare dossiers for trials.
As if he had had enough of the situation, Captain Frederick asked
for suggestions. Mine startled them. "Free Taruc and Alejandrino."

It was compromise beyond anything they had considered.
"On what terms?" Captain Frederick asked.

"Whatever they demand. Free them and work with them—
the way we have worked with the USAFFEs. One's no better than
the other."

They were all doubtful, but the captain was willing to find out
what could be done. He told us to hit the sack and went to find
Colonel White.

By the next morning the Army had softened. So did Taruc and
Alejandrino when they heard how close we were to a shooting
war. If that came, the Army would be forced to declare martial
law. I spoke to them as earnestly as I could. "We are asking you to
work with us."

They asked their same question: "In jail?"

"No. Outside."

"No restrictions?"

There had to be restrictions, the Army insisted, but the Army wanted to save lives. The Army was willing to compromise. "You will have to sign an agreement. We will make it as easy on you as the Army will allow."

They asked to be left alone for a few minutes. Confident, I went to the guard and signed for their release. When I went back they shook hands with me. They would do what the Army asked. I reminded Alejandrino that he was still the mayor of Arayat. As such, he had a special responsibility to the Commonwealth Government. He only nodded.

When we walked through the courtyard some prisoners yelled "*Mabuhay*" at them. Others begged me: "Please take me. I am good, Joe. I no do nothing." Silently José Banal watched them go, his hands gripping the bars.

In the office with Captain Frederick they were friendly and less demanding than I had expected. Almost lightheartedly they signed an eleven-point agreement, the conditions harsher than I had expected: Huk squadrons will surrender their weapons; kidnapping and liquidating will end; *palay* will no longer be confiscated; their loyalty to the American and Commonwealth governments will be observed. The agreement was dated 15 March 1945; the two had been in jail since 25 February. They shook hands with Captain Frederick as if he had done them a friendly favor.

In the parking lot, where passersby could see, they shook hands, calling me Captain Frederick also. With misgivings I watched them go—two little men, nonheroic in their *barong Tagalogs,* khaki pants, wooden sandals. They had done what they thought we wanted, had said what they thought we wanted to hear, in characteristic Filipino fashion. In the same Filipino fashion they could regard the agreement as a piece of paper and forget it. I followed them to the market and watched as crowds gathered around them. I felt the control we had bargained for slipping away.

To be fair to Taruc and Alejandrino, as well as to reduce violence, we all agreed that the USAFFEs would have to give up their anti-Huk campaign and serve only as ordered by the United States Army. Expecting help, I went to Don Pablo. He was arrogant and angry. USAFFE informers had already told him that Taruc and Alejandrino had been released. It was a mistake. There would be nothing gained, and lives lost. He knew them well and distrusted them. His distrust included me. He accused me of being on the side of the Huks, of being radical, anti-Filipino, against the American interests in the Philippines. He could consider my traveling with Huks only as betrayal.

While we argued, the sound of beating and screaming rose from the guard room. I ran down and found two USAFFEs in uniform beating a young man. I stood over him. "What's he done?"

"Huk spy, ser. We are investigating him."

"By beating him?"

"Only if we beat him will he confess."

"If he confesses—if he is a spy—what will you do?"

"Kill him. It is the order."

The man stood up and clung to my hand. "Please, ser, pity me."

I did. Poor devil. Poor devils. Poor Filipinos. Caught. Caught. Caught. In a conflict thrust upon them.

I took him to San Fernando jail for safety. Then I wrote an angry report against Don Pablo and his USAFFE guards and the special privileges given him. I ended it with a demand that the Army reprimand him by taking away the guards and machine guns.

Before Taruc and Alejandrino left San Fernando, informers told us, they swore they had not signed an agreement, and that they were free without condition. Later, the kind of report we had dreaded came in. Huk squadrons were gathering in the Candaba swamps. Other Huks were with Taruc and Alejandrino in *barrios* near Mount Arayat, and Kandating had become a headquarters. The agreement had been broken.

"What did you expect?" cynical agents asked. "Commie bastards. You won't find me busting ass over them again."

Captain Frederick came back from G-2 and called me in.

Colonel White had been forced to take action against me. Don
Pablo had written General MacArthur and had named me the most
dangerous American in the Philippines. He demanded that I be
stripped of my duties and investigated for subversion. The letter
had been bucked down through channels to Colonel White for action. I was not allowed to see it. His action was light; he did not
reprimand me but he did put me on warning.

In the middle of the night a band of Filipinos had overpowered
Filipino guards at the Army dump near Bacolor. Cases of rifles and
ammunition were missing.
"Huks or USAFFEs?" I asked the guards.
"Who knows?" They shrugged. "Such things happen."
"With the help of the guards?"
"Oh, no. We are the friends of the Americans."
Friends or not, they had let another hundred or so rifles go
underground for one side or the other.
The Army responded decisively. Don Pablo lost his guards.
American soldiers replaced Filipino guards at installations in Cen-
tral Luzon.

FIVE

MOUNT ARAYAT was sanctuary and symbol of strength to the Huks, as it had been to bandits and *insurrectos* through the centuries, at least as far back as the Spanish conquest. Huks had another shield in the ring of *barrios* scattered haphazardly around the base of the mountain. Traditionally, *barrio* people never betrayed a dissident. Traditionally, the hunted on their way to the mountain drew their help in the *barrios*. It was a matter of trust, an unspoken compact almost indestructible. The CIC learned early to go not to the *barrios* for informers but to the towns, to the lower fringes of the elite, to the eager servants of the Nacionalista Party. It was no surprise to us that Taruc and Alejandrino went to the *barrios* near Mount Arayat, no secret to them that the CIC would follow them there.

On a bright, hot afternoon late in March, I drove along the main street of the Arayat *población* looking for a place to set up an office. I passed the market, quiet in the time of siesta, and the massive gray stone church and *convento*. Outwardly, Arayat was a village sleeping in the sun, untouched by armies that passed first to the west and then to the east, back and forth, up and down. But too many cross-currents had been left for it to be only a village sleeping in the sun.

I stopped at the concrete *municipio*. Men in civilian shirts and shorts came from the luneta and crowded around the jeep. My voice was hard, my question deliberate. "I want to see Mayor Alejandrino."

From the sullenness in their eyes they might never have heard of him. It was as I expected. The dot in a half-circle on my jeep told them I was the CIC and their enemy.

A man leaned out a window. "I am the mayor." He also looked at the insignia. "You are the CIC?"

"Yes. I will be here for a few days or weeks and need quarters. Can you help me?"

He came to the door. "You will investigate?"

"Yes."

"Ah, yes. It is known the CIC would come." He did not say how it was known. "I have the house for you."

He came to the jeep and shook my hand. Then he sent a man at a run to see that the house was ready. He would go with me. "I myself will show you Arayat."

Huk mayor or not, he had been elected and I had to work with him. I turned the jeep halfway around; the gray stone church was between us and the gray-green slopes of Mount Arayat. Some Spanish priest had planned well when he chose the exact spot, the exact wall angle for limning church against mountain so that they appeared linked, inseparable, both dominating. We paused for a long look and then drove slowly past the market. Seeing the mayor with me, people stopped to shout "*Mabuhay*" and lift their hands.

"They are glad the CIC is here," the mayor said. "They suffered much from the Japanese."

He held out his left hand to show three crooked fingers. "I myself have suffered. I was a violinist. To save himself, a man I knew told Japanese soldiers that I was a spy for the Huk. They caught me here, near the rice stall there, with my violin. They stepped on it and broke it. When I would not confess, they broke my fingers with bamboo."

He had to be a Huk, he told me with no apology. When Casto Alejandrino would no longer be the mayor, the people had elected him. He was proud to follow Alejandrino. Alejandrino and his family before him were *haciendados* with rice and sugarcane fields. They could have gone to Manila but had chosen to stay in Arayat. Alejandrino had taken the oath of office with clenched fist. This mayor, too, had been sworn in with a clenched fist. He gave me a quick look. "To show the people."

His words and manner showed him to be of practiced, but not innate, cunning. I would trust him only as much as needed to work with him.

We drove the few blocks to where the main street became the road west to Mexico and San Fernando. At the edge of town we came to a two-story house with wide verandahs and an iron grill balcony. I could see past the pillars of the foundation to where back steps came down to a garden with grapefruit and mango trees. I could see men and women hurrying down the steps, carrying their sleeping mats, pots of food, little children. Squatters, the mayor explained. The owner had gone to Manila with his family.

The mayor went ahead of me through parlor and dining room, large rooms with high ceilings, the furniture looted, the bare mahogany floors oiled and rubbed to a dark red. The owner had lived well. We went up a polished mahogany staircase to a large room with mahogany paneling and floor. Sliding doors opened out onto the balcony toward Mount Arayat, making the mountain seem close enough to touch.

"It is good for us, this mountain," the mayor said. "When the Japs raided we hid in the mountain—there and in the swamps of Candaba."

We leaned on a railing looking at the slopes shimmering in the heat.

"Will you go with me to the mountain?" The question was abrupt. "We will go there?"

I wanted to go. I wanted to see the cave the Huks called the Flying Fortress, the field that was their Mariveles, their Corregidor, any of their mountain hideouts.

"I would like to go. When?"

171

"It might be on a day before Easter." In three days Holy Week would begin. "It might be better later. Many people come to Arayat for Easter. The faithful come for the rituals and parades. Many come only to see the *penitentes* torturing themselves for their sins."

I asked about the Huks, those no longer faithful.

"They will come, but not to the church. We do not go to the church."

I asked about Taruc and Alejandrino.

"They will come, but not to the church."

I asked again about Taruc and Alejandrino.

He became irritated. "You know. They are in the peace and pacification."

"Where?"

"Somewhere in the *barrios*. It may be in San Luis, where Taruc lives. You will go there?"

"Not yet. I need more time in Arayat."

He was glad that I would stay. In Arayat I would see people living in peace, a Huk peace.

After he had gone I stood on the balcony and watched the sun set in brilliant red and blue that faded to pale pink and lavender on the mountain slopes. I felt the presence of the mountain, a primeval presence, with the stirrings I had felt in early dawns when both the Southern Cross and the Big Dipper made the sky dramatic.

As the light faded, as the mountain disappeared in blackness, the people seemed nearer. There were voices, soft, lilting voices from the street, of buy-and-sell merchants going from the market to their homes in the *barrios* and of young people with lighted torches in some kind of pre-Easter parade. The mayor was right. This was peace, not war. Only in peace could the people be so serene. Yet it was a Huk peace, tenuous at best, fragile, depending on a balance between gentleness and violence. I was glad the Army had sent a Filipino-American soldier with a tommy gun to be my bodyguard as well as my driver.

Before sunrise men at the door woke me with cries of "*Japon! Japon!*" A Japanese soldier was in a *barrio* not far away. I was the

CIC. They wanted to show me what they did to the enemy. We would go in the jeep? As we went they told of Japanese soldiers who came down from the mountain to steal food. There were others, stragglers from Manila, trying to get to the Japanese lines. People in the *barrios* feared them.

When we got to the *barrio,* Huk soldiers had already shot him. He lay among the bamboos, his face contorted with pain. In one hand he had two raw sweet potatoes, in the other an egg, which he had crushed in his convulsion. I pulled his fingers apart and found them squeezing a chicken not ready for hatching. Blood seeped down his shirt but he was still breathing. The Huks wanted to shoot him again. I wanted to get him to a doctor. The nearest, they told me, was Robert Golding, an American *mestizo* in Arayat. We hooked a slide to the jeep and dragged him to the *municipio.* While the doctor was on the way, the Jap died on a desk, his mouth open. A Filipino stuck a C ration biscuit between his teeth and everyone but the mayor laughed. He was displeased, not at the mockery but at the blood that had dripped on the floor.

Later in the morning, I drove past a market alive with people, and fragrant with tropical fruits, sugarcane juice and *muscovado* sugar, and Indian corn roasting over charcoal braziers. Easter pilgrims were gathering. I passed the church slowly. A few old women, their faces half-hidden in black mantillas, crept out of the cave-like doorway. I studied the structure as I had studied many church structures in the Philippines, the hand-hewn stones, the hand-mixed mortar raised into walls and towers and arches. How many days and months and years of compulsory, unpaid labor had gone into raising that pile of stone? What burdens of forced donations? What could a priest say that would justify such a house of God surrounded by nipa huts? For generations people had answered such questions with anticlericalism. Now Huks were bolstering their strength with anticlericalism so violent that priests, afraid to go out, had become prisoners in their own rectories.

I drove through rich farm lands and took a road that gradually ascended the slopes of Mount Arayat. As I climbed I watched the broad expanse of Central Luzon to my left, stretching to the deep blue mountains of Zambales. This was the richest plain on Luzon, the southern part a design of rice paddies and tropical growth that overlapped, in a jagged line, the lengthening fields of sugarcane to the north. This was the land that landlords—among them the Church, the Jesuits—had struggled to possess. This was the land the Huks would wrest from them.

Where the first slope leveled out I came to a deserted, overgrown park. I walked around an empty swimming pool with walls so cracked that rainwater ran out as it fell. I stopped at a pavilion with rotting roof and broken floor. It was a natural resting place for climbers who wanted to go higher. Here, generations of people in rebellion against the fixed order must have paused on their way to sanctuary—Aguinaldo's men, the Santa Iglesias, *insurrectos* on one side or the other—and now the Huks. From here they could take the trail that zigzagged upward into rain forest, ending where? One branch would go to the cave called the Flying Fortress.

Slowly I took the jeep over loose gravel and rain-washed ruts, up till green growth made two dense walls. Where the road narrowed to a trail, a Filipino with a tommy gun stopped me. He was young enough to be trigger-happy. "You will not go up."

"Why?"

"*Japones.*"

"Who are you?"

"I have the honor to be a soldier of the Hukbalahap. We are the *barrio* guards. *Japones* come down to the *barrios* at night and steal. We watch for them and kill them."

Our orders were to disarm and arrest such men as this young guard. "How many guards are there?"

"Many, ser. They patrol around the mountain."

One guard might have been disarmed, but not many. Feeling both prudent and cowardly at leaving things as they were, I went back down to Arayat and stopped at the church. Inside, it was a wide, low-vaulted space, with no pews and an altar stripped of vessels and ornaments. On one side was a blue-robed statue of the Virgin, and beside it a Jesus in the robe of the Augustinians. On the other side was a Joseph in the yellow of the cuckold. Stations of the cross still hung on the walls. Two old women in black were

174

making the stations on their knees, on a stone path worn smooth by generations of knees.

I found the priest not in the church but in the *convento*. He was Spanish, middle-aged, and afraid—afraid the Huks would kidnap and kill him because of their hatred for priests. They complained that priests charged higher fees for the sacraments than they could pay. Priests had to charge more, he explained, because of Japanese inflation. The occupation had been a sad thing for the Church. Before the war Pampanga had been a center for the faithful. There had been a falling away, but there were still many devout ones, even among the Huks. He did not understand what the Huks did. They were present at saints' days in the *barrios* but they did not come to Mass. He talked sadly of how they robbed and killed. "Will it ever end?"

"Will they come for Easter?"

"They will come but not for Mass. They are now the enemy."

From him I went to Major Gabriel, an officer in the Philippine Constabulary before the war and an informer for me from my first night in Huklandia. Now, in his home, in the middle of the day, he quoted openly from speeches Taruc and Alejandrino had made in the *barrios*. They had urged people to beware of enemies within the Allied Forces, especially the CIC. They were more anti-CIC than anti-American but belligerent enough for him to recommend that soldiers enforce law and order in Pampanga. The Huks had challenged the Army. The Army had to take control where the Commonwealth Government could not.

"You mean martial law?"

He did.

Alejandrino's father, Felipe, gave up his siesta to come to my house to talk about himself and his son. He was a landowner, soft-spoken, educated, respected. He was also a brother of the José Alejandrino who had led a detachment of Aguinaldo's guerrillas against the Americans. Later Felipe had become an agitator for peasants' rights. From him, Casto Alejandrino had inherited some of the social leanings that made him a Huk.

175

This man of the middle generation recounted the strife he and his family had lived in for half a century, since the revolt against the Spaniards. In all his years there had been but short periods of peace. The strife had been worst under the Japanese. "We had to have the Huks."

He paused as if waiting for me to object. I did not. He said quietly, "I am honored that my son was part of it from the beginning."

Quietly he came, quietly he left, a man of the upper class, educated in the Spanish Catholic tradition, brought up in the *cacique* system, concerned that wrongs against the people should be righted. He was telling me that he had aligned himself with what the Huks wanted—a classless society.

Apprehensive at all I had seen and heard, I went to San Fernando and reported to Captain Frederick. He thought my worry over speeches given by Taruc and Alejandrino was exaggerated. He had seen Taruc and found him friendly and cooperative. He was sympathetic to the problems the Army had to deal with. Almost apologetically he told me that Taruc was giving a *merienda,* a feast, for him on Saturday, the day before Easter. I urged him to pass it up. He would not. Colonel White had approved.

I repeated my request for soldiers to be stationed in Arayat over Easter. There would be none. Colonel White was afraid the sight of them would stir up trouble.

I went back to Arayat, feeling very much on my own.

• • •

6 April 1945. Good Friday came and the streets and market were busy with buyers and sellers, and noisy with the cries of young men hawking roasted corn and the boiled eggs with half-formed chickens inside that they called *belot-belot.* I drove through *barrios,* observing the people as they came—bands of young men and women singing songs; families, the men walking ahead, the women following, carrying children and straw bags of food and cooking pots—all walking as if they had been compelled to lay down whatever they were doing and follow a call to Arayat. They

were like the people in the mass meeting at San Fernando, but their temper was different. They had few banners. If they had weapons, they were hidden under shirts that hung outside their trousers. Their faces wore a different look—the expectant look of the faithful making a pilgrimage to watch the procession of the *Nazareno*, the "dead body" of Christ.

I went to the *municipio* to ask the meaning of what I saw.

"The faithful are coming," the mayor said. He meant Huks.

At the *convento* I asked the same question.

"The faithful are coming," the priest said. He meant the Christians.

Two pilgrimages were converging on Arayat, either capable of forcing a confrontation. In the crowds I could not tell which was Huk, which Christian, which was both, or which wavered between. Some declared their identity. Young men and women were passing out leaflets. On Easter Sunday there would be a mass meeting in the *luneta*. Taruc and Alejandrino would speak. I took a leaflet and sent it to San Fernando. The Huks had broken their agreement. Some kind of confrontation was inevitable, and I needed help.

Back on my balcony I watched an armed squadron marching in from the direction of Mexico. The leader dismissed them in front of my house and they scattered down side streets and toward the market. With no one but myself to bitch to, I goddamned the Army from General MacArthur down. The driver returned from San Fernando with no message for me. I sent him back with a revised estimate of the situation and a plea for soldiers.

The people had separated into two crowds, one in the *luneta*, the other toward the church door—two groups unmistakably divided, with little mingling. Both were quiet, orderly, with few smiles or sounds of laughter. Both seemed to be awaiting the stroke of noon, the beginning agony of the Passion.

A stillness came over the people when a bell tolled the hour for observing. The priest, called earlier to the church to pray, had prayed and then locked himself inside his house. A second bell, and the crowd shifted. Huks, whether with weapons or banners, remained in the *luneta* and on the side of the street toward the *luneta.* The other group moved nearer the church. Trained in the same catechism, each side set its own limits on observance. I stood across from the market, where I could see the church, the *municipio,* and the *luneta.* Stalls were left untended. Doors to stalls and houses had been shut. By the time the Passion had ended, people had lined the street to watch the saints go by, as their fathers had watched before them farther back than anyone could remember—to the early days when Spanish priests had first brought their saints and rituals to replace or be superimposed on those of the pagan.

Far away, on the road from Santa Ana, there was a flourish of trumpets and drums and then violins in a Filipino tune set to the measure of marching feet. Watchers, jostling each other, erasing lines that had separated them, filled the street, leaving only a narrow path for the procession to pass through.

Almost as if a command had been given, another separation took place. Young men with banners and rifles withdrew and regrouped themselves into a solid bank along the fronts of stores and houses. Their faces were stern, disciplined; their eyes showed a mixture of curiosity and disdain for what would pass before them. Nearer the path of the procession a ragged line of old men and women waited, seemingly aware of religious tensions brought on by approaching rituals but not of any other. Their eyes were turned toward the sound of music, eager for the glimpse that would set the rejoicing in the rite of Easter.

The Christ, his robes old and shabby, led the procession, his cart drawn by twelve boys in *abaca* shorts and piña cloth shirts. As the Christ came nearer, eyes brightened, lips moved in prayer, as if the people were seeing a new Redeemer—not the same plaster Christ that stood near the altar week in, week out, through the year. No uproar greeted Him, only the whisperings of prayers, a sound like wind in leaves heard in the silences of music. Old men and women crossed themselves and genuflected. Huk soldiers stood in rows, rigid, watching with no sign, no show of emotion at what was passing before them.

Six boys in black tuxedos and six girls in white *tiernos* that looked like bridal dresses followed the Christ, marching two by two, with arches of flowers raised. The difference between the marchers and the viewers was more complex than mere difference in dress, or difference in manner between dwellers of *población* and *barrio*. The difference was ethnic—the *mestizo* mixture. The *barrio* people were strongly Malayan, with their broad faces and dark brown skins. Those from the *población* had touches of the Eurasian through the infusion of Spanish and Anglo into Oriental blood—their skin lighter, even to yellow or pink, their features less broad, more delicate. The difference was also in class: the marchers were remnants of the once ruling upper class, the viewers were the lower class, isolated, ruled.

After the Christ came the Virgin, called by the faithful Mary, Queen of Flowers. As she passed, serene in her blue silk, people leaned toward her in trance-like adoration. The Christ they worshiped; the Virgin they idolized, so much so that priests warned them against the perils of Mariolatry, the perils of confusing the Virgin with their pagan earth mother.

Huk soldiers, who had rejected the Christ, relaxed holds on banners and weapons as the Virgin went by. The Joseph in his faded yellow passed almost unnoticed. The people had spent their emotion on the Christ and the Virgin.

Musicians, men and boys, came, marching in step but not in formation, playing songs of love but not of worship, secular tunes not of the church, among them "You Are My Sunshine." They were followed by men holding aloft bamboo poles on which cardboard representations of the objects of the Crucifixion had been nailed: the cock that crowed thrice, the spear that pierced His side, the jar that held the vinegar, the sponge that was raised to His lips, the nails. Taller than the rest was a hand with fingers extended, a brown hand edged in blood red. It was the last symbol before the coming of the *penitentes*.

By custom the *penitentes* added the spectacle of blood—their own—to the parade of saints. This practice of flagellation was a remnant of the old Church practice when public penances were imposed on public sinners. In Arayat every year men flayed themselves through the streets, some for public display but most out of personal contrition. This time there were only two, one old, one

179

young, obviously father and son. Both were stripped to loincloths. Each carried in his right hand a bamboo stick strung with bits of glass. With the regular beat of the drum, each flayed himself, over the right shoulder, over the left shoulder. They had started with the music and now, an hour later, their backs were covered with cuts from which blood oozed. Blood ran down their legs and dripped from their bare heels. With each blow their fingers dipped blood and dragged it across their faces and chests. Neither looked to right or left.

These were not the usual *penitentes,* friendly Filipinos told me. The two men had been Huks. It was known that they had been members of a liquidation squad. It was said that they had foxholed many puppets and collaborators and buried them at the place called Mariveles. They were no longer Huks and this was their way of showing penance for the things they had done.

The procession ended at the church, and I went to see the priest. He talked to me briefly and grudgingly. What I had seen was a veneer of old Catholicism, much of it not sanctioned by the clergy. There were also elements of ancient pagan ritual that he could neither explain nor condone. He could not lend his presence or his blessing.

In the night, while I was still on my balcony puzzling over the crosscurrents—cultural, religious, political—that had erupted and would continue to erupt in violence, two messages were brought to me. The first was brief: Huks had liquidated the *penitentes.* The second was longer and conciliatory: Luis Taruc wanted me to come to the *merienda* for Captain Frederick. It was a way for us to meet as friends. It would be a great honor to him and Luz, his wife, if I would only come.

Before daylight an informer woke my bodyguard. The *penitentes* were dead, liquidated, but not buried. Their bodies lay beside a *barrio* road on the way to Santa Ana. It was a Huk warning to deserters.

"If you would only see, ser," he said to me.

I would, and I took the mayor with me.

The bodies were where he had said I would find them, lying

180

in dirt and scrabbly grass, pitifully small, bloody, slashed by bolos. The mayor claimed not to know who had done the slashing. Houses were in sight but we found no people. No one wanted to be seen near the *penitentes*. The mayor showed no feeling for them, but he did say they would be buried before the day was over. He did not say where, nor did he mention Mariveles. His office would not make an investigation. That would be done by squadron leaders— Americans should leave it to them. I did, but I sent another plea to Sixth Army for help.

On the *luneta,* young men and women were decorating a platform with red paper streamers and hand-printed placards. There would be a mass meeting. Juan de la Cruz and Guan Yek would speak. Huk soldiers paraded in front of the *municipio.* In the *población* alone there were enough weapons in sight for a fire fight. Resentful at being left alone in the confrontation shaping up, I decided I had to go to the *merienda.* Captain Frederick had to know what would happen. The mass meeting had to be called off, if not by Taruc and Alejandrino, then by Sixth Army. People on the roads had to be turned back.

As I went south toward San Luis I met groups of *taos* in their *abaca* shorts and shirts, sandal-shod, bareheaded except for a few in the rain hats they wore in the fields. They plodded along, making way for the jeep. They barely looked at me. Farther from Arayat I saw only a few on the road, walking slowly, at a pace that would bring them to Arayat at night, or in the early morning.

Farther on, before and after Candaba, the nipa huts were old and jammed close together on a road that followed the river. I slowed down and looked through doors and windows that were nothing more than rectangles cut in thatched walls. At the sight of the jeep, children ran up bamboo-pole ladders and out of sight. Women squatted in the sun, picking lice from each other's hair. The men I saw were old, too old to walk to Arayat.

Below Candaba I came to a *barrio* with hammer-and-sickle banners leaning against walls. A propaganda cadre had stopped to take food from the people. There was one frame house in the *barrio.* Half a dozen men and women with rifles and a machine

181

gun squatted in the yard and on the porch. When I picked up speed to pass them they leaped into the road and stopped me. A young man came close. "Where do you go?"

"A *barrio* of San Pedro." I lied to keep from saying San Luis. I knew of no San Pedro in that direction but saints' names were scattered like sharks' teeth in Central Luzon.

"Why do you go?"

"To see the *barrio teniente*."

"You are the CIC?"

"Yes."

"You will arrest the Huk?" His voice was defiant, menacing, daring. Others from the cadre stuck their heads inside the jeep on either side. I had to say no. I could see their eyes and hear their snickers. "He will not arrest us."

A woman came to the door. She had been crying and her voice trembled as she spoke. The leader interpreted for me. "The rice is cooked. She asks that you will eat with us. You will come?"

His voice was at the same time condescending and mischievous. I knew why. They had confiscated the food from the woman and forced her to cook it for them. It was a joke for them that the American would eat confiscated food.

"Come," he said to the others. "The CIC will eat with us."

"I am late—"

"There is time."

I yielded because he had a pistol on his hip and a hand on his pistol.

The house was better than others in the *barrio*, but not much. There were no beds, only sleeping mats stacked in a corner, and no chairs. There was a small fire on a sand-covered table and two earthenware pots. Cadre men and women squatted around the pots. With their fingers they took a ball of rice from one, chicken or vegetables from the other.

"You will eat," the leader said to me.

I took a piece of chicken and a slice of boiled coconut. We squatted on the porch and ate and the woman watched sadly from the door.

"She is glad we have come," the leader said. "She is a friend. People give us what they have."

The most I could do for the woman was to write a report—in septuplicate.

Other members of the cadre came from houses along the road with their guns and banners. They were again ready for the march.

"We will go now." The leader shook my hand. "We are a propaganda cadre for the mass meeting. There is a play. It is called *The Passion of the Workers.*"

Glad to have suffered no more than humiliation, I followed the river a few miles and parked on a bluff beside Captain Frederick's jeep. On the other side was *barrio* Santa Monica. Here Spanish soldiers had mistaken picnickers for guerrillas and had annihilated them. Here the Santa Iglesias had held out against the Spaniards and then the Americans. Here Taruc had been born and nurtured. His house was here, among the trees.

The *merienda* was on the river in a flotilla of *bancas* and barges, all filled with people in bright-colored shirts and dresses. In one of the barges I could see Captain Frederick, lounging with young women companions, with oarsmen moving them slowly upstream. On one side was a boat with pots and trays of food, on the other a boat with musicians and singing girls. If Captain Frederick could be blandished, Taruc had provided the proper blandishments. With Taruc in the lead, the boats moved toward a landing.

I honked and yelled till a man in a *banca* put out from the landing. I climbed down a steep path and was at the water when the *banca,* thin and straight, hand-hewn from a single log, pushed against the sand. The man spoke no English but he steadied the *banca* for me to get in.

By the time we crossed the river, the *merienda* had progressed to a grove of palms and mangoes. Near the center of the party Captain Frederick and the *Supremo*, equals for the moment, sat on a wicker settee eating ice cream. The *merienda* had brought them close together. They were convivial and jovial and neither asked why I had come. Taruc greeted me cordially, almost affectionately, and introduced me to his wife by her real name, Ena, not by her alias, Luz. She had often passed me at the jail without speaking. Now she was a gracious hostess. Captain Frederick, red from the sun, flushed from nipa palm wine, rose and made a speech. It had been a great occasion, a day he would not forget. It was good for Americans and Filipinos to know and understand each other. He said nothing about the broken agreement.

I asked Taruc about the mass meeting. His attitude not toward Captain Frederick but toward me changed. The meeting had to be. It was a movement of the people and not a breaking of their agreement. The Huk leaders had to go and answer the people. I waited for Captain Frederick's order to call the meeting off. He did not. Less than decisively, he said that I would be at the meeting and he would expect no problems.

I made myself clear to Taruc. "If I have to arrest you, I will arrest you."

Driving back to Arayat I passed squadrons carrying signs: EASTER MASS MEETING, ARAYAT. On the *luneta* and around the church were others handing out leaflets. As I went past, people stared at me angrily, defiantly. I sent one more request for soldiers and weapons.

I parked at the *municipio*. The doors were locked. I looked across at the church. The doors were open. I went in—into shadows tinged red and blue. A few women in black dresses and black mantillas were making the stations of the cross. The stone floor was worn smooth, the plaster grooved where fingers touched at the moment of prayer.

In darkness I walked in and out of the church twice, surrounded by people waiting for Easter morning, more people than in any other year, informers told me. As usual, some were coming to greet the Christ; not as usual, many more were coming to salute the enemies of Christ.

• • •

I was on the streets again before the gray mists lifted, drawn to the church to watch the rise of the Easter sun, and to witness a pageant not of the clergy but of the folk, a pageant portraying the meeting of Jesus and Mary before the others discovered that the stone had been rolled away. Not to be found in the Bible or in Church interpretations, it was a hybrid of primitive belief and ritual mingled with Christian belief and ritual brought by Spanish priests. The pageant, as old as the time of man on Mount Arayat, was in the semi-primitive mind a mystical union of mountain and swamp and fertile plain, on which an imagined story of the Christ and the mother of the Christ had been grafted. In their adoration of the mother image the people felt intuitively that Christ would have given the message of Resurrection to Mary first. Called *Sallibong,* the meeting of the two, the ritual has Christian trappings that cover but do not entirely conceal what had grown up among the people.

I could hear the shuffle of people going to the church, or to the *luneta.* I walked among those who had slept where they were, on the ground. In the gray light their faces were stolid, their eyes downcast but showing no fear from the night, no fear of what the day would bring. Huk banners floated red in the first touch of sun. Soldiers guarded the *luneta* and speaker's platform with rifles. At the church a crowd waited, quiet, expectant, not for the Mass— there would be no Mass—but for the pageant. Out of habit the ritual would for a while bring together non-Huks and Huks—or in the words of priests, the Christ and the Communists, the anti-Christ.

The church doors opened long enough for young women in white *tierno* dresses and young men in tuxedos to come out and, walking two by two, begin the procession toward a chapel half a mile or so away. I walked not in the procession but at one side. A crowd waited at the chapel doors. Toward the end of the procession two carts were drawn up, one carrying the Jesus, unchanged, the other the Virgin, completely hidden by a black robe. I wanted to ask the priest the meaning of it all but he was not there. Priests did not interfere with what the people did; neither did they approve.

Young men pulled the carts toward the chapel and halted the Virgin just under the ledge over the entrance, with the Jesus facing her. I could feel but not understand the suspense of the people crowding forward; I could hear but not understand the words repeated in an unfamiliar ritual.

185

As if performing a priestly function, a young man appeared at a window above the door and stepped out on the ledge. He carried a long galvanized wire with one end bent into a hook. With the crowd waiting, he leaned down and with the hook lifted a fold of the Virgin's robe. The cloth was old; threads ripped out. The hook broke loose, the cloth fell back. A distressed taking in of breath surrounded me. After a pause he tried again. This time the hook caught. Slowly the black was lifted, slowly the blue of her robe showed. People became excited, as if they were seeing her for the first time. At last the black of her mourning was lifted. At last she stood before them in her shabby splendor, face to face with the Jesus, the two meeting where the stone would be rolled away. At the moment of their meeting, the silent announcement of His Resurrection, the worshipers—their faces exalted—genuflected, made the sign of the cross, prayed.

Then in a sound of rejoicing the doors were opened and the carts were pulled into place side by side. Women in white, men in black took places before and behind the carts. Slowly the carts were moved forward, slowly the chapel was filled. At last the images were before the altar, side by side, their escorts around them, like a wedding party.

The ritual over, people drifted away toward the market or *luneta*. I went with them, asking questions about the pageant as I went, only to discover that I had missed a part of the drama. There was an old belief that the robe lifted on the first try was a sign of good crops, the robe snagged a sign of bad crops. This time a mischievous angel hidden under the cart had snagged the robe the first time.

I looked for the soldiers. They had not come. I was left to go it alone in a crowd much larger than the one at San Fernando. There was a saying among informers: it is the trick of the Huk to create a crisis and at the facing of it to fade away. This looked like a different kind of crisis.

Toward 1100 I went to the *municipio,* to a large room with windows that gave me a full view of the crowd and platform. Major Gabriel's son came to interpret for me. Taruc and Alejandrino, in khaki uniforms, were on the platform. Ena Taruc was

186

nearby. So was Alejandrino's wife. Guards with rifles had posted themselves around the *luneta*. Men and women from propaganda cadres sang and danced and raised their hands in clenched-fist salutes.

A few minutes before eleven the priest closed the church doors. The market became quiet, deserted, as crowds were drawn to hear a declaration of Hukbalahap independence.

Alejandrino spoke first and there were shouts for Guan Yek and G-Y as he stepped forward and raised a clenched fist. It was a long speech, sometimes rambling, sometimes passionately incoherent, and young Gabriel struggled with translation. When the Huk leader chose to make it so, the speech was clear and to the point. Huks had fought the Japanese and the Japanese had retreated. Now he was there to speak not of war but of the peace that Huks had fought for. It was the same peace Roosevelt had argued for at Teheran—not a peace for America or Britain or China but a peace for every nation, a peace for the world, and in Central Luzon a peace that would end injustice to the oppressed, which Alejandrino defined as the peonage of rents and debts. He had words of praise for Roosevelt, words of blame for American imperialists and their Filipino puppets, and words of anger for their tools, the CIC. He let his anger rise as he described the massacre of Huks at Malolos as a fascist atrocity engineered by the CIC. I wanted to remind him of Huk atrocities I had seen, and of the two flagellants, dead, murdered. But there would be no chance for rebuttal. His high-pitched voice became more strident and more emotional. When it seemed that he might pause he changed to English.

"Americans say I speak treason. They will put me in jail again." He pointed to the window where I stood watching, listening. "The CIC is there in the *municipio*. He will arrest me." He reached his clenched fist up. "Americans will arrest me but they will not kill me. They are afraid. They only hide in the *municipio*."

He had dared me to confront them. Slowly I worked my way from the *municipio* to the platform and stood below him, close enough for him to see the anger rising in me, close enough to be taking up his dare. He stepped back. Taruc stepped forward.

187

Taruc's voice was calm but his speech, without mention of the agreement, was a repudiation of the eleven points as an insult to the Hukbalahap and to all of the United Front. Quietly he reminded the crowd of Huk beginnings and of decisions made at Cabiao. The struggle had been long and costly in lives, but the Japanese had been driven out. Now the fight against collaborators, puppets, and anti-Huk landlords had to be intensified if the revolution was to lift oppression from the poor, if the people who farmed the land were to have a fairer share, if the United Front was to create a classless society. Without raising his voice he warned that, aided by the American Army, reaction was rising in Central Luzon. The people had to resist no matter how many USAFFE or American soldiers were sent against them. The revolution had to go on.

The two stood together with clenched fists raised. When the shouts of "*Mabuhay,* Juan de la Cruz" and "*Mabuhay,* Guan Yek" had died down, Taruc and Alejandrino stepped down from the platform. As they faced me an armed cadre came nearer.

"How did you like my speech?" Taruc asked.

"Not very much."

A crowd and the cadre closed in around us.

"You broke our agreement," I said, keeping my voice low. "You know I will have to arrest you."

"Yes."

At this moment they could have resisted. I followed their eyes to the ranks of soldiers in a crowd that seemed tensed for a confrontation. When I thought they would grab my pistol and carbine, Taruc touched my arm.

"It is not safe to arrest us here." In the tenseness of waiting he and Alejandrino talked in whispers, their heads close together. Taruc spoke: "We will come to your house at five. It will be safe for you if you arrest us there. You can trust us to come. You will be alone?"

"Yes."

We shook hands. The propaganda cadre cleared the platform and began taking places for *The Sorrows of the Philippines.* As I went to my jeep there were no greetings for me, either friendly or hostile. A crisis had been created. They were letting it dwindle away.

Through the afternoon I watched from the balcony as armed squadrons and Easter pilgrims passed on their way to the *barrios*. By four o'clock the street was deserted. The way was wide open. At five o'clock I saw them coming, Taruc and Alejandrino side by side, marching in an uneven military cadence. Scarlett O'Hara kept a dozen paces behind them. When they came nearer I could see their faces, like masks. She was crying.

I met them at the steps and shook hands with them. There was no sign of anger or animosity from either, only a gentle handclasp, a quiet submission to what I suspected was their own sense of fate, or to a feeling that the Huks would be stronger if they were in jail. Or they might have been counting on help from Captain Frederick.

"We are ready," Taruc said.

The driver brought the jeep. I expected them to say something to Scarlett O'Hara but they left her standing silently at the side of the road.

They wanted to talk and said so. The three of us sat on the back of the jeep, with me in the middle, touching on either side, shoulder to shoulder, hip to hip. As the jeep pulled away we heard wails from Scarlett O'Hara but they did not look back.

When we were nearing Mexico, with Mount Arayat a shadow behind us, I said what I had to say. "Thank you for keeping your word."

"It was only for you," they said. "You did not like what you had to do."

Neither did they. It was the war. We talked of the irony that had brought the three of us together, two the sons of sharecroppers, one the son of a landlord. The war was ending on the one hand in a battle to maintain the status quo ante, on the other in a battle to open up new political alignments. Alignments such as the United Front, they added, which was broad enough to accommodate Huks, socialists, Communists, even Chinese Communists from the mainland who had come as advisers and organizers.

I asked the question I had asked many times before. "Are you members of the Communist Party?"

Before, they had said no; now they said yes.

"For how long?"

Taruc answered. The two men had worked with the socialists under Pedro Abad Santos and with labor groups in Central Luzon and Manila. The harder they had tried to organize, the tighter the restrictions from Malacañan. The *taos* were getting poorer, the landlords and the Church richer. Communism promised social reform in a classless society. Deeply disillusioned, despairing, they had become card-carrying members, and then students in Moscow. It was there that their commitment had been made.

"Where did you get the money?"

"From America. Collected in New York and brought by way of San Francisco to Manila—"

"The couriers? The Lavas?"

"Not only the Lavas. There were many friends in America who wanted to help young men like us. The war came and our funds from America were cut off."

"What about money from China?"

"That is not for us to talk about."

Only now were they abrupt. Only now did they let their resentment show—resentment at the Army, at the way the Army had treated them with broken promises and money to their USAFFE enemies.

"Why did you let me arrest you? You could have hid on Mount Arayat or in the Candaba swamps."

It was the Army. The Army had ways to hunt them down, and would. They admitted their sadness at going. They knew the isolation and loneliness of prison. If they only had books.

They asked to see Captain Frederick. We went to his office but could not find him. They wanted to wait but I decided not to. If he wanted to, he could see them in jail. The only book I could find for them was an Army paperback of *The Education of Henry Adams*. I gave it to them.

Signing in at the jail was brief. They had been there before; my authority was not questioned. Their stay in San Fernando would be short, the guard told them, as they would be treated like prisoners of war. They would go the next day on a shipment to the prisoner of war camp at Calasiao. They were shocked. So was I. I had expected Bilibid. Calasiao was the first stop on the way to Iwahig Prison on Palawan Island.

Good-byes were also brief. Alejandrino shook my hand and went with the guard. Taruc held my hand in a tight grip and looked me steadily in the eyes, not accusingly, only sorrowfully. It was a silent moment of empathy between us and, for me, a bewildering search for what made him the man he was. The guard came and he was gone.

Captain Frederick was at his desk when I reported in. He knew what I had done but did not countermand my action even when he heard they were on their way to Palawan. Nor did he want to see them. We stood facing each other across the desk, in a mutual but wordless acknowledgment of what the Army had made us—shits. We shook hands and I was on my way back to Arayat.

The streets were quiet when I drove past the church and *luneta* and back to my house. Toward midnight, when I was watching from the balcony, I saw a signal flare rise high on the slopes of Mount Arayat and hang like a brilliant star. It could have been Japanese stragglers. I worried that it was Huks reassembling.

Early in the morning a young man named Sandico from Candaba was at my door asking for help to find his mother. She had been missing a whole day and he was afraid she had been kidnapped. He did not know why. She was a landowner but she had been kind to Filipinos and Americans, and she had divided her *palay* with the Huks when they asked for it.

"Where can we start?"

He thought we should investigate in the *barrio* Candating. He had heard that Huks there had a *personal disgusto* against her.

We crossed the Pampanga River in a *banca* and hiked along edges of the Candaba swamp till we came to the home of the *barrio teniente* of Candating. He was in his forties, dark, short, an ex-sailor in the American navy who walked as if he was still trying to get his land legs. He was certain that Mrs. Sandico was not in

Candating, but there was a place near Mount Arayat called Correg-idor, where Huks liquidated their enemies. He seemed knowl-edgeable in his urging us to go there, and obliging. "One of my men will show you the way."

First there were things to show us. He had been an armorer in the navy and was an armorer with the Huks. The Americans had taught him well. He brought out a rifle with a plumbing-pipe barrel, hand-whittled stock, and hand-manipulated plunger. Un-able to sight with it, I asked about its accuracy. He did not tell me; he showed me. He raised it to an angle through a window and chipped bark on a tree. With the roar still ringing in my ears, I left.

The guide beside me, Sandico on the back seat, I took the road from Arayat to Magalang. If we did not find her at Corregidor, the guide said, we would go to Mariveles. He knew that more than a hundred collaborators and puppets had been foxholed at Mari-veles. Corregidor turned out to be rice paddies with no sign of fresh digging. Farther along the road we left the jeep and crossed rice paddies till we came to what had been a sugarcane field close to the west slope of the mountain. Before we had gone far, a man who might have been a guard stopped us and talked with our guide in Capampangan. The man went ahead and we followed. Inside the field we came to a new grave. I wanted to dig into it but the man passed it and others. I counted seventeen. The man stopped at one that looked like the others, but fresher.

"Here," the guide said.

They dug with bare hands and lifted out the naked body of a woman. From her son's cry I knew it was Mrs. Sandico. Her hands had been tied behind her back and her skull crushed. A bamboo club was buried with her. Somehow the Filipinos knew that seven men had taken turns beating her till she was dead.

All this for *personal disgusto*?

I left the son with the body and went to the *municipio* for help. There was little interest and no help. Who could know in what way she was the enemy?

"Can someone help take her body to Candaba?"

"Her son can get help in Candaba."
I sent my driver.

Later I found the mayor of Arayat and the men who always seemed to be around him in a friendlier mood. "You have seen what we call Corregidor and Mariveles?"
"Yes."
"It is said you went to the mountain."
"Only to the park. A guard stopped me."
"Ah, that is so. You will also go with me?"
A chance to see their Flying Fortress. "When?"
"Today. After the siesta."
I had to report the Sandico case at San Fernando but there would still be time. "I will go."
The Sandico case was only one of many. Huks were reacting to the imprisoning of Taruc and Alejandrino. Captain Frederick did not want me to go up on Mount Arayat, no matter what kind of information I might get. "You'll get your ass shot off fooling around up there." He said it jokingly but he sent me to the colonel with the question.
Across his desk from me, Colonel White listened to my report on the Sandico case. When I asked about the trip to Mount Arayat he did not answer at once. I argued that I should go. I might be in danger but I did not think so. He did, but he was still uncertain. He left his desk and walked to the door with me. Still without a decision he walked with me through the open area toward the headquarters tents; for the moment we were a tall colonel and a short sergeant brought close by the Huk. Abruptly he stopped and put his hand on my shoulder. I could feel the anxiety in his voice. "I order you not to go."
He followed it with another order: I must close the office in Arayat and return to San Fernando at once.
Worried as I had not been before, I drove through Mexico with helmet on and rifle beside me. When I was passing through a swamp two or three miles outside Arayat I heard rifle shot and then

a burst like a small fire fight. Ambushed. To my left and within easy rifle range half a dozen men were firing at me. Bullets whizzed close. I floorboarded the rest of the way to Arayat. It may have been Japs. It may have been Huks. I never knew.

Felipe Alejandrino was waiting for me at my house, looking old and sad but not angry.

"They have been taken to Calasiao?"

"Yes. I am sorry. I did not expect it."

While I packed he stood in the room with me. With the pride of a father well pleased in his son he talked of their nobility in choosing prison over surrender. There was much for them to fight for and they would not give up.

He had a question to ask. Casto's wife had told him that when they came to be arrested she had chased me around the house with a butcher knife.

"Is it true?"

"No, sir."

I was sad to see him go.

• • •

MacArthur pardoned Manuel Roxas—*por favor* pardoned him.

It was in mid-April, when the battle for Okinawa had been underway two weeks, when José Laurel was safely in Japan, when the Japanese defense of Baguio was crumbling, when the guiltiest of the puppets were deserting to the Americans to save their hides, that MacArthur pardoned Roxas. With one pen stroke he undercut six months of Counter Intelligence Corps work, and created internal problems that would last long after Philippine Independence Day, 4 July 1946.

We had enough documented evidence in our files to hang Roxas—or at least to imprison him for life. At the beginning of the Japanese invasion he had been Minister of Finance in the Commonwealth Government and a MacArthur favorite. Before the Japanese reached Manila, MacArthur had commissioned him a brigadier general in the United States Army. When Quezon and Osmeña escaped to Corregidor, they and General MacArthur, as Roxas claimed and MacArthur confirmed, had left Roxas behind as a caretaker of the government. For a time he was in hiding from the Japanese; for a time, a prisoner of war. Then, at the request of Jorge Vargas and Benigno Aquino, and on the ground that he would be useful, the Japanese released him. He was useful indeed in matters political, in a relationship that at least outwardly was personal and cordial. Among other services performed, Roxas was chairman of the puppet Economic Commission and thus food czar for the whole of the Philippines. In the eyes of the CIC his worst crime was that he prepared, wrote, and signed the constitution of the puppet Philippine Republic. That placed him second to Laurel on the CIC list, and high on the list of puppets Washington had ordered purged.

We thought we were prepared for Roxas when he and José Yulo, Chief Justice of the puppet Supreme Court, were brought to our office in San Fernando. He was taller than the average Filipino, with a Spanish thinness of face, in his fifties, slightly nervous, and, under the circumstances, extremely arrogant. We expected that after a preliminary interrogation by Captain Frederick he would be transferred to Bilibid Prison, where the full case against him could be developed. With three of us agents in the office as witnesses Captain Frederick called Roxas in. He refused to undergo interrogation.

Nettled, Captain Frederick repeated his question about collaboration. Imperiously Roxas turned the question into statements in his own defense. He reminded us that in 1941 he had been senator-elect. Through General MacArthur's reestablishment of the Commonwealth Government he was now senator *bona fide*. He expected to take his place in the Government when he reached Manila. Like hell, we thought. He told stories of his heroic escape from the Japanese and of the work he had done with them, work we called collaboration.

"The mere fact of service under the Japanese is not conclusive evidence of collaboration," he said. It was a matter of survival. "A man could not afford not to collaborate."

He had also been a part of the underground, he claimed, a part of the guerrilla movement. He had had to collaborate publicly in order to work with the guerrillas. He cut off questions with a demand that he be allowed to talk to GHQ.

195

We were not prepared for General MacArthur's action. A limousine he had sent arrived. The driver delivered a suit box with a new uniform and a star. Roxas had arrived a prisoner; he departed a brigadier general in the United States Army. We watched him go but did not salute.

"Goddamn it," we swore. "Goddamn it to hell."

It was entirely MacArthur's doing. As far back as Hollandia he had told Colonel Thorpe, "I'm taking the business of dealing with collaborators away from the Philippine government and giving it to you." Disaffected CIC agents mocked with "the general giveth, the general taketh away, goddamn the general."

The GHQ press release only increased our anger. Favoritism was blatant: "Among those freed is Brigadier General Manuel Roxas, former Speaker of the Assembly. Four members of the Philippines collaborationist cabinet have been captured. They will be confined for the duration as a matter of military security and then turned over to the government of the Philippines for trial and judgment." Five men taken together, one "freed," four "captured." José Yulo, one of the four, understood the machinations.

With no mention of President Osmeña, perhaps without consultation, MacArthur had freed the president's strongest political opponent. The meaning was not lost on Filipinos, especially on officials of the puppet government, including those named as captured: José Yulo, de las Alas, Quintin Paredes, and Teofilo Sison. Roxas was on the way in, Osmeña on the way out. There was also something for them. Even if their investigations were continued, even if they were confined in prison, General MacArthur had opened an escape hatch. Manuel Roxas was on his way to a hero's welcome in Manila. The others could hope to trail behind.

CIC work suffered in general. In some areas it was near collapse. Agents who had made thousands of arrests and were working on thousands of investigations saw little reason to go on.

José Yulo remained with us, quiet, patient, uncomplaining. No one in our outfit could see in this gentle, white-haired man a threat to military security. Hoping to keep him out of Bilibid, Captain Frederick arranged for him to be kept in my personal custody.

He had to eat with me, sleep in a cot beside me, go to the latrine with my eyes on him. In three days of debriefing we talking about the problems of survival under the Japanese, the kind of men who had made up the puppet government, the destructiveness of war on Filipinos. He had not seen Manila. It grieved him to think of Manila.

At first I thought he was as guilty as José Laurel or any other man who had held high office in the puppet government. As hours together went by I saw him as collaborator but also as a man of conscience—intelligent, informed, pro-American, with no criticisms of us for our defeats, no outward resentment that he would be in jail while Roxas was in a seat of favor and honor. It was true, he told me, that the first meetings of what became the puppet government had been held in his house. In the chaos following the departure of Quezon and Osmeña and the beginning of Japanese occupation he had hoped to maintain the Commonwealth Government, a hope destroyed by the Japanese and by ambitious Filipinos eager to serve them. To remove himself as much as possible from politics he had allowed himself to be made chief justice of the Supreme Court. If he had to collaborate, collaboration from the bench was more acceptable to him.

Almost shyly he mentioned his wish to visit his *hacienda* and see his people—not his family but the people of his *barrio*. He had been away a long time; he might be gone longer. It was a *barrio* of Floridablanca. Captain Frederick agreed that I should take him.

We went on the road to Bataan and at Guagua turned toward the Zambales Mountains. Sugarcane fields stretched away from either side of the road. As we came nearer to Floridablanca we could see the walls of the sugar *centro,* owned in part by the Yulo family. It was the *barrio* he wanted to see. From the *población* we went on a dirt road that stopped at a clear-running stream. We forded it and walked on a carabao trail to the *barrio.* Two men saw us and came running and shouting. They knelt before Yulo and kissed his hands. Then they ran ahead of us, and as they ran people came from their huts. An old woman, barefoot, hurried down a pole ladder, knelt, and kissed his hands. Where the huts were thickest we stopped in the road. Families gathered around him, their words strange, the meaning clear. They were like children greeting a father who has been away a long time.

The *barrio teniente* came and they talked of harvests and plantings. The *barrio* belonged to Yulo. He asked my pardon. There were so many things he needed to know.

They offered us rice and fruit. He asked for something to drink. They had only milk and brought us two glasses freshly drawn from a carabao.

He tasted his and said, "Warm."

It had animal heat and felt thick in my throat. He emptied his glass. So did I. Both of us said *salamat po.*

Shadows from the mountains fell across us and it was time to go. People trailed after us till we reached the edge of the *barrio.* After they had turned back we met a family of Negritos on the trail, little people, pygmies, the grown men about four feet tall. They saw Yulo and ran to him, laughing and crying and talking a language that was not Capampangan. They were people of the mountains, he told me, nomads who, in their roaming, came often to the *barrio* for food. It was harvest time for *camotes,* sweet potatoes, and they had been digging some for themselves.

"They love you," I said when they had passed on.

"I own the land. I am responsible for them."

"The *cacique?"*

He smiled. "I am the *haciendero.* It is the *cacique* system here. The *teniente* is *cacique* for me."

His tone was matter-of-fact. Thus it had been under the Spaniards and before the Spaniards. He could not change it.

On the way back I asked about the Huks and the Chinese squadron in Floridablanca. He knew there had been Huks there but not on his *hacienda.* "I did not know this Luis Taruc. It is a pity the Huks have caused so much trouble with the people."

They would cause more, I wanted to tell him, if they kept on fighting a system where Spanish colonialism was so tightly held onto. I did not.

With a feeling of regret I watched the next morning as MPs took Yulo and others to Calasiao. Their next destination would be Palawan.

• • •

When José Yulo moved out of the cot next to mine, Sergio Osmeña, Jr., son of the president, moved in, also in my custody. He
had been arrested on charges of using his buy-and-sell business
in Manila to equip Japanese troops fighting Americans. He was
young, urbane, politically connected, contemptuous of the ac-
cusations. Like other men of the *ilustrado,* he could recite his secret guerrilla connections, not as a soldier but in their intelligence
operations. He did not have an ID card but there were men in Manila who would vouch for him. He was in the buy-and-sell, but he
had done for the Japanese only what he had had to do.

"The Americans had been defeated and my father was in
Washington. The Japanese occupied Manila. What could I do? I
sent my family to the provinces and worked in Manila. When the
Americans invaded I went to the mountains." It was true that he
had surrendered to American soldiers in the mountains.

"Did you get rich in the buy-and-sell?"

He shook his head. He had made money but it was Japanese
invasion money and worthless. He had nothing for his family. He
sat on the edge of the cot and there were tears in his eyes. "If I
could only see my father. It is so long since I have seen my father. If
I could only go to Malacañan."

His father was not likely to see him, we knew. His father was
obeying orders from Washington. He would not intervene to save
his son from Bilibid. Sergio, Jr., was bitter. General MacArthur had
freed Manuel Roxas, but his father was too honorable to lift a finger for him.

In the ironies of war, Sergio, Jr., was sent to Bilibid, where he
was a political liability to his father. Yulo, Taruc, and Alejandrino
were sent to prison in Palawan. Taruc took up his early trade as a
tailor and worked for other prisoners, including José Yulo.

With Taruc and Alejandrino on Palawan, entirely shut off
from communication, the Huks turned to Mariano Balgos, alias
Tony Callentes, who had been third or fourth in command. Our
informers had some information on him. When we were sweeping
through Pampanga on our way to Manila he had offered Huk soldiers to fight against the Japanese, with the reservation that Huk
guerrillas would be recognized separately from the USAFFEs. On

advice of USAFFEs, the Army refused his offer. Afraid of being arrested, Balgos went underground and did not come when the Army sent out an order for him. Informers reported that he was in a new campaign of confiscation and liquidation in an attempt to hold together the organization built by Taruc and Alejandrino.

One day an informer came to me, out of breath from running.

"Mariano Balgos is in the market. It is a meeting. You will see him talking to the people."

I went at once and saw him in a group of men and women the size of a squadron, or larger. He was speaking in Capampangan, in a haranguing tone, stirring them up. When he saw me at the edge of the crowd he stopped speaking and, pushing his way through, ran. I ran after him, calling him by name, telling him I only wanted to talk to him. He kept running. I could not overtake him but I kept him in sight, out of the market and across the street. He hesitated in front of a frame house and disappeared through an open door. When I went inside there were only some frightened women and children. No, they had not seen a man come through. No, they had never heard of this Mariano Balgos.

"What about Tony Callentes?"

They had never heard of a Tony Callentes.

I searched the house but did not find him. He had escaped to the *barrios*. I would not find him in the *barrios*.

I had to make my way back through the market, past huddles of men years younger than I, and bear the contempt in their eyes.

SIX

FOR TWO MONTHS I had spent all of my time and energy on Huk conflicts, and had lost more than I had gained through recommendations that had backfired, through alienation or criticism from Filipinos and Americans alike. It was no consolation that all sides had lost more than they had gained. Uncontrolled Huk squadrons were on a rampage of revenge. Philippines Civil Affairs Units reinstated prewar officials, often without investigation, only to have them jailed by the CIC. The Commonwealth Government, slow in reorganizing, had no means for policing Central Luzon. The time had passed for the Army to establish effective martial law. The people no longer wanted it. They were weary of war and fighting. CIC agents were frustrated 'over failures and over contradictions at GHQ. It was easier for the agents to sit on their butts than to go out on the carabao trail. I agreed with them but I had to make one more try, this one as much as possible on my own.

The idea of recruiting a Hukbalahap regiment for the United States Army sounded bizarre but I wanted to try it. So did Captain Frederick after I had presented my plan in detail. Why not? USAFFEs had been inducted by the hundreds or thousands. No one knew how many. Rosters changed daily. Wasn't it only fair to give the Huks the same chance?

Together we presented the idea to Colonel White. The Huks would be bought soldiers, but no more so than the USAFFEs already in the Army, we reminded him. There were advantages. Every Huk taken by the Army would be taken away from a squadron. And there were advantages for the Huks. Once the roster was official they would be on Army pay and their families would be guaranteed Army benefits. Paying them would remove some of their resentment and make them more willing to accept military discipline.

Colonel White worried about costs in money and supplies. The outlay would be large, the gains not guaranteed. Our only argument was that the same had been given to the USAFFEs. We waited while he went to another office, we thought General Krueger's. He returned with a question: "Who will be your commander?"

I named the only one I thought we might count on—Bernardo Poblete, El Mundo, José Banal. My evidence was slight. As a young man he had served as a private in the United States Army. As military commander of the Hukbalahap he had carried on extensive campaigns against the Japanese. Out of loyalty to Taruc and Alejandrino he had surrendered at the jail, when he was field commander of the Hukbalahap in Pampanga Province. He was still a prisoner in San Fernando jail, and a cooperative one. More persuasive than anything I could say was a passage in a letter he had sent to General Krueger 5 February 1945: "And in closing, permit me to reiterate the loyalty of the Hukbalahap and of mine to the United States of America and to its armed forces."

With so little to go on, Colonel White gave me the power to release Banal and to offer him an appointment as a full colonel in the United States Army, with full pay and privileges. His outfit would be called the Huk Regiment. It was a risk, but one, we felt, that had to be taken. If he failed us, we could send him to Palawan.

The jail had not changed in my absence. The gallows, now double, seemed permanent in the courtyard, the shadows of the two arms blackish gray on the gray earth. José Banal, in the cell with his son, had changed. He looked older, smaller, frailer. Prison pallor was on his face, dejection in his eyes. He squatted with his back against a wall. Tomás squatted beside him. Without moving they waited for the door to be unlocked and for me to enter. Then they stood and shook hands.

Quickly I told them why I had come. "It is a plan for a Hukbalahap regiment in the Army—the same as the USAFFEs but not under the USAFFE." José Banal looked skeptical. I used the persuasions Colonel White had provided. "Your soldiers will get American uniforms. They will be paid like American soldiers. They will fight with Americans against Japs."

He wanted Tomás to repeat what I had said, what I was asking of him. I took his hand again. "I want you to be colonel of the Huk regiment."

Disbelief was still in his eyes. He took Tomás by the hand and led him to the back of the cell. They talked quietly in Capampangan and came back to me. Tomás spoke. "Why do you ask this of my father? He is old and in prison."

"The Army needs his help. He is trusted by the people. The Americans trust him."

"Why? When he is in jail?"

We had come to know him and respect him. There were other reasons. I brought up the case of the renegade Briones, a Huk squadron leader. When he had been tried and found guilty of rape, torture, and murder in the name of the Hukbalahap, José Banal had driven him out. In that case he had been just. The Army had faith that he would deal justly with soldiers under his command.

If they would go, I promised, we would work together, recruiting, equipping, training. He would wear the eagle. He would not be against Huks, only for the people. He had questions and I answered them. Yes, Tomás could work with him as his executive officer, maybe as a major, maybe as a lieutenant colonel. Yes, there was time for him to talk to Tomás. Yes, I would take him home at once.

A new look came into his face, an eagerness to be on his way. The release signed, we went to the jeep. Tomás had a question:

"What is the pay of a soldier?"

"Fifty dollars a month. A hundred *pesos*. Plus allowances."

From his look I knew that, bought or not, he was convinced. His father agreed.

I left them at an isolated hut in a *barrio* of Minalin. I did not ask for their word that they would be there the next morning. There seemed no need to.

I had left Tomás in the doorway. He was in the doorway when I returned the next day. I climbed the bamboo-pole ladder and he took my hand. José Banal stood behind him in the middle of the room. Both were in American uniforms, khaki, cut down but not enough, the kind of tailoring they could get in the black market. José Banal took my hand.

I expected a yes. "Not yet," Tomás said.

José Banal stared at me for what seemed a long time and turned away. Slowly he went toward a shed room.

"Come, ser," Tomás said.

I followed him to a room without windows. Light sifted through bamboo-slat walls and *cogon* grass thatch. In a manner of deep conspiracy José Banal led us to a small closet, darker than the room. They squatted together. I knelt on one knee. José Banal leaned close and began talking in a voice too low to penetrate the bamboo walls.

He was afraid, afraid of the USAFFEs, and more afraid of men like Briones in the Huk. The Huk regiment was no longer a secret. Threats had come in the night that he would be liquidated, and he believed them. He had helped to build the discipline of the Huk soldier. It was treason to go against it and take the side of anyone the Huks considered the enemy. Through the night he had been thinking. The war would soon be over. The Japanese had lost in the Philippines, and would go on losing. In a year American control would end; the Philippines would be free. The Huks would have to change their tactics from the military to the political. What they had done in war they could not do in peace.

Suddenly he reached under a pile of sleeping mats and brought out a Japanese revolver. He handed it to me, butt first.

"My father took it from Bataan," Tomás said. "It is for you, to show that he will follow the discipline of the American Army."

Solemnly they shook hands with me in a strange and likely to be dangerous compact. Solemnly they talked of how to raid Huk squadrons for recruits. Many would follow José Banal as they had followed him before. Soldier's pay would bring others. Others who had a *personal disgusto* for their leaders would enlist. If they were attacked by a strong squadron some recruits would run away. There was a plan. Each recruit would have to turn in a gun before he could be accepted. Squadrons would be weaker, discouraged, and more likely to take revenge.

There would be danger but we had to go to the *barrios* and explain to the people that the Huk regiment would not be against them; that José Banal as commander of the Huk regiment was as much their friend now as when he had been their El Mundo, Huk military commander. Would I go with them? They would be my bodyguards.

"Yes."

First we must go to the *población* of Minalin. There was a priest in the church, Padre Daniel Castrillo, a Spanish priest, a good priest, a priest of the people. He would be our friend. So would the Huk mayor. The *municipio* would be our recruiting center, the *luneta* in front of the church our bivouac and drill field.

I went and waited for them in the jeep. When father and son came out, José Banal had pinned old-fashioned eagles, old enough to have been in the Spanish-American war, on his collar tabs. Tomás had the gold leaves of a major. Self-consciously they saluted me. They had assumed that I was a captain and began calling me "Captain Blowens." They asked to be called not Poblete but Banal in honor of the regiment.

Father Daniel was in the church, saying a funeral Mass for a child. We waited and watched the people bring out a small white coffin, place it in a *carreta,* and form a sickly-looking procession to the cemetery.

José Banal touched my arm. "Padre does not charge for the funeral. Many priests must have the money first—some the prewar money. It is sad for the *tao* to bury without the Mass."

205

Father Daniel, a hearty man with graying hair, came to us. He shook hands with the Banals, gave each an *abrazo,* and turned to me. "Ah, an American friend."

He took my hand and put his arm around me in a half-embrace. His loose white cassock draped my shoulder. "Welcome, welcome, my friend." He stepped back and I felt as if I was passing inspection. "You have come to me, and I have not yet seen an American in Minalin. Is it something you need?"

I started telling him but he interrupted. "In the refectory. Will you come to the refectory? Perhaps you will have a drink?"

In a small sitting room—dining room we drank nipa palm wine and I told him about the Army plan to raise the Banal Regiment. He was glad. The Huks were his friends but there had been too much trouble. José Banal was the right man to lead it.

"We want to make Minalin our headquarters," José Banal said.

Father Daniel reached for my hand. "The church is yours, my son."

He took us to a large bedroom with windows above the church door looking out on the *luneta.* "This will be yours, my son. You will be safe here."

I looked out. The Banals had chosen well. In front of the church, on either side, would be the bivouac area and beyond it the drill field. The *municipio,* at the west end of the *luneta,* was large enough for storing supplies and equipment. A community artesian well would furnish water.

"We have not spoken to the mayor. Will he agree, Father?"

"The mayor is Huk but he will be friendly. Minalin is friendly, loving. The Banal Regiment will be welcome. When will you come?"

"22 May."

That was the date we had agreed on for the induction. On that day, if our plan worked, the troops would assemble.

Father Daniel walked to the jeep with us. After a final *abrazo* he said to me: "Will you bring the white bread? For so long I have not seen the white bread."

"Yes, Father, for all you are doing for us."

When we went back to San Fernando, Captain Frederick and

Colonel White were waiting. They looked at Colonel Banal's eagles and could have laughed, but did not. Rank is to be respected. The Banals mapped out our plans for recruiting, chiefly in Pampanga, among the people they knew. We told them that basic training would combine what José Banal remembered from the hitch in his youth, and what I remembered from basic training at Camp Wallace. Not the best, I apologized, but I knew nothing better. Colonel White ordered an officer to issue supplies and equipment, to be delivered to me in Minalin early on the morning of 22 May.

CIC agents, claiming that the Army had gone soft on the Huks, were less than sympathetic. I was a Huk lover and had gone over to the Huks. They were skeptical, in their jokes unkind. Some found the whole idea ludicrous. To them it was not the Banal Regiment but "Captain Blowens's Army."

Mike Horowitz, my master sergeant and friend, summed up their feelings. "What kind of an *opéra bouffe* war is this anyway?"

• • •

Our journeys, as they reached out farther day by day, took us on paved roads north and south from Angeles to Calumpit, east and west from Arayat to Dinalupihan, and once, because I wanted to go, south on the coast of Bataan past Cabcaben till we could walk on the Mariveles battlefield and see Corregidor across a strip of Manila Bay. We passed through the *poblaciónes* but our work was in the *barrios* with the *taos,* and José Banal brought me as close to them as ever an outsider—barred by language, by customs, and by the now blurred distinctions between East and West—could approach. Often I had to stand by, waiting, while the Banals talked and argued with Huk leaders or *barrio tenientes.* At times my bed was a blanket on a mat on a bamboo-slat floor, with a family sleeping in a row near me, as many as three generations sleeping together, with the night noises of as many ages. Once my bed was a table in a jail, with the table pushed against the door and bodyguards keeping watch.

It was a happy time to be in the *barrios.* The work of the harvest was over, the last strips of *pancit,* rice noodles, were drying in the sun. It was the time of festivals—the *barrio* festival honoring the name saint, and *Las Floras de Maio,* The Flowers of May, for

207

Mary, Queen of the Flowers. The *taos* were parade-loving, ritual-loving, Mary-worshiping. Day and night, sometimes late at night, we saw their flambeaus and stopped to watch. No matter how poor the *barrio,* the young people paraded with arches and flowers, with band music and singing—music of the islands, often touched by the rhythms of Spain or by American popular tunes, with "You Are My Sunshine" the most popular. Priests thought these observances pagan in origin with overlays borrowed from the Spanish Church. In the *barrios* people told me that they were simply something that had always been done.

It was also a time of uneasiness. The rains would come; they had to come for the rice planting. Rivers would overflow and flood the paddies. Then would come the backbreaking work for men and women, for children barely old enough to work—transplanting rice seedlings by hand, with the back bent, the feet always in water. It was the way they had always planted. It was also a time of danger. The rainy season was the season of typhoons, and half a dozen or more could be expected to come sweeping in, destroying houses, taking lives. Houses did not matter so much. They were flimsy and could be rebuilt from the ground up in a few days. Loss of a house was not necessarily an act of fate. Loss of life could be, and no matter what the priests said, the people retained a strong streak of fatalism.

Fatalism, always a deterrent in efforts to rouse the people, operated against any persuasion the Banals could offer, either in the *que sera sera* mentality of the totally illiterate or in the disillusionment over hope offered, fulfillment denied. At times the Banal Regiment seemed doomed but we kept on going. After a few days I could not remember the people I had talked to, the hands I had grasped, the times I had said "I'll meet you in Minalin."

Couriers came from the *barrios* of San Luis and Candaba. They delivered their messages and departed, leaving a silence that could only mean trouble. On the road, away from other ears and eyes, we sat in the jeep and went over the things they had to tell me. The Banal Regiment and José Banal's orders were being challenged by Huk officers who had served under him, led by Mariano Balgos and advised by Vicente Lava. Balgos had appointed a Huk named Esting to succeed José Banal as military commander in Pampanga. In a meeting Huks had approved the creation of a special force to liquidate deserters and "opportunists." By opportunists they meant any from the United Front who accepted positions in the United States Army. There were offers of rewards for anyone who would foxhole José and Tomás Banal.

"Do they mean me, too?"

They did.

The Banals did not question their intentions. Still we went on, José Banal in a kind of desperation, I because I knew nothing else to do. There was one change. I would not sleep again in the *barrios*. Before dark I would go to San Fernando or to the church in Minalin.

Late one morning we came to where a dirt road stopped at a river. With cigarettes we hired a *banca*, polished till it shone black as ebony. José Banal stepped in first and knelt in the bow, his eyes turned downriver, the direction we would go, his hands pressed against the wood, as if they had been carved from the same piece. I squatted in the center and grasped the smooth rim on either side. A *banca* tips easily. Tomás knelt in the stern and with slow, gentle paddle strokes moved out into the stream.

The river drifted sluggishly through swamps of nipa palm and tropical growth that matted and fell into the water. Smaller rivers, crisscrossing the larger, made a watery network of vistas deep into jungles where, the Banals told me, only strange birds and monkeys and boa constrictors lived. Rounding a bend, we came up to a barge drifting down to market in Manila, loaded with green and white vegetables. A man with a pole kept the barge near midstream. A woman knelt on the bamboo deck beating clothes with a paddle. As she finished a garment she dipped it in the river and hung it to dry on the thatched shelter above the cargo. As the *banca* glided past, José Banal spoke to the man about the Huk regiment. The man was friendly. He would pass the message along: Minalin, 22 May.

Toward noon Tomás guided the *banca* to a bamboo landing at a path that led through red earth out to the rice paddies. It was the place of Bongue, the harelipped one, a Huk leader, one that José Banal thought would be a sergeant in the regiment, if he could be persuaded. Tomás tied up to a bamboo post and we waded through high grass up from the river. After a narrow strip we came out on flat land ridged and furrowed for rice. Not far away, the huts of a *barrio* showed through vegetable gardens and banana palms. We skirted the *barrio* and came to a nipa hut set in an open, clean-swept place.

Men armed with bolos and rifles squatted in the shade. Among them was a man with a harelip holding a white gamecock in his arm. Both had the look of a fighter. The harelip split over long teeth. His nose was large, high-bridged, in a face bony and angular. He had been a Macabebe scout and may have inherited his looks from Mexican Indian ancestors.

Bongue, stroking the feathers of the gamecock, listened earnestly to José Banal. Without changing from Capampangan he spoke to Tomás. Tomás repeated, "He says we will eat if we will only enter his house."

José Banal went up the bamboo-pole ladder first. My boots slipped on the polished bamboo, my carbine slapped my thigh. Smiling a friendly, split-lipped smile, Bongue waited for me to regain my balance and then followed me.

The room was large, the thatched walls clean, the bamboo uprights and slat floor polished a rich brown. In one corner was a Singer sewing machine, in another a hanging mirror with curtains drawn to keep out lightning during the monsoons. Six cheap American-made chairs had been hung upside down from the rafters. Bongue brought one down for me. I was the first American to honor him by entering his house and he wanted me to use it.

A woman called from another room. We followed Bongue and stood around a hand-hewn *nara* table. He passed me half a coconut shell. I filled it with rice from an earthen pot and with a wooden ladle spread pieces of chicken and mango over it. There were no knives, forks, or spoons. Watching the others, I rolled balls of rice on my fingers and picked out pieces of chicken and mango. They laughed and told me it was the way of the *tao*.

After nipa palm wine drunk from coconut shells José Banal

210

and Bongue talked, Bongue in short questions, Banal in long, sing-song answers. Bongue was willing to listen to all Banal's arguments but he was cautious. To go with José Banal was to go against comrades he had fought with for three years. There was also Mariano Balgos. It was a dangerous thing to go against Mariano Balgos.

When we had to go he still had not made up his mind. We would have to leave without an answer. It might be that he would come to Minalin.

In the office in San Fernando there was a message for me to report at once to a lieutenant in the adjutant general's office. Worried that there was another report from Don Pablo, or that because of the Huk regiment I had stepped over some boundary invisible to me, I went. The lieutenant was abrupt but efficient. He asked me to sign a paper. It was for an honorable discharge at the convenience of the Army in order that I might be commissioned a second lieutenant in Military Intelligence. The paper was a surprise and a shock. In Australia, in my most disaffected days, I had read a directive on combat appointments. I could never pass one specific statement: "Efficient performance of duty not involving actual combat, even though in a combat area, is not sufficient to warrant recommendation under this authority." It had to be a mistake but I signed. It was dated 2 May 1945.

The lieutenant was in a hurry. "Raise your right hand and repeat after me."

I raised my hand and repeated after him:

I do solemnly swear that I will support and defend the Constitution of the United States against all enemies, foreign and domestic, that I will bear true faith and allegiance to the same; that I will take this obligation freely, without any mental reservation or purpose of evasion; and that I will well and faithfully discharge the duties of the office upon which I am about to enter; SO HELP ME GOD.

I had no reservations. That was what I had been doing for three years.

The lieutenant shook my hand and I went on my way, but not fully rejoicing. My years of trying to be a half-assed gumshoe were over, but so was my freedom as a special agent. Now I would be tied to desk jobs, signing reports in septuplicate. And a barrier had been placed between me and the other agents, the age-old barrier between the officer and the enlisted man. As much as we could, we would remain the same to each other, but they knew and I knew that I could never invite them to the officers' club for a drink.

Major Frederick, the leaves on his tabs new, congratulated me approvingly. He should have. He wrote the recommendation. Soon we were on our way to the officers' club to celebrate his promotion and mine. At the bar, officers who for almost a year had observed the distinction of rank between us now slapped me on the shoulder and bought the drinks. There were other things to drink to. Berlin had fallen. The war in Europe was all but over.

On the street Major Frederick took my hand and with as much affection as the Army allows said, "By God, you made it."

In Minalin the next morning, when I went to meet the Banals, they saw the bar on my fatigue cap. They were puzzled and then reticent. Tomás spoke for both. "We are sorry, ser, that you were busted in rank. Was it because of the Huks, ser?"

They could not comprehend my explanation.

• • •

22 May 1945. Huk Day to Army skeptics. It was midmorning when, after hurrying and waiting, the supply convoy rolled through San Fernando and turned south toward Minalin. I took the lead and kept an eye on the road ahead and on the trucks and weapons carriers behind. When we turned off the Manila highway I scouted ahead for Huk squadrons or any gathering in a *barrio*. At Minalin the drivers would unload and turn back. I, one American, would be left with the supplies, with only the Banals and whatever recruits had turned up to guard them. On my word alone I had been issued enough guns and bullets to start a small war, if we were raided by USAFFEs or Huks.

After I had turned off the main highway I saw a young man in

212

shorts and a hat large as a small umbrella crossing rice paddies. He was carrying a gun but did not look like either a USAFFE or a Huk. A recruit? He stopped, looked at the jeep, and started walking in the direction of Minalin. Soon there were other men on the road, some in shorts and rain hats, a few in shirts and pants made from Japanese or American uniforms. They were coming in from the hills, from the swamps—from any direction to the road to Minalin. Before I reached the *población* I had counted enough men to know the Banals could cull out some kind of regiment.

More men waited with the mayor at the *municipio*. On the *luneta* José Banal and his staff, Bongue among them, were marking out bivouac areas. Proud, erect, military in new khaki uniforms, they saluted me and then shook hands. They had already counted enough recruits to begin putting together a regiment. The trucks rolled up to the *municipio*. Father Daniel came from the church and embraced me with a special blessing.

There was no time for delay. Selections had to be made, supplies unloaded and issued, and pup tents set up. The mayor set a table and chairs in front of his office. As a recruit came forward Tomás Banal took his gun, whether it was an Arisaka in good condition or a plumbing pipe mounted on a piece of wood. José Banal interrogated them and passed the approved ones to me for the roster.

"No Huk names," I told him. "Only real names, real places." Then I thought of the investigations that might have to be made. "You'd better add Huk aliases for the ones who have them."

By late afternoon two hundred men, tested, approved, sworn to loyalty to the United States Army, waited in line to sign for their uniforms and supplies. I checked the supplies and saw that for a time it would be a barefoot regiment. Supply had sent shoes in sizes eight to twelve. Filipino feet came in fives and sixes. Then the test of their trust and mine came. We began piling in a truck the guns they had brought in, most of them old, rusted, barely good enough to be melted down for pot metal. In faith they had given them up. I had to have enough faith in them and in the Banals to put new ones in their hands. It was too late to turn back. Nervously I gave the order to issue uniforms and weapons.

213

At a command from José Banal men stripped in the street. Making a game of discarding their civilian clothes, they threw them to whoever among the onlookers could catch them. Then they filed slowly through a side door of the *municipio*. They went in naked; they came out in green fatigues and armed with rifles or carbines. The crowd laughed and cheered as José Banal marched them single file across the *luneta*.

Men who had no weapons to turn in or who had been rejected by the Banals stood around the table. One by one they pleaded with me. "Ser, if you will only put me on the rooster."

I counted the names on the roster. We had two hundred and had turned away half a hundred more. Others came. I took their guns but had to turn them away.

I heard the first "Forward, march" and went to watch the first drilling, if it could be called drilling. The officers were awkward, the enlisted men more so. They all belonged in an awkward squad, but they were all we had. They were awkward when they fell in, awkward when they fell out, ragged but willing. When darkness came, four rows of pup tents, twenty-five to a row, had been set up, two rows on either side of the church door. The kitchen crew were handing out cans of C rations. To a squad at a time Tomás Banal was reading the Articles of War in English and translating to Capampangan.

When I went to my room Father Daniel was waiting for me, white-shrouded on a stool at the window, looking out on the rows of tents, watching the regiment take shape. He rose and embraced me. "My son, it is a good thing you are doing. I watched the people today. It was a great change that came over them. You gave them hope at a time when they had so little. All day I watched for the hammer and sickle. Not one did I see."

He put his hand on my shoulder. "Tomorrow the Mass will be said for you. You are to come only if you want to. You are my friend." There was sudden humor in his voice. "You brought me the white bread."

When he had gone I sat on the stool and looked out onto the *luneta*. It was a strange sight, made stranger by the shadows of armed guards on the perimeter and two at each church entrance, and by the sound of their feet in wooden sandals as they walked their posts.

As I watched and worried that a Huk attack would come in the night the shadow of a soldier appeared below me. He stopped and raised a bugle. The first notes of taps sounded on the still air. Clear and true the notes rose, phrase after phrase, and at each pause echoes floated back from jungle swamps. *All is well.* The climax was reached, and the tones drifted down to the final phrases: *Safely rest* and, softly, *God is nigh.* With faith and gratitude I wrapped my mosquito net around me.

The sharp, staccato sounds of reveille woke me and I went to the window. The bugler stood alone on what was now the drill field. Father Daniel was entering the church for early Mass. A peaceful night had passed into a peaceful day. I went to Mass; the two of us had the church to ourselves. I sat in the shadows. Ghost-like in the light of one candle he read the ritual in Latin. At the door he took my hand. "I prayed that you will be safe. You will not take chances?"

"No, sir."

By sunup the officers had assigned the men to squads and were teaching them saluting by the numbers, the manual of arms by the numbers, drilling by the numbers. José Banal went from squad to squad in a continuing inspection. We had to be ready for an inspection by Sixth Army.

Rumors had spread. A name on the roster meant rewards in American dollars. More volunteers came and added their weapons to the pile. To get rid of so many guns the Army had to bury them.

A message came from Major Frederick. Sixth Army had set the inspection date. Whatever training could be done on the double must be done on the double. The men were already on the double. Officers shouted themselves hoarse, driving the men, driving themselves. The shape of the regiment changed daily as José Banal learned the men and what they could do. He promoted or busted in rank on standards that were his own. If there was complaining I never heard it. At the end of each day they passed before me in review, the command "Eyes right," solemnly given, solemnly received.

New recruits reported that Huk squadrons were organizing in the *barrios* to march on Minalin. Some recruits had been threat-

215

ened with death if they joined the Banal Regiment. The guns that would destroy the Banal Regiment would also be turned on them. CIC reports from Sixth Army were just as alarming.

I worried. José Banal remained calm. To him the threats were a sign that the Huk organizations were weakening. His officers agreed with him. Bongue smiled his split-lip smile. "Let them come."

José Banal doubled the guard at night.

•   •   •

Reveille sounded clear and sharp. Inspection day. When I looked out I saw what had become the morning routine: Father Daniel opening doors for early Mass, José Banal coming from his cot in the *municipio,* soldiers gathering around stoves in the field kitchen for chow. Steps were lively. The Army had said snap to and they were doing their best. Inspection was set for 1100.

The seven o'clock Mass was for the Banal Regiment. The church was still shadowy when I took a seat in a front pew. A few men and women knelt in the pews behind me and there was a hushed whisper of prayers. From the outside the church looked old and gray. The inside was a darker gray except for colored mosaics decorating a low dome and ceilings. Father Daniel came to the altar, gave me a quick glance, and began the ritual. Unable to understand his words, unfamiliar with the ritual, I knelt and with closed eyes listened to the assured tones of the priest, the mumbled responses of those who worshiped with him in a centuries-old coming together. The only discordant sounds came from outside, where drill masters shouted orders and troops counted cadence. At the end of the Mass, Father Daniel, in English, spoke of the feeling of peace in Minalin and read a prayer for the Banal Regiment. Only a few soldiers left off drilling to hear him.

From 0700 to 0900 the troops drilled back and forth, up and down the *luneta,* some by permission in their underwear because they wanted to keep their uniforms fresh for inspection. At 0900 they had a dry run for Father Daniel and me, complete with a manual of arms and an eyes-right salute as they marched past. José Banal stood with us for the salute. Then he himself took the field and

216

put them through an inspection of arms that was weak on precision, strong on determination. At 1000 he gave final instructions and ordered the men to check their tents and uniforms.

At 1100 I heard jeeps pulling through the swampy stretch of road at the edge of Minalin. They made a wide sweep past the *municipio* and came to a stop near the church. Major Frederick, followed by Lieutenant Ripley and Special Agent Horowitz, stepped down and strode forward. Major Frederick was crisply military in suntans, crisply military as he took salutes from Colonel Banal and his officers. He was deferential when he shook hands with Father Daniel and thanked him for supporting the Regiment.

Methodically he inspected the rows of pup tents. Methodically he snapped tent ropes and counted personal equipment and gear laid out on the ground—methodically but uncritically, even when ropes sagged under his hand. Then, with me at his left, the Huk officers a pace or two behind or to the side, he marched from the church door to the troops lined up on the drill field at attention. With a sergeant counting cadence the soldiers marched the length of the field and back. It was basic drilling, but they did it with less than precision. On the manual of arms they were nervous. They were more nervous when Major Frederick went down the lines inspecting arms. What I had expected happened. A man dropped his rifle.

José Banal, with an animation I had not seen in him before, took charge and put the troops through drills taught in his own basic training but long since discarded. At a rapid cadence he commanded them through "Squads right" and "Right by squads." Then his voice became a high singsong as he led them through the "First file to the rear, march" and "Second file to the rear, march" of the Marine Drill. There were mistakes and a pileup but no cliffs to march them over.

In the final maneuver Colonel Banal took a place with us but a little to the rear—the respect of the colonial. The troops, in columns of four, marched by at "Eyes right." Major Frederick, with no show of emotion, took the salute. I took it with him, but I let my pride show. In the recruiting days I had referred to them jokingly. Now they were my friends.

When he had dropped his hand in the final salute Major Frederick smiled at me and said, "Good-o." They had passed inspection. Major Frederick knew and I knew that anything else would be a political fiasco.

The troops dismissed, Major Frederick complimented the officers and me. Abruptly he announced their orders. "You're shipping out. The trucks will be here at 1600."

"Where to?" I asked.

"Cabanatuan."

Cabanatuan. Nueva Ecija province. Next to Pampanga the strongest Huk territory. Juan Feleo was the Huk governor. Mariano Balgos was operating out of there. The Army knew the situation.

"Is this a deliberate Army snafu?"

Major Frederick did not think so. The Army had put soldiers on alert for an attack on Minalin that never happened. Soldiers would be kept at ready, but for the moment the fight seemed to have gone out of the Huk. He explained Banal Regiment's mission. They would be mopping up behind American soldiers, capturing or killing Japanese soldiers trying to regroup. The emphasis was on killing. It was a difficult assignment, dangerous but necessary. The Army had assigned the area to them with full responsibility. They were there as soldiers. Civil law and order would be left to the Commonwealth Government. If they encountered Huks it was better to remain neutral.

"Understand?"

"Jes, ser," Tomás Banal said.

Major Frederick commended me on the regiment, shook hands with the Banals, and left.

From my window I watched the soldiers strike tents and pack equipment. Then there was a policing up and they were ready to load. Father Daniel crossed the *luneta* to the *municipio* and joined the crowd gathered to see them go.

When the last truck was out of sight and I was packed, I went to the *municipio* to thank the mayor. The crowd was still waiting. The mayor came out and in an impromptu ceremony placed on my head a rain hat as wide as my shoulders. Some of the onlookers said *"salamat po"*; some cheered. He had made me an honorary *tao* and probably an honorary Huk. In the midst of a laughing crowd I shook his hand and thanked him. Father Daniel embraced me and blessed me and walked with me to the jeep.

He was also leaving Minalin. He would be a priest at San Augustin, the only church left standing in Intramuros.

"My friend, I will say the Mass for you and the Banal Regiment in San Augustin Church."

• • •

8 May 1945. V-E Day. I was out on the carabao trail with the Banals when President Harry Truman issued his proclamation. Intense relief spread among Allied Forces all over the Pacific. No longer would we be a second-class operation. Invasion of the Japanese homeland became a possibility, planning a necessity. On 25 May 1945 a plan for the invasion of Kyushu Island was put into effect by the Joint Chiefs of Staff, scheduled for 1 November 1945. The code name "Olympic" was top secret but it was leaked by someone in GHQ. Disaffected GIs pounced on it. "Is he going to play God now? He can already walk on water."

The date of their decision was auspicious. On 26 May vast sections of Tokyo were laid waste by American bombers in a kind of total annihilation the world had never known before.

On 1 June 1945 or thereabouts I received a VOCO to report at once to the 441st CIC Detachment at GHQ in Manila. It was followed by a telephone call from Captain Edward F. McLaughlin. He had been appointed plans and training officer for the CIC in Operation Olympic, and I was to be his assistant. Leaving Major Frederick was not easy. In the abruptness of change in the military, I left him in his office and never saw him again. In the unpredictability of the Army I was being placed near the center of potentially the bloodiest battle of the war, to serve under the only other officer with whom I had worked for any length of time. One day I was on the carabao trail, the next in a well-furnished office in the Uy Suy Bin building in Manila.

Officers with a knowledge of Japanese customs, institutions, and language would have been a better choice, but in the early hysteria of the war we had sent the ones we had off to fight and die in Italy. Two Anglos would have to muddle through. Our consolation was that the ground attack would be under General Krueger and the Sixth Army.

An overriding question was the kind of defense they could mount. We knew their sea power had been diminishing since the Battle of the Philippine Sea. Their air power had been reduced to sporadic response to Allied attacks and to the fanatic *Kamikaze* pilots. They would have to depend on depleted ground troops and whatever defense civilians could muster.

Another question had to do with their will to continue to fight. On this I had to prepare a report. With a curiosity near morbid I read ATIS translations of documents captured on Okinawa, and evaluated as rapidly as possible the changes in attitude that I found. Individually, at least, their faith was shaken, but not their fanaticism. They knew and had known for months that they had lost the war. The defeatism expressed in New Guinea had infected soldiers stranded on Pacific islands, isolated, not under attack, as virulently as it had those retreating on Leyte and Luzon. Only after their devastating defeat on Okinawa had the infection become widespread in Japan. There the antidote was the Emperor, as he had been on far-flung battlefronts, and no more effective. Ritual suicide as a way out reached staggering proportions. One diarist described an example that can stand for all who made this ultimate escape from the humiliation of defeat, this ultimate sacrifice for the Emperor:

Alas! the stars of the generals have fallen with the setting of the waning moon over Mabuni. . . .

The pale moon shimmers bluish white over the waters of the southern sea, but on Hill 89, which juts abruptly from the reefs, the rocks and boulders are dyed crimson by the blood of the penetration unit, which, with burning patriotism, rush the American positions for the last stand. The surrounding area displays a picture of concentrated fireworks; bursts of naval gun fire, flashes of mortar and artillery fire, to which is added the occasional chatter of machine guns. . . .

Gathered around their section chiefs, members of each

section bow in veneration toward the eastern sky and the cheer of "Long live the Emperor!" echoes among the boulders. . . . The faces of all are flushed with deep emotion and tears fall upon ragged uniforms, soiled with the dirt and grime of battle. . . .

Four o'clock, the final hour of Hara-kiri; the Commanding General, dressed in full field uniform, and the Chief of Staff in a white kimono appeared. . . . The Chief of Staff says as he leaves the cave first, "Well, Commanding General Ushijima, as the way may be dark, I, Cho, will lead the way." The Commanding General replies, "Please do so, and I'll take along my fan since it is getting warm." Saying this he picked up his Okinawa-made Kuba fan and walked out quietly fanning himself. . . .

The moon, which had been shining until now, sinks below the waves of the sea. Dawn has not yet arrived and, at four-ten, the generals appeared at the mouth of the cave. The American forces were only three meters [*sic*] away. Four meters away from the mouth of the cave a sheet of white cloth is placed on a quilt; this is the ritual place for the two generals to commit Hara-kiri. The Commanding General and the Chief of Staff sit down on the quilt. . . . the time for the honored rites of Hara-kiri arrives. At this time several grenades were hurled near this solemn scene by enemy troops who observed movements taking place beneath them. A simultaneous shout and a flash of the sword, then another repeated shout and a flash, and both generals had nobly accomplished their last duty to their Emperor. . . .

All is quiet after the cessation of gunfire and smoke; and the full moon is once again gleaming over the waves of the southern sea. Hill 89 of Mabuni will live in memory forever.

For nearly a hundred years Americans had thought of the Japanese, when they thought of them at all, as inscrutable Orientals, slant-eyed, unemotional, insular and insulated. The few who had read the Tanaka Memorial—with its boast that the invasion of Manchuria was the beginning of a hundred years' religious war with the aim of bringing the eight corners of the earth under one roof, with the Emperor-god at the roof pole—ignored or refused to believe what they read. Instead of seeing it as a declaration of a holy war, Americans dismissed it as fantasy. In the American mind, the victory of the "banty Japs" over the "shanghai Russians" was a fading memory still favorable to the Japanese. Little men from a little country had overcome big men from a big country. The fact that these little men had by 1941 overrun Korea, Manchuria, and many Chinese provinces was of little concern to Americans deep in the Depression and blissful in their isolationism.

Pearl Harbor forced Americans to consider the kind of enemy we faced. The image of the inscrutable Oriental disappeared in the boasts and ranting over their great victory. A wide streak of emotionalism appeared and became more apparent in national and individual outbursts as the Japanese progressed from victory to victory, to the Equator and south. Emotionalism with a different tune appeared as defeat followed defeat. As disillusionment set in, Japanese soldiers relieved tensions in threats against the "hairy Americans" and in romantic poems to be wept over. The more the tide of war turned against them, the more emotional their outbursts became. Theirs was a war for the Emperor. Let the enemy come. They would fight him on the beaches. Old women with nothing but bamboo spears would fight him on the beaches. Victory or suicide—these were the alternatives set by national tradition and fostered by neighborhood associations organized for the purpose of thought control.

Americans had contempt for them, for their size and superstition, but not for their fighting ability. A little man behind a big gun can be as deadly as any other, and deadlier on his own soil. For the ritual of *seppuku*, self-immolation, American soldiers had no understanding, nor for the kind of thought control that would make Japanese soldiers jump off a cliff in a group for their Emperor.

However seasoned CIC men were in combat, as agents they needed intensive training to deal with an alien, conquered people, whose language they did not speak, whose psychology in victory or defeat they did not understand. But training resources were meager, time short. At the end of eight weeks all agents had to be with their units making final preparations for embarkation. To each agent we could spare one week of intensive training and no more. Our answer was a school like Camp Ritchie, in Manila, under the best staff we could assemble. It was approved.

Every weekend one class was flown out, another in, with agents from as far away as Hawaii, New Guinea, Australia. For five days, almost around the clock, the agents absorbed what they could of lectures on Japanese government, Japanese psychology, Japanese geography, Japanese extremists like the Black Dragon Society. Their incentive to learn was great, based as it was on fear of the foe they would have to face.

I shared their anxiety. My orders were to land on the beach at Muyazaki in the third wave on the first day.

• • •

Reports on the Banal Regiment were better than I had hoped for. They had completed mopping up in the Cabanatuan area and had received a Sixth Army commendation. I wanted to see for myself.

On a Sunday morning Lieutenant Dana Creel and I went to Cabanatuan and to the warehouses the regiment had made their headquarters. The Banals met us, saluted, and took us through rooms that had been converted to barracks. Morning inspection was over. Soldiers in uniform stood by their cots and saluted as we passed. Not a man had been lost in the mopping up.

The Banals took us to their quarters for Filipino-style bourbon and a lunch of rice and vegetables and C ration meat for a viand. At ease as he had never been before, Colonel Banal gave his report. It was good; Sixth Army had lived up to the agreement. Supplies and pay had come on time. They had plenty of guns and bullets. He and his officers had been treated with the respect due their rank.

"Any trouble from the Huks?"

No attacks, but there had been banditry in the *barrios,* maybe Huks confiscating *palay,* maybe ordinary thieves. Some Huk leaders had respected him and his soldiers and had guided them to Japanese hiding places. He had heard of no kidnappings or liquidations in Nueva Ecija, and it was safe for landlords to return to their homes. People were glad the Army had sent them to Cabanatuan.

"What about Pampanga?"

That was a different story. Huks angry because they were co-operating with the Army had gathered in Pampanga and there had been skirmishes with the USAFFEs. The Army would not return them to Pampanga. Only that morning they had received new orders. They were to dislodge Japanese soldiers holed up in the tunnels on Corregidor. They knew it was a more dangerous assignment, but they would be ready when the trucks came.

"We will meet on Corregidor?" Colonel Banal asked.

"Yes."

I went to Corregidor the next Sunday, this time with a colonel from quartermaster who had scrounged a launch. He did not care about the Huks. He was on his own pilgrimage to a place he felt had been dishonored by defeat, but honored by the men who had lost their lives there. It was still "The Rock," but he talked of it as a national monument.

The Banals met us at the North Dock and took me on an inspection trip, first toward Malinta Hill and then to their quarters in a bombed-out building that had been a part of Fort Mills. Colonel Banal had been made commanding officer but the island had been bombed out, as Intramuros had been bombed out. In a pounding from sea and air that began the last week in January, Americans had turned stone and concrete fortifications around the fort and on the outer rim to piles of rubble. Blasts were strong enough to level small heights. The Rock itself had been diminished by scars and craters.

After Pearl Harbor, when defeat in the Philippines was inevitable, Americans had taken refuge in the tunnels. When the Americans had returned, Japanese took to the same tunnels. When American paratroopers arrived with their napalm bombs and flame-throwers, Japanese soldiers in suicidal desperation blew up themselves and their ammunition dumps. By the end of February, Corregidor had been declared secure, but in June the last Japanese survivors had not yet been dug out. Soldiers of the Banal Regiment were fighting it out with them deep in the tunnels. Colonel Banal wanted to show me.

We went to the Malinta Tunnel first. MacArthur's last stand had been made there, with Quezon and Osmeña, officers, nurses, guards—the entourage of GHQ. From there the last radio reports had come, reports of death and heroism, of Army nurses serving beyond the call of duty. Corregidor became second to Pearl Harbor as a name to inflame Americans. And to inspire bitter humor. Here General MacArthur became Dugout Doug to hundreds of thousands of GIs. Here soldiers helped perpetuate a song that had come from other bottled-up comrades:

> We're the battling bastards of Bataan:
> No mama, no papa, no Uncle Sam,
> No aunts, no uncles, no nephews, no nieces,
> No rifles, no planes, or artillery pieces,
> And nobody gives a damn.

Corregidor the invincible fell to the Japs. The Japs in turn defended and lost. Only by spectacular derring-do did General MacArthur escape from a hole without a second exit. The Japs would not escape. Banal's men were seeing to that.

The main tunnel was safe for us to walk in, but not the laterals where there was fighting. We went anyway, with bodyguards leading us, moving cautiously in the darkness, guiding ourselves with hands on the wall. Far in, where there was a stink of gunpowder and death, we saw the flash and heard the sound of an American carbine. Farther on, a Japanese mortar shell exploded. Harsh echoes reverberated around us.

Colonel Banal took my arm. "It is not safe. We will go."

He ordered his men to cease fire and hold where they were. Starve them out. Let them surrender or die.

In the afternoon Tomás Banal took me to a promontory commanding the entrance to Manila Bay, an eagle's nest high above the water. At a gun emplacement two American 210s had been knocked from their mounts. They lay like logs. Never again would they guard Manila Bay.

The place was peaceful. We sat on a cannon and rested, with

the Pacific stretched out before us. I studied the debris at my feet and shuddered. These jagged concrete foundations, these cannons, had been part of the final Japanese stand. These were the leavings from American bombings—fragments of uniforms, bits of straight black hair, fragments of bones, no longer carrion, only bones bleaching on a dry crag. I had walked in on the remains of Japanese soldiers. I would have to leave the same way. The knowledge was shattering but clarifying, not in the sounds of war but in the silences, not in the humanity but in the desiccating lack of humanity.

• • •

The Doolittle raid, a morale booster in and out of war zones, became a symbol of what Allied planes could and would do to the Japanese homeland, but results were not entirely optimistic. Precision bombing on railroads and factories had disrupted but not destroyed the Japanese will to defend to the death. Intensive bombing of residential sections in Tokyo had been only slightly more effective. Even the massive raids on Tokyo on the night of 5 August had failed to make them give up. It was starve them out, we thought, or rout them out with the ever-essential foot soldier. We were making plans for the latter, not quite believing persisting rumors of more deadly tools of war.

I was walking toward the Escolta, the business section of Manila, when I heard of the raid on Hiroshima, first from soldiers and civilians shouting in the streets and then from Army radios blaring from every military building. *The atom bomb*—newscasters and communiqué writers savored the words. The years of work and secrecy at Los Alamos, the Manhattan Project, made manifest at last.

6 August 1945. A day for the world to remember. The American answer to Pearl Harbor, to be celebrated not as a day of infamy but as a day of exultation. A blow too devastating to exaggerate. A city almost totally destroyed, a civilian population dead or maimed, innocent victims in the ultimate of total war. The next advance would be toward world obliteration. In the first moment of shock, people were so stunned that they could comprehend only quan-

titatively—the qualitative study of the impact would have to be the work of philosophers and humanists.

To war-weary soldiers, chances of going home seemed brighter. Gangplank fever, endemic under the point system for rotation, became epidemic as rumors spread of what the bomb had done. Under such a disaster Japan could not go on. In a day, a week, at most a month, it would all be over. We could hear the music of the gangplank rising.

In the office, still working on plans for Operation Olympic, I read communiqués and intelligence reports on Hiroshima and what had happened to the people of Hiroshima. A question gradually insinuated itself: Should we have dropped the bomb? The GI answer was, Hell, yes. Why not? It was a military solution to shortening the war. Why not set fire to the yellowbellies? The Japs would have done the same if they had had the bomb.

Meanwhile we studied Japanese maps and pinpointed landing beaches. "The war's not over, not by a long shot," we answered as we prepared assignments and orders.

7 August 1945. President Truman broadcast a message heard around the world, a message and a threat. The message was the fact of the atomic bomb, with a force of more than twenty tons of TNT, a "harnessing of the basic power of the universe."

For the Japanese the threat must have been ominous: "Let there be no mistake: we shall completely destroy Japan's power to make war."

A GI response: "Good on you, Harry."

A GI observation: without fanfare Tokyo Rose had gone off the air.

Perhaps too stunned to speak, Japan remained silent, while odds against survival increased.

8 August 1945. The Soviet Union declared war against Japan and planned to begin the invasion of Manchuria the next day.

9 August 1945. American flyers destroyed Nagasaki with the second atomic bomb.

10 August 1945. From all our study of intelligence reports, we knew that the Japanese situation was deteriorating rapidly. Japan had no recourse but to accept the terms drawn up on 16 July 1945 at Potsdam by the United States, the Soviet Union, and Britain. Japan offered to surrender "without prejudice to the Emperor's position." The Emperor's position was a stickler. Without him the *Hakko Ichiu* tradition would go down the drain. With him, the seeds of war expressed on the Tanaka Memorial might lie fallow but would not die.

The bomb on Nagasaki had increased American cockiness and determination to blow the divine-wind mindset into nothingness. "If we've got another one," American soldiers argued, "let's drop it. Let's blast that little tin god Emperor."

11 August 1945. The United States sent a secret message stipulating terms of surrender. While the Japanese pondered, or stalled for time, plans for Operation Olympic went on, with little shift in emphasis. The only way to overcome their fanaticism was to grind them into the earth.

Soldiers boasted, "We'll fight them on the beaches. We'll smear them on the beaches."

13 August 1945. With the Japanese still trying to save the Emperor's hide, the air attack was renewed. A third atomic bomb had not been manufactured, but there were plenty of other bombs and plenty of planes to drop them. On the thirteenth a thousand planes flew over Tokyo alone. It was their last raid.

15 August 1945. The Emperor broadcast the Imperial Rescript of surrender, which included a characteristic Japanese face-saving understatement: "Despite the gallant fighting of the Officers and Men of our Army and Navy, the diligence and assiduity of Our servants of the State, and the devoted service of Our hundred million subjects—despite the best efforts of all—the war has not necessarily developed in our favor, and the general world situation also is not to Japan's advantage. . . ." There was an added plea for the Japanese to cultivate ways of rectitude and to foster nobility of

spirit. Nowhere in the broadcast was there a sign of remorse—apologies are not for gods—or a repudiation of *Hakko Ichiu,* or a sacrifice of national ambition. The dream of the world under one roof with Japan at the roof pole was submerged but not abandoned. This gem called peace had a noticeable flaw. General MacArthur, never imperial, ever imperious, had decided that the Emperor should keep his position.

By chance I was in the Escolta when the word of surrender came. A major earthquake could not have brought people to the streets faster. Americans and Filipinos met each other, embraced each other, yelling, laughing, crying, in an orgy that spread through streets and houses and ships in the harbor, an orgy of drinking and dancing in a frenzy of relief from doubt and dread and fear. Sailors stripped off their middies and threw them to Filipino girls. Soldiers ripped off buttons and chevrons in a rush for civilian anonymity.

Gears of war had to be reversed. We were going into Japan not as invaders but as occupying aliens. Old plans had to be scrapped. New orders had to be cut. There was no time for training. We would have to muddle through.

One order cut was my own, giving me forty-five days for rest and recuperation at home before reporting for duty in Japan.

At the end of the day, on my way to visit Father Daniel, I walked in the arcades of cloisters that had been destroyed in the battle of Intramuros. In the midst of this destruction I could not even imagine that of Hiroshima and Nagasaki. By then, my own mind had been made up. The bomb should not have been dropped.

• • •

One afternoon, when I went for my daily check of Americans recovered from the Japanese, I found the name of John M. Owens, Jr. Peapicker's ordeal was over at last. He had been recaptured on Formosa and was on his way to Manila, where he would be transferred immediately from Nichols Field to a hospital near Cavite. The answer to my request to meet the plane was, "Try the hospital tomorrow."

I was on the road early. On my right was the blue of Manila

Bay, on my left miles and miles of war materiel, ready and waiting for an invasion that would never take place. Operation Olympic had been scrapped. Useless now, trucks, tanks, weaponry waited to be cast into the sea or to rust away under jungle growth. An incalculable waste of war.

The hospital was a cluster of temporary buildings set in a park-like grove. Men, more like skeletons, shuffled along the walks. Men too weak to walk lay on cots in overcrowded wards.

"Yes, John Owens is here," a nurse told me. "He's taking a physical."

I went to the building she had pointed out to me and walked past a line of naked, scarecrow men moving slowly past a line of doctors. No Peapicker among them. A corpsman showed me a dressing room. "Try there."

Seven or eight naked men were waiting on benches. Not one looked in the least like the gangling boy I remembered. I went inside. "Is Owens here?"

A voice answered "Here," and with difficulty a man got to his feet—not a man but a caricature of a man, with a face as round and puffed as a Mandarin's, a thin chest over a bloated belly, spindly legs swollen close to bursting at the ankles. He came closer.

"Well, I'll be damned." The voice was his. "What are you doing here?"

The words I had planned to say no longer seemed right.

"Looking for you."

"Well, you found me—what the Japs left of me." His hand closed over mine without a grip. "How's everybody at home?"

He had been three years in almost total isolation. I told him the little I knew about his family and gave him a letter I had just received. He read it through with no show of emotion, and read it through again. "How's Grandma?"

He meant my mother. "She died in April."

There was a kind of gasp in his throat and tears in his eyes. "Grandma's dead?"

"Yes."

He sat down and lowered his head. "It's been a long time."

230

A long time and so little that we could say to each other.

I was relieved when a corpsman called them out and took them to the examination line. I walked beside him. The examination was superficial, but some results were predictable. He had a severe case of beriberi. Too little food. Too much rice. An officer tapped his chest. Some ribs had broken.

"How?"

"The butt of a Japanese rifle." A Japanese soldier had beaten him and he had had no medical care.

"On the Death March?"

Not on the Death March but in one of the many prisons he had been in.

We came to the end of the line. From first to last the medics treated him gently. He knew and we knew that rescue had barely come in time. He was a casualty of war, not counting the four years he had lost, or the years he would lose regaining his health, if he ever did.

"How soon can he go home?"

We had to go to the personnel office for the answer. Within a matter of days he would be flown to California for a month or so of recuperation. I was relieved. His family would not have to see him as I had seen him.

They gave him a pass to go to Manila. He dressed, but there was no uniform that would fit his distorted body. The fatigues he wore were strained at the middle and hung like bags above and below. His shoes were sizes too big but he could not lace them around his ankles. His step was as infirm as that of an old man.

In Manila the food we urged on him was too rich. It nauseated him and made him incontinent. Asleep, he woke us with nightmares. Awake, he talked of the Death March and Cabanatuan and Bilibid and of cruelty beyond our comprehension.

Anger at the Japanese rose in me. I had last seen him as a handsome, intelligent college student with the world before him. He had enlisted not so much *pro domo* as for adventure, and had become a victim of atrocity. By any definition, Japanese atrocity was different from German atrocity only in numbers.

• • •

231

The wind-down of war was underway, the final dramatic flourish yet to be orchestrated. General MacArthur, now Supreme Commander of Allied Forces in the Pacific, responded to the news of surrender characteristically: "I thank God that this mighty struggle is about to end." He would stop hostilities and bloodshed at once, he pledged. He spoke no word of or for the dead. To those who had survived he gave a pat on the head and a sermon: "The magnificent men and women who have fought so nobly to victory can now return to their homes in due course and resume their civil pursuits. They have been good soldiers in war. May they be equally good citizens in peace."

In the final drama General MacArthur would go to Tokyo, but first the Japanese would have to come to him in submission if not in reverence. In an exchange symbolically called "Bataan" he ordered the Japanese representatives to travel to Manila on 17 August 1945 on special planes and by designated routes. The Emperor asked for more time to get the message of surrender to his widespread forces. The general generously granted it. Not until 19 August could the emissaries reach Manila. They arrived duly and, after exchange of credentials at the airport, were taken into Manila by a route that showed the materiel strength of the Allied Forces and the destruction of the city. The first step of surrender was dramatically played out. Time and place of the final act were tentatively agreed upon.

28 August 1945. The first American troops landed in Japan, met not by a hostile but by a docile, mind-controlled people. The Emperor had spoken. They would obey.

30 August 1945. General MacArthur arrived in Japan aboard a C-54 with "Bataan" prominently displayed on the nose.

2 September 1945. The final drama of the signing was played out on the deck of the battleship U.S.S. *Missouri,* again with symbolic rituals carefully observed. I listened to the official broadcast but the event seemed anticlimatic, partly because bilingual exchanges were slow, partly because the broadcasters themselves

lacked the fire that battles had inspired in them. In any case, the war was over at last. General MacArthur opened his final statement: "Today the guns are silent. A great tragedy has ended. A great victory has been won. . . ."

In the treaty signed, some of history had been forgotten or ignored when it should have been remembered. In the ending of one war, seeds of others lay concealed. Japan had lost the first phase of her hundred years' war, but nothing in the treaty required her people to give up their commitment to the belief that the world is destined to be under one roof with Japan at the roof pole. They had kept their Emperor, his divinity only slightly diminished. They are Oriental. They can bide their time.

For Filipinos the end of the war was the beginning of a perilous political aftermath. On 23 August 1945 General MacArthur ordered the release of all interned Filipinos—some two thousand on Palawan alone. In addition, some six thousand cases were still pending. In one official act he ended the investigative work of the CIC in the Philippines and left thousands of Filipinos in a political or legal dilemma. The Americans compounded the problem by contending that the release was not an indication of either innocence or guilt—that could be determined only by the courts of the Commonwealth Government. Seeing a way out for themselves and using the pardon of Manuel Roxas as precedent, some of the most flagrant collaborators argued their release as proof of innocence. The *ilustrado* began deserting President Osmeña and aligning themselves with Manuel Roxas in a political party he was forming. Ironically, perhaps with tongue in cheek, Roxas called it the Liberal Party.

Guerrilla leaders like Ramón Magsaysay and Ferdinand Marcos became a new part of the *ilustrado*. Favor with the United States Army had given them a power and arrogance that before the war had belonged only to the elite.

By accident or contemptuous scheme, members of the *ilustrado* and of the Huks had been thrown together at Iwahig Prison. No matter their political alignments, they had had to tolerate each other. The treaty signed, President Osmeña proclaimed a general

233

amnesty for all Filipinos charged with collaboration with the Japanese or with anti-American activities. General MacArthur had killed the collaboration issue. President Osmeña buried it.

On 17 September I was transferred to a repple depple outside Manila to wait for water transportation. With my case of gangplank fever intensifying at the prospect of getting out, I went for a last tour of Manila. With some show of hope, people were rebuilding, but for many the materials were boxing cases, scrap galvanized iron, and thatch. In Intramuros bulldozers were still pushing up rubble. Inside San Augustin Church I sat near the front for the Mass Father Daniel was saying for me. The Mass over, he embraced me and blessed me.

In the afternoon I was in the tent city of the repple depple among hundreds of officers waiting for transportation and lining up as loudspeakers called names.

18 September. My name was called, not for transportation but for visitors at the gate.

Before I got to the guard station I saw José and Tomás Banal standing outside. As I came closer I saw they were not wearing insignia. They looked sad, defeated. Solemnly they shook hands.

"Ser," José Banal said, "we have come to you for help."

"Why?"

Tomás spoke. "The Army disbanded our regiment. They took our weapons and supplies before we left Corregidor. They left us only with our uniforms."

His father could no longer wear the eagles. Their pay had been cut off. They were left with nothing.

Another disillusionment for me. "Did they give a reason?"

"There were Americans against us. When we had cleared the tunnels they said there was no mission for us. They said everything was in the hands of the Commonwealth Government, but they would not let us in at Malacañan. Can you not do something?"

I could not. I could not leave the repple depple or telephone anyone at San Fernando. Major Frederick was no longer at San Fernando.

"There is Huk trouble," Tomás said. "Taruc and Alejandrino have been released. Scarlett O'Hara is organizing a cadre in Quezon City. They are confiscating and liquidating in the *barrios*."

He held my hand and begged. "If you will only go with us, ser."

The loudspeaker was blaring names. Mine might be among them. I had to go. I took José Banal's hand. "What will you do now?"

Tomás answered. "We fear, ser. We are no longer of the Huk. They have sent word. We are the traitors. The trial has been held. We are to be liquidated. We will go to the *barrios* and hide as long as we can. Who knows how long?"

They had walked out from Manila. With a last "Good-bye, ser," they went. I watched them go—father and son, father old and frail, son young and strong—both, I was convinced, condemned to die. This I had done to them. No, not I alone, I consoled myself. The war? The Japanese? The Spaniards? The Americans? The Americans, yes, knowing little or knowing much of what they were doing. These and all the furies let loose by war.*

19 September 1945. In a slow-moving convoy of personnel carriers from repple depple to ship, in a Manila Bay sunset of red, purple, gold, I thought of the Philippines more than I thought of home. Bitterly I recalled what cynical Americans had named as the four freedoms of the Philippines: freedom to starve, freedom to stagnate, freedom to revolt from democracy, freedom to go from one political form to another until chaos or authoritarianism rules.

I had arrived in the Philippines in darkness; I was leaving the Philippines in darkness.

---

*In 1949, when Mrs. Geronima Pecson was in New York, I asked her what had happened to the Banals and to certain other Filipinos. She replied that the Banals were all right; a report from another source, a short time later, said that José Banal had been killed.

235

CITATION FOR LEGION OF MERIT

Second Lieutenant *WILLIAM A. OWENS,* 02026827 (then Technical Sergeant), Military Intelligence, United States Army. For exceptionally meritorious conduct in the performance of outstanding services in Luzon, Philippine Islands, from 13 January to 1 May 1945. Landing in Lingayen Gulf with the 306th Counter Intelligence Corps Detachment, Lieutenant Owens assisted in the re-establishment of civil government in the numerous liberated municipalities through which he passed in the drive to Manila. Soon after arriving in the Philippine Capital, he thoroughly exploited enemy records and documents and conducted an exhaustive study of the puppet government during the occupation. The results of this survey provided the Counter Intelligence Corps with invaluable information on the activities of the puppet government and grounds for treason cases against specific officials who had collaborated with the Japanese. After the liberation of Manila, Lieutenant Owens accompanied his detachment to Central Luzon where he instituted a complete study of various recalcitrant guerrilla organizations, which, by their obstructionist and terroristic activities, constituted a grave threat to the security of our forces. He operated a Counter Intelligence Corps Office in the heart of the most troublesome guerrilla territory and through his broad knowledge of the political aims and tactics of radical forces, successfully prevented all attempts to preclude the re-establishment of lawful government. By his outstanding courage, noteworthy resourcefulness, and forceful treatment of agitators, Lieutenant Owens made a distinct contribution to the continued effectiveness of Counter Intelligence activities and to the expeditious restoration of civil authority in Luzon.

INDEX

239

place, 85, 127, 133, 157, 159, 160, 166, 171, 191

Candating, 191–92

Cannibalism, 4, 24, 55, 66

Capampangan (Pampangan) language, 139, 145, 150, 155, 156, 158, 192, 198, 200, 203, 210, 214

Castrillo, Padre Daniel, 205–6, 213, 214, 215, 216, 217, 218, 219, 229, 234

Catholic Church: and Communists, 185, 190; and Hukbalahap, 174; and pagan rituals, 152, 180, 185, 208. *See also* Missionaries; Santa Iglesias

Catmon Hill, 2, 4, 6, 8, 10, 13, 26, 35, 36, 37, 40

Chingi, 113, 114

Clark Field, 68, 81, 84, 159, 160

Clausewitz, Karl von, 14, 92

Clerkin, Father Michael, 74

Cokinos, Jimmie, 116

Collaborators, 54–55, 72, 85, 88, 100, 102, 117, 197; in Commonwealth Government, 105, 106, 145; and General MacArthur's orders, 61–62, 84, 194–96, 233–34; and Hukbalahap, 133, 180, 188; priests as, 74–75; and puppet government, 38–40, 42–45; three kinds of, 104. *See also* Spies

Coloocan, 89

Commonwealth Government (Philippines), 145, 164, 175, 194, 195, 197, 201; collaborators in, 105, 106, 145; and Filipino internees, 233; and Hukbalahap, 141, 155, 165, 218, 234; and Japanese, 108; and Leyte, 17, 58; and Philippine Republic, 73, 103, 105

Communism: in Philippines, 153–54, 189–90; and U.S. Army, 126–27. *See also* Hukbalahap

Communists, Chinese, 153, 189

Corregidor, 1, 8, 67, 68, 105, 108, 120, 158, 194, 207; Banal Regiment at, 224–25, 234; fifth column at, 21; guns captured at, 70; survivors of, 80, 99

Counter Intelligence Corps: and Army, 13–14, 19–20, 24, 31, 32, 77, 211–12; in combat, 1–32, 51, 71, 90–91, 222; and entrance into Manila, 83–89; and Filipino culture, 57–58; and Filipino

guerrillas, 34–35, 54, 56, 57–58; 441st Detachment, 219; and interned Filipinos, 233; interrogations by, 38–39, 40, 42–44, 54–55, 56, 73–74, 96, 98, 128, 132–35, 136, 139–40, 142, 148, 195; and Japanese culture, 47–50, 222–23; morale of, 20, 25, 30, 35–36, 59, 62, 65, 164, 196; Ninety-sixth, 35, 37; and priests, 148–49; 306th, 61, 83. *See also* Hukbalahap; Leyte; Luzon; Manila; Sixth Army

Creel, Lieutenant Dana, 223

Dagami, 33

Daguitan River, 54

Dagupan, 71

Damortis, 70

David, Don Pablo Angeles, 130, 136–38, 139–41, 147, 148, 166, 167, 211

Dayang-Dayang, 134

Death March, 8, 79, 94, 113, 137, 162, 231

de la Cruz, Juan, *see* Taruc, Luis

de las Alas, 196

Dewey, Commodore George, 102

Doolittle raid, *see* Tokyo, bombing of

Du Bard, Colonel Horton, 75

Dulag, 8, 16, 19, 21, 23, 24, 25, 26, 36, 38, 41, 44; air raid at, 50, 51–53, 55; Christmas in, 59–60; General MacArthur at, 32–34; Kamikaze attack on, 49, 50; naval bombardment of, 2, 14–15; refugees in, 17, 40. *See also* Leyte

Duncan, Louis, 70, 100

Edwards, David, 90, 93

Eichelberger, General, 22, 83

Eleventh Airborne Division, 50, 81, 117

Emperor Hirohito, 2, 4, 47, 48, 49, 100, 111, 220–22, 228, 232

English, Jim, 24

Faustino, 36–37, 39, 40

Feleo, Juan, 153, 218

Fil-American troops, 79, 107–8

First Cavalry Division, 10, 81, 83, 86, 115, 117

Floridablanca, 197–98

Fort Sam Houston, 8

Fort Stotsenburg, 81, 84

Frederick, Captain Harold: as commander of 306th Counter Intelligence Corps, 61, 70, 78–79; and Hukbalahap, 124, 127, 128, 129, 135, 136, 141, 144, 154–55, 165, 189, 190, 201–2, 206–7, 215, 217, 218, 234; and José Yulo, 196, 197; and landing on Leyte, 4, 5, 10, 11; in Manila, 92–96, 100, 101, 104, 105, 106, 107; and Manuel Roxas, 195; *merienda* for, 180, 181, 183–84; ordered to San Fernando, 109; and Owens, 15, 18, 21, 27, 36, 41, 44, 77, 81, 160, 164, 166, 176, 191, 193, 212, 219; as planning officer for Luzon invasions, 45; and priests, 148, 149, 152; and XXIV Corps, 13, 14, 16, 19, 20, 24, 25

Gabriel, Major, 175, 186
Gaydon, Corporal, 90
Geneva Convention, 6, 98
George F. Clymer (troopship), 1–9
Golding, Robert, 173
Gorman, Ed, 13, 21, 22, 25, 26, 30
Greater East Asia Co-Prosperity Sphere, 50, 66, 101, 109
Guadalcanal, 1, 17, 47, 120
Guagua, 141–43, 145, 148, 197
Guan Yek, *see* Alejandrino, Casto
Guerrillas, 5–6, 108, 109, 114; and CIC, 34, 37, 51, 54, 55, 67, 70, 72, 107; USAFFE, 85, 87, 88, 89, 127–28, 129, 138, 141, 145; and U.S. Army, 56, 57, 58, 76, 80, 99, 155. *See also* Hukbalahap
Guzman, Captain, 72, 73, 76, 77

Hagan, Father William, 74
hara-kiri (seppuku), 47, 48, 221, 222
Hiroshima, 226–27, 229
Hodge, General John R., 14, 19
Hollandia, 45, 73, 91, 96, 97, 196. *See also* New Guinea
Horowitz, Mike, 67, 74, 207, 217
Hukbalahap (Huks), 84–85, 113–14, 126; aliases among, 127, 128, 130; history of, 133–34; Japanese attitude to, 129; and *Kempei Tai*, 129; leaders of, 128–36, 146–48, 153–59, 161–62, 165, 166, 169–72, 175–77, 181, 184, 187–91,

196–200; and priests, 148–52, 173, 175; propaganda of, 150–52; and Spanish colonialism, 198; vs. USAFFE guerrillas, 87, 88, 89, 127–28, 129, 145, 155, 164, 166, 167; and U.S. Army, 82, 84, 124, 129; women among, 127, 134. *See also* Banal Regiment; Mount Arayat
Hunter, Woody, 62

Ilocanos, 58, 78
Imperial Rescript, 47, 49, 228. *See also* Japanese soldiers
Infiltration, 30–31, 32–33, 34, 41, 76–77
Insubordination, 19, 20, 23
Intramuros, 119. 120, 121, 122, 219, 224, 229, 234. *See also* Manila
Irwin, Colonel John N., 21, 22, 23, 25
"I Wanted Wings" (Navy song), 60

Japan: CIC crash training courses on, 222–23; defeat of, 228; *Hakko Ichiu* tradition of, 228, 229; Samurai tradition in, 6; surrender of, 228–29, 232–33. *See also* Tokyo, bombing of
Japanese soldiers, 4–5, 15–16, 47–48; American attitude to, 47; and American soldiers, 47; atrocities of, 24–25, 74, 75, 76n, 96, 100, 119, 231; attacks by, 29, 49; and battle for Manila, 90, 93; code of, 24, 48; and Corregidor, 224, 226; devotion to Emperor of, 2, 4, 47, 48, 49, 131, 161, 220–21; 222; diaries of, 17, 47, 49, 65, 71, 74, 220; emotionalism of, 222; and Filipinos, 73, 88, 119, 120; and Hukbalahap, 172–73, 174; morale of, 4–5, 65–66, 220; and nuns, 96–97. See also *Banzai*; *Kamikaze*

Kamikaze, 48–79, 50, 51, 68, 95, 220
Kangleon, Colonel Ruperto, 34
Kano, Hisamichi, 111–12, 113, 114–16
Kavieng, 75n
Kempei Tai (Japanese military police), 15, 18, 26, 41, 72, 73, 79, 93, 147; and Hukbalahap, 113, 128; interrogation methods of, 54; and prostitution, 61
Krueger, General Walter, 31–32, 81, 82, 83, 86, 112, 202, 220
Kublai Khan, 48

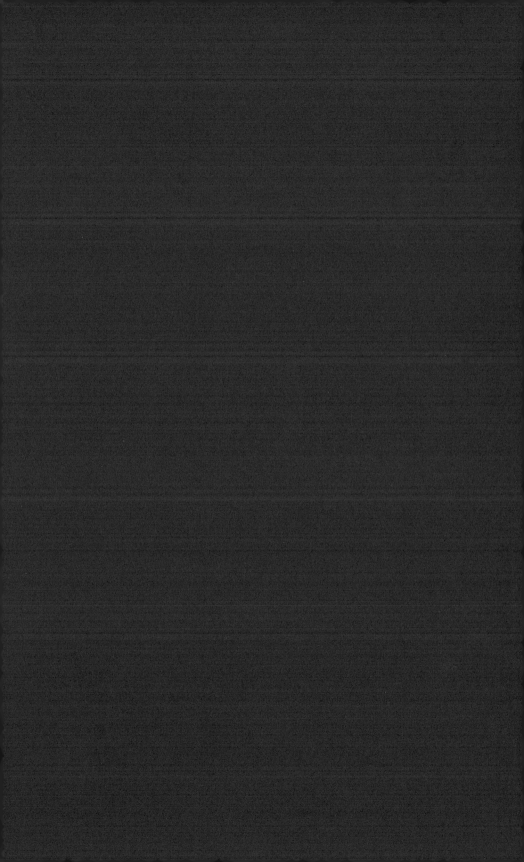